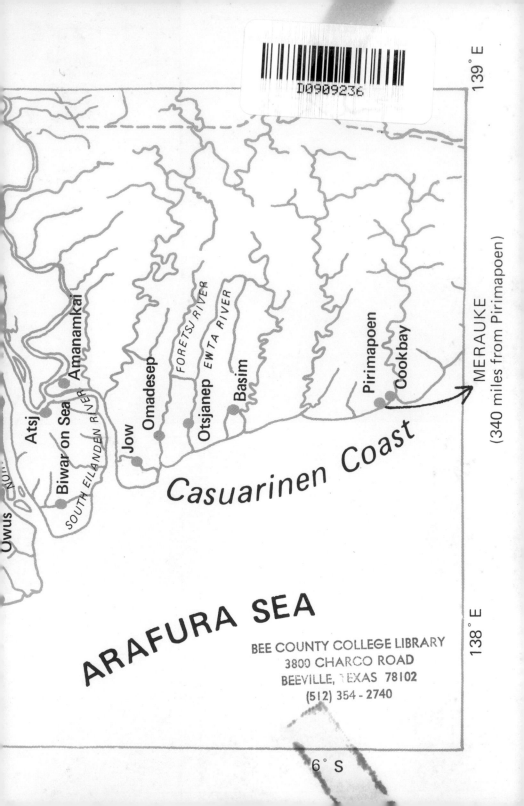

139° E

MERAUKE
(340 miles from Pirimapoen)

Pirimapoen

Cookbay

FORETSJ RIVER

EWTA RIVER

Amanamkai

Omadesep

Basim

Otsjanep

Jow

Atsj

Biwar on Sea

SOUTH EILANDEN RIVER

NOIL

Owus

Casuarinen Coast

ARAFURA SEA

138° E

6° S

The Search for Michael Rockefeller

Books by Milt Machlin

NINTH LIFE with William Read Woodfield

THE PRIVATE HELL OF ERNEST HEMINGWAY

THE SEARCH FOR MICHAEL ROCKEFELLER

The
Search
for
Michael
Rockefeller

MILT MACHLIN

G. P. Putnam's Sons   GPPS   New York

Contents

I. Michael Rockefeller   7

II. Donahue   13

III. Father Van Kessel   89

IV. Dias and Lapre   152

     Bibliography   249

     Index   251

Illustrations will be found following page 128.

Acknowledgments

I have tried to include credit in the text for all the people who generously gave of their time and cooperation in the preparation of this book. I would particularly like to thank Jim Anderson for his help and understanding during difficult days in New Guinea. I would also like to thank Stuart Inder, Keith Willey, Robert Gardner, Karl Heider, Father Van Kessel, Tim Ward, Count Herve De Maigret and his wife Pamela, and others who provided valuable information and made their time available to me. Thanks are also extended to Qantas Airlines for assistance in the air travel aspects of my New Guinea trip. Most of all, I would like to thank the pseudonymous John Campbell.

I would also like to express gratitude to my publisher at *Argosy*, Harry Steeger, and my editor, Hal Steeger, for their understanding, cooperation and aid in the preparation of this book.

M. M.

I. Michael Rockefeller

MICHAEL ROCKEFELLER at twenty-three was the most restless of Governor Nelson Rockefeller's three sons and two daughters, and the most promising.

A fourth-generation heir to the fabulous dynasty founded by great-grandfather John D. Rockefeller, young Michael yearned to learn about life at the other end of the social scale. Summers he worked in a Puerto Rican supermarket or as a hand on his father's Venezuelan ranch.

Graduating from Harvard *cum laude* in 1960 (the year his father failed to get the Republican Presidential nomination), he still didn't seem ready to settle down in the business and political world of the Rockefeller dynasty. He enlisted as a private in the Army and put in six months, and then, still apparently looking for adventure far from the world of finance and government, Michael joined some friends who were traveling to New Guinea in an expedition sponsored by Harvard's Peabody Museum.

"It's the desire to do something adventurous," he explained once, "at a time when frontiers, in the real sense of the word, are disappearing."

Certainly New Guinea was a true frontier. The 1,500-mile-long island 10,000 miles from New York still contained vast unexplored areas and many savage tribes who had not encountered civilization as we know it. Headhunt-

7

ing and cannibalism were extensively practiced in some sections.

The Peabody expedition brought Michael, who had signed on as a sound technician, to a world whose primitive savagery was a far cry from Cambridge or the Pocantico Hills of Westchester County, where Michael had been reared.

The mission of the group was to film and record the customs of New Guinea's little-known tribes. The expedition's assignment was in the Baliem Valley of Dutch New Guinea (the island was bisected by the 141st parallel into two colonial administrations, the eastern half administered by the Australian government and the western half by the Dutch).

Natives of the valley, said the Dutch, had only recently been educated away from incessant tribal warfare and headhunting. The Peabody expedition, which included Michael's Harvard friends Robert Gardner and Sam Putnam, spent six months in the primitive mountain areas. The rugged life appealed to Michael's restless spirit.

At summer's end the expedition's activities were concluded, and after six months in New Guinea Michael returned to New York in September, 1961.

During the Peabody expedition he had become intrigued by the fabulous artistic talents of the natives of the Asmat coast some 500 miles from the valley in which he was working and briefly visited the region. He decided to return almost immediately to collect the artifacts of this remarkable people, living along the half-submerged southern coast of Dutch New Guinea, for the Museum of Primitive Art in New York, which had been founded by his father and of which he had been named a trustee.

In New Guinea he was joined by René Wassing, a thirty-four-year-old Dutch ethnologist and expert on primitive wood carvings.

The area to which they were traveling was known in native dialect as "the land of lapping death"—probably because of its topography, a steaming mass of surging muddy rivers, swamps and tidal flats infested with a teeming population of sharks and saltwater crocodiles and plentifully supplied with mosquitoes, giant beetles, some as large as a man's palm, and other insect pests.

Within a month of his arrival Rockefeller had amassed an impressive collection of the grotesque primitive carvings for which the area was famous. The trade goods he had brought—axheads, knives, tobacco and cloth—were eagerly sought by the natives who were still barely emerging from the Stone Age. A single axhead in some areas could buy the labor of a small village for a day.

Another source of artistic interest in the Asmat area was the fantastically decorated human trophy heads which formed an important part of the native religion and culture. Though the government said headhunting had been halted in recent years, decorated heads were still available, and Michael was anxious to acquire some for his collection.

The Dutch were not enthusiastic, however; they were afraid that the Rockefeller team might stir up dormant urges on the part of the natives. One administrator claimed that members of a local tribe had approached him and asked if they could go headhunting "for one evening only, please, sir."

"We had to warn him [Rockefeller] off," the administrator told newsmen, "as he was creating a demand that could not be met without bloodshed."

Travel in the Asmat is mainly by boat. There are no roads, very few airstrips or available airplanes, and the marshy mangrove jungles are in many cases impassable even to natives. To facilitate transportation of the heavy loads of trade goods and artifacts needed for the expedition's collection trips, Michael had acquired a 40-foot catamaran made up of two native dugout hulls lashed together,

9

surmounted by a small shelter cabin and powered by an 18-horsepower outboard—*under*powered, many thought, for the heavy loads involved.

On November 18 Michael and Wassing set out in the catamaran from the mission outpost at Agats. The boat appeared to be heavily overloaded, and the pair were warned that where local rivers joined the sea, tides 20 feet high surged 75 miles upstream in places, with a force that could swamp even the expert native canoeists. Michael promised to watch out for the dangerous seas, and the two men departed for the village of Atsj, 25 miles down the coast. With them they took two native guides who had been given the Christian names of Simon and Leo by the missionaries.

About three miles offshore, the boat, crossing the mouth of the Eilanden River, was swamped by the rough seas which drowned its outboard and left it helpless in the rush of the tide. Simon and Leo, both excellent swimmers, decided to swim to shore for help. Wassing and Rockefeller stayed with the boat through the night. On the next day when help had not appeared, Michael became convinced that Simon and Leo had been lost in the treacherous shark- and crocodile-infested waters and decided his best move was to try to swim ashore himself. Wassing, who was a poor swimmer, urged Rockefeller to stay with the boat, certain that help would arrive when the Crozier fathers became aware that they had not returned when expected. But, Wassing told reporters later, "Rockefeller's restless nature made it impossible for him to endure our drifting around."

Michael stripped to his shorts, tied his glasses around his neck, attached the red jerrican in which they had carried extra gas and the outboard's fuel tank as floats, and dived into the sea. Wassing watched until all he could see were the three dots of the swimmer and his two floats.

As far as was known, it was the last time Michael Rockefeller was seen alive.

Meanwhile, the two native boys had in fact reached shore and alerted authorities to the disaster. Dutch Colonial Governor P. J. Plateel ordered a giant search for the missing men. Boats, airplanes, marines and thousands of natives beat the bush for the lost pair. The Australian government lent the assistance of helicopters. The U.S. Seventh Fleet even offered the services of its aircraft carriers. Governor Rockefeller and Michael's twin sister, Mary, flew by regular airlines to Honolulu where they chartered a jet for $38,000 to fly them to New Guinea's nearest jet strip (to this day the only jet flight ever made from Honolulu to Biak). In Biak they were transferred to a DC-3 which flew them to Merauke, the local Dutch colonial headquarters and the post from which the search was directed.

On their arrival at Merauke the Rockefellers were given the news. Wassing had been picked up by a Dutch flying boat which had spotted him clinging to the capsized catamaran some 20 miles offshore. The Rockefellers and search directors questioned Wassing closely, anxious for some clue to the possible fate of Michael. Wassing said he had done everything in his power to dissuade young Rockefeller from leaving the catamaran. "I warned him about the crocodiles. I told him I could take no responsibility for him."

Michael's last words to him, said Wassing, were: "I think I can make it."

But the days stretched on, and no word was heard from the missing Rockefeller heir. A reward of 250 sticks of tobacco was offered—enormous wealth to the natives. An estimated 1,000 canoes probed the many tributaries and miles of mangrove and mud coastline without results. A jerrican which was thought at first to be Rockefeller's was found, but Wassing said that he didn't believe it was theirs. After ten days the governor and his daughter, haggard from strain and emotion, boarded their charter plane to return to civilization. *Newsweek* magazine commented: "All the evidence pointed to Michael's being dead—yet until his body is found, it is impossible for any man, and especially for his agonized father, to put aside the thought that possibly, Mike is alive somewhere in the lagoons, along that cruel coast."

But the years have stretched by and still there is no word of Michael Rockefeller. The governor and the world became convinced that he had died somewhere in the Arafura Sea.

II. Donahue

1

In October, 1968, Ethel Klock, the switchboard operator at *Argosy* magazine, where I was employed as executive editor, rang my office and announced that there was a man in the reception room who wanted to talk with me.

"He says he can't give his name and he doesn't have an appointment, but he has to talk to you. He's a very rough-looking character."

I was busy that morning wrapping up our December issue and irritated that the man had come unannounced. I called Jean Russell, one of my assistants, and asked her to go out and get rid of him.

When Jean had not returned in ten minutes, I began to worry. I called the switchboard and asked if the man was still out there.

"He's still here, and Jean can't get him to leave," she said.

It was annoying, but I was afraid that the man out front might be one of the occasional violent eccentrics who call at our offices. I went to the reception office with the intention of evicting the unwanted visitor.

The man to whom Jean was talking was a rough-looking customer all right. He was about five feet ten, stocky and muscular. He was wearing a blue tank jacket, of the sort usually favored by merchant seamen, and suntan workpants.

His jaw was heavy, blue and unshaved, and he had a deep scar on his forehead. Jeannie seemed perplexed and concerned. I felt protective and a bit angry.

"OK, mister," I said, "what's your problem?"

"You Machlin?" he asked.

I nodded.

"I got important information, and I can't tell it to nobody except you."

"Write it down, and I'll read it as soon as I can get to it."

"I got to leave this afternoon," he said in what I took to be a Cockney or Australian brogue.

"Mail us the story, mister," I said. "I promise I'll read it. Now if you don't mind. . . ."

"Look," he said suddenly. "Suppose I told you that I saw Michael Rockefeller *alive* only ten weeks ago?"

It worked, all right; he had me hooked. Actually, I was well informed on the fate of young Rockefeller because only the previous month we had published an article reviewing his tragic disappearance.

"OK." I signaled him to sit down and sent Jean back into the office. "Let's have it."

The man looked around apprehensively.

"Look, I'm only doin' this because I don't like to see an innocent bloke in a mess. I could get in a jam over this."

"Where did you see Rockefeller and when?"

"I saw him on an island near New Guinea. Actually I saw him twice. Once about eighteen months ago and once just over two months ago."

"Why didn't you report it to the authorities? Why come here?"

"That's it, mate. I *can't* go to anyone official. I'm sort of— well, not in a position to deal with the authorities. Look, I just want to give the information to someone who can do something about it and get out of here. I can't afford to stay around too long."

I was still highly doubtful of both the man and his story, but intrigued enough to listen to more. I asked him to give me all the details of the story that he could recall.

"Can't we go someplace else?" he asked nervously.

I got my coat and took him down to the Blarney Stone bar on Third Avenue. Was this a con game just to get some drinks or a few bucks, I wondered. I had been taken like that before, but I'm usually willing to gamble a few dollars on a possible good story. Much to my surprise my visitor, after picking a corner chair where he could watch the early lunchtime crowd, refused a drink. He refused a sandwich or lunch as well, accepting only a cup of coffee. "I'm too nervous to eat, mate, and I can't afford to let myself get drunk."

His name, he said, was John Donahue. He was a Tasmanian and in town only for the day.

"Merchant seaman?" I asked.

He hesitated. "That's nothing to do with it. You want to hear the story?"

I nodded.

It all started, Donahue said, eighteen months before—or perhaps with World War II. Donahue had been in the Australian Army—Seventh Division—during the New Guinea campaign. I was interested in this because I had been through almost the entire New Guinea campaign myself in a U.S. Army signal battalion attached to General George Kenny's Fifth Air Force. I had spent more than a year on the island, and while I was no expert on its habits or geography, I was well enough informed to trip up anybody who was lying about having actually been there. In fact, my outfit had worked closely with some units of the Aussie Seventh. I asked some questions about the battles of Buna, Lae and Salamaua and the famous march over the Kokoda trail across the hump of the Owen Stanley Mountains. (This had occurred fairly early in the war when it looked for a moment as though the Japanese were going to push right down into the Australian mainland.) His answers checked. One thing was sure so far, and that was that the man knew something about wartime New Guinea. A bit more interested, I asked him to continue with his story.

Before coming to New Guinea, Donahue said, he had fought with the Seventh in Benghazi, Tobruk, and Palestine. This, too, checked with my knowledge of the history of the division.

After the war he had stayed on in the islands, making a good living by scavenging military supplies left behind by the Americans. He acquired a 90-foot island trader, and packed it with matériel left on the beach by the advancing Yanks. A jeep could bring $5,000 in those days, though he had to cut it into two parts to load it aboard ship.

From this activity he drifted into smuggling and then piracy, preying on ships crossing from the Far East to Australia and the Fijis, among other places. Chinese and Indian traders with cargoes including transistors and wristwatches from Hong Kong, as well as alcohol and tobacco, were his principal victims.

As outlandish as this sounds, the piracy bit of his story was also corroborated by information I had. Only the year before, en route to an assignment in Vietnam, I had passed through Manila, where the newspapers were full of stories of the activities of modern pirates and hijackers operating in the Sulu Archipelago and the China Sea. Singapore, too, had almost daily reports of piracy and hijacking of cargoes, In both places these activities are a major problem today.

I asked if he had any associates.

He replied that his gang had varied in size and composition from time to time.

Just over seven years before our talk, Donahue said, he and two "cobbers," Jeffries and Lang, got into really serious trouble. They were operating a fast launch filled with contraband running along the coast between Hollandia and

Wewak when they were intercepted. I listened with interest. My outfit had participated in the liberation of Hollandia from the Japanese.

Dutch patrol officers hailed their boat and signaled that they wanted to come aboard.

"You have to understand that I am a smuggler, not a killer," Donahue explained seriously, "but we were not about to get caught with the cargo we had aboard. Some of us fired on the patrol, and we took off and managed to lose ourselves. Later we found out that we had killed one Dutch constable and two natives.

"Me and my mate, Lang, was named in a murder indictment for that job—it was the first time that we were in really serious trouble, but by that time we were wanted for one thing or another by the Australians, Dutch, British, French and I guess about every government in the islands. So you can see that when we ran into the Rockefeller kid we weren't exactly in any shape to go to the authorities about it."

First contact with the young American came, said Donahue, just eighteen months earlier when his boat put into a tiny seldom-visited island on the north coast of New Guinea for water and food.

"The *north* coast?" I asked. "Rockefeller was lost on the *south* coast."

Donahue was unperturbed.

"Who was with you when you landed on this island?" I asked.

"The same two mates who were on the boat when we shot the Dutchman."

"Can I talk to them?"

"Well, Lang is still hiding out from that murder charge. Jeffries is in jail in the Fiji Islands for smuggling alcohol and brandies, but I doubt if he will talk because he doesn't want to be connected to the killing. He's named only as John Doe on the murder rap."

The three men, Donahue said, had been on a gunrunning trip through the Solomon Sea which borders northeastern New Guinea. As usual they avoided legitimate ports and put in for water and food supplies at tiny seldomvisited islands which dot the area. They remained on good terms with the isolated local populations of these islands with small payoffs of trade goods such as trade tobacco, cloth, razor blades and knives. None of these islands had any whites on them, and there were no radios to signal the arrival of the gunrunners to authorities. In any event the natives were not that friendly with the government, so Donahue and his friends were relatively safe. Often they would leave caches of fuel near the isolated beaches, Donahue said.

"What was the name of this island?" I asked.

"It was called Kanapua or Kanaboora—something like that. Hard to tell when you hear it from the natives. I can tell you where it is, though. It lies around a hundred and fifty degrees longitude by eight degrees south latitude."

The preciseness of the information and the fact that he was willing to name other witnesses, at least one of whom could probably be reached—the one in the Fiji jail—gave his story considerably more credibility. I began to listen with serious interest, taking notes as I went.

The island, Donahue said, contained two small native villages on the site of an abandoned coconut plantation which had once belonged to an Australian named Medwick. One village contained about 200 people, the other about 65. Also living on the island were a couple of Japanese fishermen—holdovers from the war—probably deserters from the imperial forces.

One of these Japanese, who had worked for Donahue as a packer, offered to show the three smugglers a white man who was living secretly on the island, captive of the villagers. After reassuring themselves that the man the Japanese described was unarmed and was not a missionary or government agent, the three smugglers agreed to see him. They were led to a thatched hut on stilts, similar to the others in the village, though a bit neater and better kept. The hut was at the outer edge of the village but, other than that, undistinguished in design from the rest of the native dwellings. The Japanese called into the dark thatched doorway: "Mastah, men here to see you!" From the hut emerged a tall, fair, long-haired white man with a long sandy beard. The man was dressed only in a native pareu of red trade cloth. He hobbled painfully, apparently barely able to walk. His right knee joint was swollen as big as a cantaloupe. His left leg below the knee had apparently been broken and set so badly, Donahue said, that he could see the bone pressing against the flesh.

"The man was excited, I could see that," Donahue said. "He was squinting at us something fierce. I reckoned he had real bad eyes, but even at a distance he could tell we were whites by our clothing."

The bearded figure struggled toward the visitors, extending his hand.

"I am Michael Rockefeller. Can you help me?"

The three Australian smugglers were shocked and excited. They brought food, tobacco and supplies from their cache and sat down with the stranded famous heir.

"How did you get here? We're more than a thousand miles from where you were lost," Donahue said.

Rockefeller, according to Donahue, told the following story:

Afraid that the catamaran on which he was drifting with René Wassing would be swept farther and farther out to sea, he decided to swim for land while it was still in sight. He tied the two fuel cans to him as floats, launched into the water, and headed for the trees he could see on shore in the distance. After what he estimated to be about six hours he reached the tree line, only to find that he was in a practically impenetrable mangrove swamp. Walking along the shore was impossible because of impassable deep soft mud, so Rockefeller had set off inland, wading and climbing over the mangrove roots which formed man-high labyrinthine tangles almost impossible to penetrate. This also checked with my knowledge of the shoreline of southern New Guinea which I had last seen twenty-five years earlier when I made a short patrol with ANGAU—the Australia New Guinea Administrative Unit which handled civil government affairs in those days. Our mission then was to visit native settlements along the coasts and collect fresh fruit and vegetables for the hospitals. As a result, I had had a chance to examine a good bit of the shoreline first hand.

Rockefeller spent several days crawling through the mangroves in hope of making some contact with the native population. At night he would climb high into the trees to sleep to stay out of reach of the sea snakes and saltwater crocodiles that infested the area. After several nights like this he was exhausted. Then, one night, a rotten bough on which he was perched suddenly gave way. Rockefeller fell out of his tree, landing with the branch between his legs. The impact broke both limbs below the knee. At this point, Rockefeller was certain that his desperate attempt to reach help had ended in disaster. He fainted from pain, and the next thing he could remember was being lifted, in enormous anguish, into a native dugout canoe. It appeared that some time after his fall from the tree a headhunting party in canoes had come upon him lying in the mangroves. They had heard rumors of the search and knew that this white man was "big medicine." A valuable capture, but they apparently had no intention of harming him. They made him as comfortable as possible in the bottom of the long dugout canoe, for a journey which Rockefeller understood from sign-language conversation would take several days. At this point he could only think of the horrible pain in his broken legs, which had been bound in leaves in native fashion.

After several days of paddling, just as they seemed in reach of the natives' home village, the canoe party was intercepted by a headhunting party of another tribe. There was a fierce bow and arrow battle, and many of the natives were killed. During the fight Michael was captured by the new group.

These natives, it appeared, were from an area near the Trobriand Islands far to the northeastern end of New Guinea, about 1,500 miles from the point where Rockefeller disappeared. I questioned Donahue on this.

"It was plenty far, but these particular natives are famous through the Pacific as being great sailors. Also, they cut off some of the distance by crossing the neck of the Vogelkop, you know—where it gets real narrow."

I knew that New Guinea was divided by a high range of mountains running east to west which ranged in height up to nearly 17,000 feet. The island is roughly in the shape of a giant bird with its head to the west toward Indonesia. I knew that the mountains ended some time before they arrived at what the Dutch called the Vogelkop—or Birdshead. But I also knew that the terrain was extremely rough, and it seemed doubtful that the natives could drag their heavy dugouts overland across this narrow neck, as Donahue claimed he had been told.

Donahue shrugged at my doubts. "If you check your map, you'll see that it is all practically sea-level swamp there. I know the area well. These natives use outriggers, and when they can't paddle anymore, they flop the canoes, trapping air under them, to lug them through the marshy sections."

The details sounded authentic, though I knew little

about this aspect of native travel. Donahue continued Rockefeller's story (as he claimed to have heard it) .

The journey with his new group of captors took four or five months, not an unusual voyage according to Donahue. Rockefeller soon grew to understand that the natives were not going to kill him. They had by now heard rumors of the big search for the missing heir. They didn't understand it completely, but they felt that anyone who could cause such excitement must be "big bottle"—very valuable, since he commanded important magic.

New Guinea natives in general do not have an organized religion. They do not believe in a god or even in a pantheon of gods. Their religious ideas are more involved with magic, sorcery and a belief in the existence of spirits in various objects—in their canoes, their houses, their weapons, their art, also in nature in the animals, trees, in the sea and rivers and in the mountains. All these were occupied by spirits which could be propitiated or defeated by magic. The possession of the missing white man, the natives felt, would add enormously to their magic power over the spirit world.

Eventually Rockefeller and the war party reached the island where Donahue found him. Medwick, the planter who formerly owned the island, had returned to his home in Townsville, Australia, several years earlier, and the last missionary had also left about a year before, so the island was completely in the hands of the natives. It was out of the way and, as Donahue claimed, almost never visited by passing ships—which at any rate were few. No planes ever flew over this area either, so the hope of signaling for a rescue was slight.

The natives, Rockefeller allegedly told Donahue, treated him well. They removed all his possessions, including his much-needed eyeglasses, and kept him in a special *haus tambu*, or magic house; but they fed him well, according to native standards, on taro, yams, fish and coconut. In a sense, Donahue said Rockefeller told him, the natives had been right. Young Rockefeller possessed a certain amount of knowledge which in native eyes was "magic." He knew how to weave cloth, an art unknown on the island, and some techniques of native carving, which he had learned on the Asmat coast. These he taught to the villagers to whom he became something of an honored figure. He was treated well and with dignity except that whenever it appeared a boat might pull into the island, he was hidden in the nearby jungles.

The island itself, said Donahue, was only a few miles long and completely off the track of even far-ranging trade boats.

Rockefeller himself, apart from his still painfully mangled legs, was in fair condition, he told the smugglers. There were sores on his ankles, though, and he suffered from jungle rot on his feet, in his groin and behind his ears. (Here again Donahue struck a familiar chord. I remembered having been troubled with residual tropical fungus like that for more than ten years after leaving the islands.) Rockefeller complained as well of suffering from chronic dysentery. The smugglers offered him what medicines they had. They also offered him reading matter—paperback books which they had aboard their boat—but Rockefeller pointed out that since he had lost his glasses, it was impossible for him to read.

The three smugglers, while sympathetic toward the stranded white man, were preoccupied with their own problems. They were in a hurry to get going. Remaining even a day or an hour too long in one place greatly increased the danger that they would be spotted by a Royal Australian Navy patrol, though few passed that way.

Rockefeller pleaded with them to take him along, but they refused. All three felt, Donahue told me, that the risk of being slowed down by the presence of the handicapped American would be too great.

"We knew that we couldn't even be seen near a harbor within thousands of miles of the area without risking arrest on the murder charges. We would have liked to help the kid, but it was just too chancy."

The three men explained as gently as they could that as soon as they possibly could do so, they would get word to the authorities to come to Rockefeller's rescue, but he in turn had to understand that this might take some time since the risks were great for Donahue and his friends.

I wondered, as Donahue told me this, if the three fugitives weren't guarding their secret in hopes that they could in some way profit from it.

Donahue, Lang and Jeffries left Rockefeller dimly hopeful with vague promises of help. They were not to see him again for almost one and a half years.

The three men really felt that there was no way to report on their find without risking capture. For the next fourteen months they continued their traffic in contraband, and Jeffries finally was caught smuggling alcohol into the Fiji Islands and sentenced to several years in jail. He was deeply concerned that while in jail his connection with the murder of the Dutch patrol officer and the native constables would be revealed.

Lang and Donahue, the swarthy Tasmanian said, had ultimately put into Rockefeller's island again within the past ten weeks. They found Rockefeller more or less in the same condition in which they had left him, except that he complained that his eyesight was getting worse. The two men offered to leave him with knives and tobacco. Rockefeller refused the knives. He said that they would be taken from him anyway, because of both their potential danger as weapons and their great value to the natives.

"A man with four knives is reckoned a rich man in that village," Donahue said. Again Rockefeller pleaded with the two men to get word to authorities, and again they promised that they would do what they could.

Shortly after this visit, Donahue said he had left the island and headed for America. In New York he had seen a copy of *Argosy* which carried our story on the Rockefeller disappearance. As a result, he had come to me.

Donahue's yarn was certainly an intriguing one, and in many ways convincing. His familiarity with New Guinea seemed undeniable. His willingness to name names was impressive. Questioned about his own background, he said that he had been born in Burnie, Tasmania, a notoriously tough town on the island lying just south of Australia. His nickname he said was Bluie (this seems to be the nickname of one out of two Australians. The other one is usually Snow). In addition to the murder charge and various smuggling charges, Donahue said, he was wanted for breaking out of a Tasmanian jail.

"If I'm ever caught—well, that'll be it. I'll never see daylight outside of the nick again. I'm not about to get caught, not even for Rockefeller."

"Why are you telling me all this anyway?" I asked.

"Listen, I have been nothing but a criminal all my life. I just thought I would help someone else for once. Besides, I promised the kid."

"If you turn in this information, you probably could make a deal to have the charges against you dismissed or at least reduced."

"Listen, mate, they got so much on me in so many different countries that if one country was to spring me, another one would grab me. There's no hope if any of those blokes ever lay hands on me."

"The Rockefellers would pay you a fortune for this information," I said.

Donahue looked nervously about the bar in which we were talking.

"Look, just forget about all that. I don't need no reward, and I'm not hanging around here much more either. I could get nailed right here as well as anyplace else. I don't give a blast what you do with the info. I promised to turn it over, and that I've done."

He started to get up from the table, but I held him back.

"Wait, I have to have more details. What were the full names of your pals Jeffries and Lang?"

Donahue shook his head. "I shouldn't have told you *that* much about them. I ain't telling any more. Tell you what, though. You want to check on my story—I'll give you the names of two blokes in the Royal Australian Navy Constabulary who had the job of chasing us."

This seemed to me to be an important point.

"Once in a while we would run into them—even have a drink, when we knew we were clean and they couldn't nab us. They knew us real well—of course, that was before the murder rap. Once we were even picked up for questioning about the Rockefeller kid during the search for him."

"What are the names of the men?"

"Well, the commanding officer was a bloke named Donaldson. Don't remember his first name. The other one was O'Hara—they called him Big Jack O'Hara—he must be about six three. I suppose his right name might be John—never asked him. I tell you what, you can find out more about the island where we found the kid from Medwick. I'll give you his address—it's 14 Burns Road in Townsville."

I wrote down the information, growing excited in spite of myself because of Donahue's apparent willingness to give specific checkable details.

I asked how he thought we should go about the job of rescuing Michael Rockefeller.

"You'd have to be plenty careful. The natives are suspicious of strangers. Might even be dangerous. Best way would be to get Medwick to go back in with you. They know him—even treated him as a kind of king. He was there for a long time, and I reckon quite a few of those natives today are his kids. He's been in a few tricky operations, though. Might be a little cautious himself."

"Smuggling?" I asked.

"Let's just say that he was friendly to some of us, and we did a few things for him. But a lot of the officials wouldn't have too many nice things to say about old Medwick. He was a regular king on that island when he lived there. Made his own law. Had a shotgun, and wouldn't let nobody land if he didn't like 'em."

I asked if he could tell me any more about the island.

"Not much. I know it was a mail drop once. Maybe the postal officials could help. But you'll find it all right, with those map coordinates. They're pretty close." Donahue made to leave.

I pleaded with him to stay. There was still so much information I needed if I was to act on his story. But he refused.

"I can't stick around no more. I'm taking a chance as it is."

"Do you have any more information that will help us if we try to go ashore on the island?"

"If you can't get Medwick, O'Hara and Donaldson might be a help with an armed party. But then you'd risk having the natives kill the kid before you could get to him. They consider him a very valuable property, and they'd fight before they'd give him up. No telling what those rock apes would do.

"You gotta realize these are primitive people. Regular Stone Age buggers. Get 'em riled and they'd kill you as soon as look at you and hang your head up on a pole in their huts. I ain't exaggerating, mate. You better be careful if you start fooling around down there. Them bastards would kill you without thinking about it if they thought they could get away with it.

"Only thing that keeps 'em in control is they're afraid of the white man's guns. And maybe a little scared of his magic. They hunt heads down there for—like prestige— you ain't a man, they reckon, unless you've taken the head of an enemy. You can check this out if you want. You'll find out I'm telling the truth.

"One other thing I can remember, the islanders called themselves by a family name that sounded like Kee-ut. Dunno how to spell it. The only name they have for themselves—I think it means just 'man.' They have a real simple life there. No radios or television, just sit around telling stories at night 'round the fire or singing these monotonous songs. Sometimes they start laughing like crazy, but I can never figure out about what. Women ain't nothing in their life. Men are the whole thing. A lot of times they even kill the girl children. The heads are important, and they will even steal heads in a raid on another village because the more heads a village has, the more magic power they have."

Donahue pushed his chair back. "I really got to go now."

"You headed for Brazil?" I asked.

He smiled tightly. "I'm not saying. Might be."

"Look, we could set up an ad—a blind ad in one of the English language newspapers down there. I could arrange that you could pick up a reward if anything happens out of this, without taking a chance of getting caught."

"Skip it. I ain't looking for no reward. This is just something I had to do, and now I'm going. Do what you want with the information. Stuff it for all I care."

And he swung off down Third Avenue before I could

finish settling the check. He had accepted from me only two cups of coffee. No lunch. No drinks.

I mulled over what he had told me. Much of it was plausible. I had studied little anthropology and was not deeply versed in the habits of Papuan natives, but almost all he said checked out against the fragmentary knowledge I had picked up during my wartime stay. As soldiers we had not had contacts with any of the really primitive tribes, but I had heard stories of headhunting and cannibalism in the interior. In general, my own contacts were with the relatively educated members of the Papuan Infantry Battalion who acted as scouts and sometimes carriers and laborers. Rumor in the Army camps, picked up mostly from the Aussies, was that the natives were too primitive even to learn to drive a car. (This was disproved in later years.) On Yule Island, while visiting the ANGAU mission there, I had been assigned a native "boy" named Warupi as my personal servant. In those days it was considered undignified for a white man to carry anything, even his own hat if he wasn't wearing it. Wherever I went, Warupi, dressed in a colorful lavalava and wearing a bright flower behind his ear, would follow, often stumbling through the slippery mountain paths with fifty pounds of bananas on his back while I walked unencumbered. No matter how late we stayed up— the Australian contingent and myself—Warupi would remain crouching in the shadows ready to guide me to my hut, arrange the mosquito bar, and fix my bedding. The moment I stirred in the morning he would be ready with a canteen cup full of tea and milk. Primitive as it was, I understood what life must have been like for the British colonials.

Aside from the Australian communications unit and the ANGAU civil government, the tiny island was dominated by a French Sacred Heart mission. I visited the local bishop (who was not too well liked by the Australians) and chatted with him in my high school French. As far as I could tell, he was strongly Pétainist in his sympathy and not interested in the war or who won it. He had, however, the only supply of scotch whisky and American cigarettes in the area.

The island was peaceful, but once, when I was chatting with Charlie Robinson, the keeper of the local trade store, I noticed that the natives who had come down the Angabunga River in canoes to trade for razor blades, files and other iron implements which were just beginning to lift them out of the Stone Age, had suddenly taken fright. They gathered their belongings in packs of tapa bark cloth and trade cloth and retreated hastily toward their canoes.

"What's happening, Charlie?" I asked.

"There's a rumor that Kukukukus are coming downriver. These blokes want to be out when they arrive. Might be a bit of bloodshed. Those Kukukukus are right mean fellows. Some scientific bloke who studied them once said he reckoned they were the meanest people in the world. I don't generally worry about these other ones here. They're simpleminded really. Fight a bit among the different villages but never bother me. I'm too valuable to them—keep them in iron and cloth and tobacco. But them Kukukukus, can't tell what those buggers will do. I always keep the shotgun ready for them. Let them see it, too. That's one thing that scares 'em." With that fragment in my memory, I found it possible to credit Donahue's warnings about the savage nature of some of the natives.

As carefully as possible I examined the Australian's story. Nothing in it sounded totally implausible. Even the wildly unlikely place he said Rockefeller was being held seemed too unusual to have been invented.

But before anything else I had to check out the verifiable

parts of Donahue's story and locate the island of Kanapua or Kanaboora on a map. One thing I knew: If by the remotest flight of fancy Donahue's story should actually be true, Michael Rockefeller would have to be found. And I was determined to be the one to do it.

2

DESPITE a certain skepticism, I wanted very much to believe Donahue's story. Still, I hardly knew how to go about describing this fantastic tale to Hal Steeger, my editor.

I thought at first that we should go directly to the Rockefeller family itself, but decided against this for two reasons: First, our original story by John Godwin, an Australian journalist who had been on the actual hunt for the missing heir at the time of his disappearance, had convinced me that the approach taken by the search team was not the right one and could jeopardize the project.

There had been too much ballyhoo and general excitement. Many people connected with the search felt that if the natives knew anything at all, they would have been frightened off by the sheer mass of the search effort. A more discreet approach was called for under the circumstances. Perhaps a small and circumspect party which could elicit information without alarming the local tribesmen. Presence of police and administrative authorities who had taken an active part in the search was often enough in itself to frighten the villagers into silence.

Accounts of the actual search showed that an operation on the scale of the massive hunt staged in eastern New

Guinea just after Michael's disappearance could not be conducted without word leaking out on the grapevine all over the territory. Not only would such publicity hamper the hunt, but it probably would endanger Michael's life, if what Donahue said was true.

Second, I knew from previous efforts that Governor Rockefeller had closed himself off from all further discussion of the subject. What I had from Donahue was intriguing, but it was far from definitive. I knew that I would need something much more conclusive before I could even get Rockefeller to listen to my story. How many similar tales and rumors must have been offered to him in the years since the disappearance of his son?

I returned to my office and typed every note I had and every detail I could remember and sent it to my editor, Hal Steeger, for his files, in case my copies got lost.

Then I went to the atlas to try to locate "Kanapua or Kanaboora" island. Not a sign of it. I had my secretary, Darlene Downing, call the Australian consulate in New York to request any information on an island of that name in the approximate location. If it was as small and little known as Donahue said, the fact that it was not in the atlas was not surprising. Meanwhile, I got busy checking out what I could of the rest of Donahue's story. We asked Australian authorities to find out what they could about the existence and whereabouts of Donaldson and O'Hara, the two RAN Constabulary men mentioned by Donahue. I tried to telephone Medwick on Townsville (where I had spent part of a convalescent leave during the war) , and when I discovered that there was no phone listed, I sent the following telegram:

MR. MEDWICK, 14 BURNS ROAD, TOWNSVILLE, QUEENSLAND, AUSTRALIA

IF YOU ARE THE PERSON WHO MANAGED A PLANTATION ON

Judging from hints given by Donahue, the lure of money should be effective.

Meanwhile, inquiries to the Australian naval attaché in Washington had turned up some exciting news. There *were* two men answering Donahue's description in the Royal Australian Navy. The man described as Donaldson was Sub-lieutenant M. G. Donaldson—he was stationed aboard the HMAS *Lae*—then cruising off the Madang area of New Guinea!

Madang I knew well since it had been one of the principal air targets programmed by the Fifth Air Force. It was on the north shore of New Guinea, about 300 or 400 miles from the Trobriand Islands where Donahue alleged Rockefeller was being held.

Big Jack O'Hara was identified as a J. S. O'Hara aboard HMAS *Melbourne,* care of GPO Sydney.

The fact that these men *existed,* and particularly that Donaldson was at that moment in the actual area, supported at least part of the Tasmanian smuggler's story. This was obviously not information that Donahue could have easily picked up from Sydney newspapers or other sources outside New Guinea. It was unlikely that such obscure details could be learned without his having visited the area—and fairly recently.

Meanwhile, I was trying to find detailed maps of the Trobriand Islands area, but with little success. A check of the map I had *did* show that the neck of the Vogelkop was roughly at sea level and extremely swampy as Donahue had said. Also, in looking up information about the Trobriand

Islanders, I discovered that they had been described as the "Argonauts of the Western Pacific" by the pioneering anthropologist Bronislaw Malinowski. This too checked with Donahue's statement that the island people were fantastic long-distance sailors. In the port area of New York near South Ferry I found a map company which could supply the maps I wanted but needed several days for delivery. Meanwhile, I sent duplicate telegrams to O'Hara and Donaldson:

WE ARE PLANNING TO SEND A MAN TO DO SOME MAGAZINE STORIES IN YOUR AREA. COULD YOU CALL ME COLLECT AT YOUR CONVENIENCE IN NEW YORK CITY? I AM PARTICULARLY INTERESTED IN AN ISLAND CALLED KANABOORA OR KANAPUA AT 150.05 DEGREES LONGITUDE, 8.20 DEGREES SOUTH LATITUDE. DID A MAN NAMED MEDWICK OWN A PLANTATION ON THIS ISLAND? MY INFORMATION COMES FROM A MAN NAMED JOHN DONAHUE WHO TELLS ME THAT HE IS WANTED BY AUTHORITIES IN YOUR AREA. IS THIS TRUE?

MACHLIN
ARGOSY

There was no answer to either cable. There was, however, an answer to the cable to Medwick. Western Union said our cable had been UNDELIVERED FOR FOLLOWING REASON: STREET ROAD UNKNOWN.

So that was a cold trail too, but not necessarily a contradiction of Donahue's story. I then had the following advertisement placed in all newspapers serving northeastern Queensland:

MEDWICK—Information wanted concerning a man named Medwick, first name unknown, who operated a plantation for many years on one of the islands in the

Trobriand Group and reportedly retired to Townsville about ten years ago. This will be to his advantage.

While waiting for answers, and for my maps, I called René Wassing, the Dutch anthropologist who had accompanied Rockefeller and had been on the catamaran when Rockefeller disappeared. I was able to reach him by phone in Rotterdam, but he said little more than that Rockefeller had been a good swimmer, and it was possible that he reached shore—but if so, Wassing knew nothing about it.

Finally the map I wanted arrived—prepared by the Army Map Service, Corps of Engineers, U.S. Army, and revised by the Royal Australian Survey Corps "from all available source material and limited field work."

In the area marked Lusancay Islands and Reefs, just east of 150.01 longitude and just south of the blue line for 8.04 south latitude was a tiny island called Kanapu. A few miles away was another slightly larger island called Kanapa.

Knowing how such names are often twisted or mispronounced or have local variants, I had felt it likely that Kanapu was the island Donahue referred to. Furthermore, as he had said, it was remote from any population center and was very close to the coordinates he had given me.

I was beginning to feel I really would have to go on the hunt. The fact that the two Navy people were apparently real and that one of them was more or less in the area was persuasive. The existence of the island was even more so.

If I should go, a logical step would be to try to talk to Jeffries, supposedly in jail in Fiji. I felt that by some ruse or another it might be possible to get further information from him if I could see him in private or at any rate to get confirmation for the information I had. I even considered blackmailing Jeffries into telling what he knew by threatening to reveal his connection to the alleged slaying of the Dutch patrol officer. I wrote to L. G. Usher, editor of the *Fiji Times,* giving what details I had on Jeffries and asking his assistance in locating the smuggler. No person of that name was known, Usher replied, and no cases of alcohol smuggling had been reported recently in his paper. So that was also a blind alley. Not likely, anyway, that Donahue would have given straight information on this. Before he left me I had asked one final question:

"Is John Donahue your real name?"

"I wouldn't lie to you about that, mate," he answered.

But I had a strong feeling that he *had* lied about that.

The question now was: If Donahue had been lying about Rockefeller, what was his motive? He hadn't accepted food or drink (I've known alcoholics who have made up more fantastic stories just to get a few shots). He hadn't even nibbled at hints of money or reward. I doubted that anyone would bother with such an elaborate hoax—or even if he would, that he could find such obscure information—especially the name and location of a flyspeck of an island that was only on the most detailed maps.

As for Donahue himself, I was almost positive that his name was an alias, but to double-check, I got in touch with Interpol, the international organization which collates information on criminals around the world.

Beyond this there was little more I could check—without going to the source itself: New Guinea.

Steeger, confronted with the provocative network of confirming information I had gathered, was definitely interested in following up the story. We had worked together for more than ten years, and he had backed other extensive expeditions—two to Vietnam, one to Taiwan, several to Cuba, one to Israel, one or two to Yucatán, one to the Philippines and Japan.

By now we had decided that if Donahue's story turned

out *not* to be true, my next step should be to go to the actual village from which Rockefeller had taken his last voyage and try to find out what actually *had* happened to him. In preparation for this I contacted the Indonesian consulate in New York and explained to the consul, Joop Ave, that I wanted to charter a boat or plane from Port Moresby to proceed to Merauke, the former Dutch government outpost which had been used as the base for the Rockefeller search, and from there proceed to Agats, the village from which Michael had departed.

This was less simple than it sounded. Since Rockefeller's disappearance, and even several years before, the Indonesian government had been agitating to attach western New Guinea as a sort of *terra irridenta*. In the fifties the acquisition of this huge Stone Age island territory had become an emotional obsession with Sukarno and his supporters on the grounds that Indonesia, as it was formed after its separation from the Netherlands, was supposed to comprise all the Dutch East Indies. But Dutch New Guinea had not been included. The Dutch in the fifties had been working on a plan to grant gradual independence to western New Guinea and then, with the cooperation of the Australians, to merge the whole island into one independent state. But growing Asian and African political support for Sukarno's plan to cede the territory to Indonesia thwarted this. When Sukarno forced an ultimatum, the Dutch had to yield since the United States, Great Britain and the United Nations all refused to intervene. So in 1962—one year after Rockefeller's disappearance—the Dutch signed an agreement to turn the territory over to the United Nations for administration. A year later the territory was ceded to Indonesia with the understanding that by 1969 the population of West Irian would be allowed what was described as "an act of free choice" to decide whether or not they would remain part of Indonesia. But the way the Indonesians saw it this was not to be exactly a plebiscite. Instead 1,025 Indonesian-appointed representatives of the 800,000 known people living in the territory would have "consultations" with Indonesian officials. The preparations for this "act of free choice" were going on as I made my pitch for a special visa to enter West Irian.

What I had not known when I first approached the Indonesians was that a *special* permit to enter West Irian—or Irian Barat as the Indonesians now call the former Dutch New Guinea—was as likely to be granted as a Papuan passport to the moon. During the existing political turmoil, and in fact since 1965, the Indonesians had not been letting *anybody* from the foreign press—and few foreigners of any sort—into Irian Barat. The only exception was in 1968 when four Australians, closely escorted by Adam Malik, the Indonesian foreign minister, were allowed a brief but revealing look at the capital—Djayapura. (Djayapura had formerly been named Sukarnapura, and earlier Hollandia. Its name metamorphosed with the political tides.)

Mr. Ave said that the only port of entry to Indonesia was Djakarta, but that he would get in touch with the capital and find out what he could do about my plan to enter at Merauke instead. While awaiting his answer, I was informed by other sources that it would be a cold day in Djayapura before I ever got a permit to go there either from Djakarta or anyplace else. Going to Djakarta to enter Irian Barat from Port Moresby would take me about 4,000 miles out of the way. At this point things looked very black for getting into the area from which Rockefeller actually disappeared. The letter I received shortly afterward did little to brighten my hopes.

DEAR MR. MACHLIN,
    As per your request by telephone to send a cable requesting special permission to enter West Irian directly

38

from Port Moresby in a chartered plane, I herewith would like to confirm our telephone conversation.

As I anticipated before to you, the regulation still requires Djakarta as a port of entry for persons desiring to visit West Irian.

I have explained also that at present all planes Djakarta–West Irian are heavily booked.

For that reason the possibilities of visiting West Irian will be decided upon by Djakarta in Djakarta.

Fully cognizant of these facts you have decided to take the chance, and I sincerely hope that you will succeed.

May I wish you a very pleasant journey and stay in Indonesia.

JOOP AVE
Consul

I decided that this was one bridge I could jump off when I got to it. Besides, I had an alternate scheme for getting to the village which involved the pearl fishermen of Thursday Island off the northern tip of Australia, but I felt that this plan should wait until I got to Sydney, which was my staging area for New Guinea.

Just about this time a story under a two-column head appeared in the New York *Post* which had a distinct bearing on my plans:

WAS ROCKY'S SON
KILLED BY NATIVES?

SAN LUIS, the Philippines (AP)—A Dutch priest who led searches for Michael Rockefeller in New Guinea in 1961 said he is certain the son of the governor was slain by natives in retaliation for the killing of four tribesmen by Dutch officials. The Rev. Corneles Van Kessel said that he became convinced of the fate of the 23-year-old anthropologist about a month after he was officially declared missing and presumed dead. . . .

39

The priest, now attached to the Dutch Sacred Heart mission in this remote village on Mindanao Island, said he believes Rockefeller was found dazed in shallow water by Otsjanep tribesmen in dugout canoes and was killed immediately.

"The tribesmen had killed him as revenge for the senseless killing of four of their brothers by some Dutch officials," he said. "Those men were innocent and they were shot to death for no reason. That was nearly four years earlier, and the tribe never forgot." . . .

He said that he had made a written report to his bishop who passed it on to the top Dutch official in Southern New Guinea.

"But the officials denied it," the priest said, "because they were ashamed. They were afraid it would be learned why Michael was killed."

I was puzzled by the story. It seemed to be given little credence by the other New York newspapers or newsmagazines, none of which carried a line on the subject. Up to a point it actually supported Donahue's theory—in that it stated that Michael swam ashore and had been intercepted by natives. But suppose he *hadn't* been killed, as Van Kessel indicated, but had been captured as Donahue claimed? I wrote to Father Van Kessel in care of his bishop in the Philippines. It would not be hard for me to detour via the Philippines on my return from New Guinea, should I not, in fact, find Rockefeller. Among the questions I asked in the letter was: "What is your opinion of the possibility that the young man was kept alive?"

On February 12, 1969, I arrived at Kennedy International Airport to find it paralyzed and blanketed under two feet of snow! Two hectic days later I was on my way to Sydney.

3

SYDNEY WAS glistening in its summer sunshine when I arrived. It was a vivid contrast with the dowdy wartime city I had known in 1943, when I arrived en route to New Guinea for the first time. With its bridges and old but brightly painted buildings against a background of modern skyscrapers it reminded me very much of San Francisco—without the fog.

I planned to be off for New Guinea in less than a week, the time I estimated I would need to purchase supplies for the trip and check out some details.

At 9 A.M., a few minutes after I had checked into the Chevron Hotel in the Kings Cross section of Sydney, I phoned Jim Anderson and told him to come right over. Jim was an American expatriate I had picked to be my cameraman. He was at the hotel about a half hour later—he was a tall, rangy Kansan with a Midwest accent as thick as mom's apple pie. Jim had at this point been photographing the Pacific area from New Zealand to New Guinea for five years. During that time, though he was already in his midtwenties, he had run afoul of his U.S. draft board, which had demanded that he report to Guam at his own expense for a physical. Anderson had replied that he would be happy to come at the Army's expense or to submit to an examination at U.S. facilities in Australia. The exchange grew confused and acrimonious until Anderson resolved it all by giving up his U.S. citizenship to become a full-fledged Australian.

41

It turned out that Anderson was a perfect choice for the job. He had already been to New Guinea at least four times and was in fact in the course of preparing a book on the island. As a result, he had many valuable contacts and a very good knowledge of the field requirements for the trip.

I reviewed my notes completely with him, and we began to plan our logistics in detail. Jim agreed to draw up a full list of our needed supplies and to make inquiries on travel and hotel arrangements. Reservations for hotel space had to be well in advance, he warned me.

"You mean they have *hotels* in Port Moresby now?"

"Port Moresby *is* civilized, and so are Madang and Lae and Wewak," Jim said, "but when you get out in the boonies, where we're heading, you'll find it's all the rough you want."

I mentioned that I had read that in some parts of New Guinea cannibalism still existed. Was this true?

"You bet your sweet ass. Government guys will tell you it's all over, but I was on a patrol up in Nomad only a few months ago where they had never seen more than a couple of white fellows before, and I want to tell you the *purpose* of that patrol was to put a stop to cannibalism."

The present-day structure of New Guinea, Jim explained, involved a dozen or so frontier towns connected only by air or sea. Between them stretched thousands of square miles of mountain and bush, most of it impenetrable. We would need a full kit of camping gear—tarpaulins for shelter, cooking gear, machetes, camp cots, mosquito nets and so forth.

"What about guns?"

Jim shook his head. "Can't bring 'em in. I have a pistol I may try to ship in. It might get by customs. I'd sure like to have it. Other than that, tear-gas pistols might be a good show. They're permitted, and they could come in handy."

In New York I had acquired a list of names—people who

42

might be useful—from some of my friends in the Australian press. One of the most important was Stewart Inder, editor of the *Pacific Islands Monthly,* the most highly respected and authoritative publication in the islands.

Another was Keith Willey, feature writer and reporter for the Sydney *Morning Herald* who had written a book about his travels in New Guinea called *Assignment New Guinea.*

I was most anxious to see if I could pick up the trail of Donahue and of some of the people he mentioned.

Inder was my first stop. He generously opened his files to me and had members of his staff pull out dozens of back issues containing stories about the cargo cult, about Trobriand Island customs, and some pieces about the search for Rockefeller. Without revealing my entire purpose I tried to find out what he could tell me about Kanapu. It was one place that he had never heard of and that he doubted existed. When I pointed it out to him on the map, he could only comment that he had never been there, nor had he ever heard any talk of anybody's having been there. (So, I thought, it is *possible* that someone could exist there without the knowledge of the outside world.)

"The person who has been to every island in the group and knows more than any man in the area—or as much—is Tim Ward. He also runs the guesthouse on Kiriwina and owns the only trade boat in the islands. You'll have to charter a boat from him if you want to get out there in the Luscanays. There is no other means of transportation—no scheduled boats and no airstrips outside Kiriwina."

"What about people?"

"Several of the islands have small villages of at most a few hundred people, nothing much really. A lot of them never see an outside person for two or three years at a time."

I asked if he had ever heard of a man named Medwick—a planter who lived in that area.

43

Inder thought for a while. "I don't really recall such a man, though there is something familiar about the name."

"What about smugglers? Do you think they might come through that area—maybe use one of the islands for a base?"

"Well, it's certainly in the channel they often use."

Another point for Donahue.

Next I outlined to him Donahue's career. "Do you think I might be able to get some background on such a man?"

Inder seemed puzzled. "I think I would have heard about it if a Dutch patrol officer had been killed, but we were not always in touch with what the Dutch were doing over there. I'll give you the name of a man who was in charge of the Australian Special Branch (the Australian equivalent of the FBI) down there. He certainly should know something about your man Donahue. I also think you're in luck with the Dutch side. The former secretary to the director of the Netherlands Department of Territories is in Sydney now. I'll put you in touch with him."

It took a certain amount of persuasion, with me promising not to reveal who helped me or how, to convince the Special Branch man to talk to me. But he had never heard of Donahue. He promised to search his files and get back to me.

Pat Loosjes, the former Dutch official, was not much more help. He did not know of any Donahue being sought for the murder of a patrol officer.

"I think I would probably have heard of such a crime, but not for certain."

"It is possible that such a crime could have been committed?"

"Yes, it is possible, but I don't remember it."

"Might your government still be looking for this man?"

"Oh, no. I am certain not. We have nothing to do with the territory anymore. If we caught the man, I doubt that we could even prosecute him. We no longer have jurisdiction."

This offered no encouragement, but it didn't rule out the possibility that Donahue's story was true. He could have covered his own tracks with a fictional or semifictional account.

Next, at Inder's suggestion, I went to see Peter Hastings, a highly respected writer for the reputable weekly *The Australian.* Hastings was also editor of the scholarly quarterly *New Guinea,* had been one of the four journalists who had been into West Irian with Malik since the Indonesian takeover, and is regarded as a top authority on the New Guinea area.

I asked him what he thought of Van Kessel's story that Rockefeller swam ashore and had been killed at the mouth of the Eilanden River. (I was still not anxious to reveal my own information—partly because, if true, it was too valuable to divulge. And partly because I was a bit afraid of being laughed at for my gullibility.)

Hastings was not receptive to the Dutch priest's report.

"I was there during the search. We flew over the area many times at low altitudes. You have never seen a place so infested with sharks and saltwater crocodiles. It would have been impossible for a man to swim through all that and live. Saltwater crocodiles are particularly vicious, you know."

"Then you are convinced he drowned before reaching shore or was killed by crocs or sharks?"

"I am just about certain of it."

This was a blow. Hastings packed a lot of authority.

That afternoon I got a call back from my man at the Special Branch. No record of anyone resembling Donahue could be found—by either name or description.

Still more discouraging news.

About this time I had an appointment with Keith Willey, who had also been on the search. The area in which Rockefeller was lost, the Australian newsman told me, was the third biggest swamp on earth.

"Is it possible that the Dutch priest is right?" I asked.

"There's a lot of unanswered questions in that Rockefeller story. I heard rumors that he had stirred up the natives to fight on his earlier trip to New Guinea and that several had been hurt or killed. As a result of this, he was asked to leave and warned not to cause trouble again. I know at least part of that is definitely true from other sources."

"What part?" I asked.

"Well, I know that some people were killed during Rockefeller's earlier stay, and I know that there was a complaint about the expedition and an investigation by Dutch authorities. I also know that several of the Dutch officials in the area weren't at all happy with Rockefeller's group. It's a confirmed fact that Rockefeller returned to the States—or was sent back—right in the middle of his stay in New Guinea. But he returned only about a week later. I reckon his dad may have pulled a few strings there."

"But why do you think that he might have been killed, rather than drowned?"

"The first stories hinting that Rockefeller might have been killed by cannibals began to leak out of the territory about a year after the hunt. That hunt was a fantastic scene too, if you can imagine seventy-five journalists or so plus officials and so forth in an area that had probably never seen more than a half dozen white men at once in its entire history. A priest named Willem Hekman, I hear, reported that tribesmen killed Rockefeller the minute he swam ashore."

"Then you think he *could* have swum ashore? Hastings says the crocs or sharks would have finished him first."

Willey gave me a quizzical look. "Those two native boys made it, didn't they?"

Finally, a ray of light!

"You'll hear a lot of rumors if you're going digging into this story. Some tribesmen even claim that a young warrior has been seen wearing a white man's skull around his neck."

"Do you believe it?"

Willey shrugged. "It's a strange country. Certainly there are men who still wear skulls around their necks for their magic powers."

"What are my chances for getting back in there?"

Willey laughed. "No chance at all, mate. If there were, I probably would have been up there again myself."

I had to be careful about what I said, because my plan could have been ruined by too much gossip in the wrong places.

"I hear that there are a lot of unemployed pearling luggers up at Thursday Island," I remarked casually.

I had decided that if I did not find Rockefeller on Kanapu Island, I would return to northern Australia and proceed to Thursday Island, a raffish community of pearl divers, fishermen and smugglers off Cape York on the extreme northeast tip of Australia—a short sail from the southern coast of West Irian. The pearling business had been terrible since plastic replaced real pearl as the major ingredient in buttonmaking. (The divers mostly were after the pearl shell. Actual pearls were regarded as a bonus.) There was a good chance that for a relatively modest fee I might persuade a pearling captain to run me into a certain inlet on the West Irian shore without having to secure a visa first.

I could see that Willey understood my hint. He smiled thinly.

"I'll give you a couple of names up at Thursday, but after that you're on your own. It could be a tricky business."

4

ANDERSON AND I spent the next few days rounding up camping equipment and motion-picture gear. There was not a wide choice in cameras, but we finally settled on a hand-wound Bolex H-16 and a Japanese-made electric motor-driven Doiflex. I decided that it would be a silly economy to run short of film, so we elected to take 10,000 feet with us.

Anderson had with remarkable industry acquired an assortment of aluminum packing cases, into which we put most of our perishable gear. Film was packed in insulated styrofoam eskimos. We spent a hectic couple of afternoons in Army-Navy surplus stores, where, in addition to camping necessities, we laid in a supply of trade goods for the natives —knives, axes, small files. For my personal kit I had tropical fatigues left over from my Vietnam tours, plus a trim and useful bush-jacket suit dubbed the "TV suit" in Saigon because it was comfortable enough to wear in the tropics, but neat and dashing enough for TV correspondents to wear on camera. Most important were hard-soled canvas-sided jungle boots which are essential footgear in the tropics. Unlike the boots I had worn in World War II, which were supposed to be waterproof but often produced a troublesome case of trenchfoot with the flesh peeling from the toes in onionlike layers, these were porous. They let water *in*, but they also let it out and provided enough air so that the feet would have a chance to dry out and be coolly ventilated.

48

On February 28 our Qantas jet finally lifted off for Moresby. As we flew into the island's only jet strip at Jackson's Drome, I had some momentary overviews of the postwar city of Port Moresby through the intermittent but heavy cloud layers which were to complicate our film exposures in the future. The first thing I saw was a sprawled-out city extending from Hanuabada, the native village which had been a thatch-hut stilt city, but was now a row of tin and fiberboard huts on piers, all the way out to the airport—some 16 miles of one- and two-story tin-roofed houses—and amazingly enough a Miami-modern eleven-story skyscraper in the center of town.

I had done some homework so that I knew the city had grown from a hot buggy colonial outpost of a few hundred white administrators and traders and a few thousand natives to a hot, buggy city of more than 42,000, about 25 percent Europeans. When I had last seen Moresby, it was the only place on the island that could really be called a city. Moresby in fact is the largest city in the Pacific outside Australia and New Zealand.

The harbor around which the city was built was not discovered until 1873 by the Englishman Captain John Moresby, who is also credited with having more or less mapped the true shape of the island for the first time. From about 1884 until the First World War, the eastern end of the island was divided between the Germans—who controlled the north—and the English, who had the south coast facing Australia. Meanwhile, almost by default, the Dutch, expanding from the Netherlands East Indies, had been able to maintain their control of the western half of the island from about 1828 until the Indonesian take-over in 1962.

None of the colonial rulers did much about developing these remote and primitive islands, and what they did do was largely confined to the easily accessible coastal areas.

The interior remained, as it remains to this day, a remote little-explored mystery. In early years it was so little known that explorers would bring back fanciful reports which were swallowed without a murmur of protest since there was no one to contradict them.

A Frenchman, Louis Tregance, wrote a book called *Adventures in New Guinea* in which he claimed he had been held captive for nine years by a tribe called the Orangwoks, which rode around on small yellow-striped ponies and protected themselves in combat with gold shields and breastplates. According to Tregance, the Orangwoks' king kept as pets two tigers tethered by a twisted gold rope in front of his palace, which was in a city that boasted houses six stories high.

An Englishman named Lawson claimed to have seen huge apes, a black, white and brown striped tiger, trees 80 feet around at the trunk, and a mountain 4,000 feet higher than Everest. (Carstensz Toppen in West Irian is New Guinea's highest peak at 16,500 feet. This hardly dwarfs Everest's 29,141 feet but is still a pretty high mountain. The central range which divides New Guinea has many peaks more than 14,000 and 15,000 feet in height, and most of the passes are at least 12,000 feet high.)

While there have been considerable exploration and research in the past fifty years or so, much still is unknown about the geography, people and history of this tropical subcontinent, mainly because of the fantastically rugged and mountainous terrain of the interior. This has resulted in a population so chopped up and isolated from one another that at least 700 separate languages are estimated to be spoken on the island.

So here was Port Moresby like a sort of tropical Dawson City, gateway to the unknown territories, steaming in the sun beneath us as our Qantas jet settled into the Jackson's Drome strip, beside which I could see the long, low modern

Gateway Hotel looking like nothing so much as a California motel.

As we descended from the air-conditioned plane, the outside heat hit us like a jet from a turkish bath steam nozzle. Though the hotel was only a quarter of a mile away, I was soaked with sweat by the time we got there. Fortunately Jim's experience and talent as an organizer saved us and our twenty-seven pieces of luggage from complete disaster. Anderson had made a complete list of the contents of each case and canvas bag and had labeled them all with giant letters from A to ZZ and listed their separate contents. Example: CASE N—*Extra duffle bag, 200 yards nylon rope, two water bags, one shower bucket, one five-gallon jerrican, one spare film tin, remote-control gear, spare flashlight, plastic sheets, one box .45 cartridges, Jim's jungle boots, canteen knife, haversack, compass, utility knife.* And there were twenty-six more similar cases. All in all we were 600 pounds overweight. Native bellhops in fuzzy Papuan hairdos and red lap-laps rushed to handle the imposing pile of luggage. To my amazement none could speak English, and only a few could even struggle along in pidgin.

It was also hard to get used to being called "Mastah!" I wondered how, with all the development and progress I could see had taken place, so little attention had apparently been paid to educating the people.

I had hardly settled into my air-conditioned room when the phone rang to say that a reporter was downstairs from the *South Pacific Post,* Port Moresby's English language newspaper. He had been alerted to our arrival by the Qantas public relations man who had greeted us at the airport.

David Kennedy, the reporter, acted as his own photographer. I decided that at this point it would not be a bad idea to leak the fact that I was interested in Michael Rockefeller, without necessarily telling all the details of Donahue's information, which in my mind I was beginning to associate

51

with the tales of the Frenchman Tregance and the Englishman Lawson.

The next edition of *South Pacific Post* carried a three-
column cut of me with a three-column headline and a
one-column cut of Jim.

It said in part:

> Mr. Machlin is in the territory for a minimum of a
> month [my first estimate of three weeks had long since
> been abandoned as unrealistic] with magazine photogra-
> pher Jim Anderson, 27.
>
> The team plans to make a feature film on the territory
> and compile a series of articles on the disappearance of
> Michael Rockefeller. . . .
>
> Mr. Machlin said he had a "new lead" on Rockefeller's
> disappearance. . . .
>
> Mr. Machlin smiled and said "no" he could not reveal
> what the new lead was. . . .

I wasn't sure whether or not it was overplaying my hand
to make these statements publicly, but I was hoping that
they might lead to unearthing new clues to our story, possibly right in Port Moresby.

5

OUR FIRST job was to get in touch with Tim
Ward at Kiriwina, largest island in the Trobriand group
and the only one with an airstrip, and find out when and
how we could get to Kanapu Island.

Already I could see my vision of dashing to the Trobriands, checking out Kanapu Island and returning in a few weeks was unrealistic. Nothing moved that fast in this outpost of Empire. For one thing, there was only one plane a week to Kiriwina. Once we got there, the only way to reach Kanapu would be by native canoe or by chartering the trade boat belonging to Tim Ward. We quickly found out that there was no direct telephone communication with Kiriwina, only a radio patch via Samarai, nearest sizable settlement, a small island off the extreme eastern end of the island. This was available only at certain rare hours of the day, so even getting to *talk* with Ward was a bit of a problem.

"You're not in the world now," said the manager of our hotel. "You're in New Guinea."

Donald Hogg, a New Zealand journalist working in New Guinea, was helpful in supplying us with leads.

He quickly hit on two topics which I felt were important in determining the fate of Michael Rockefeller: magic and revenge. Both, according to Hogg and to Jim Anderson, were still important motivating factors in native life. Despite the work of missions and government schools, belief in magic was widespread and ineradicable. And of all forms of magic to plague authorities in recent years, probably none has been more troublesome than a widespread set of local myths called the cargo cult.

Almost every artifact Papuans use in their society they make themselves from materials familiar and near at hand. Native houses are built of local substances; clothes are plucked from the trees. Food is grown in the garden or hunted. Weapons are fabricated by hand from local wood, bone and stone—as are tools.

Then suddenly the white man arrives with his alien and complex technology. Out of a small box made of some odd material comes the sound of human voices and weird music. The white man says he cannot explain exactly how this happens; he did not make the box himself and cannot explain how it is made, or so he says. But the canny native is not fooled or even terribly surprised. He already knows that the world operates by sorcery—or *sanguma*. Every object has its ruling spirit—the tree, the house, the table, the canoe. These spirits must be pleased or they will not help people. The weapons or the boats must be coaxed to perform by spells and sorcery, or they will not function properly. A sorcerer is a powerful man and will not easily yield his secrets to others.

The white people controlled many unknown spirits which provided them with boats that moved without paddles, "canoes" that traveled over the ground without being pulled or pushed, and huge birds that flew in the sky and carried in their bellies people and the white man's wonderful cargo—metals that cut better than any stone or shell, containers that made fire, clothes made of some strange fiber. Until recent times there was no knowledge in New Guinea of the wheel, of metals, of the art of weaving cloth or even of the art of fermenting alcohol, so obviously the way to have all these wonderful goods was to watch the white man closely and learn the secrets of his sorcery. This was what Donahue was driving at when he said that Michael was "big bottle"—an important source of magic to his captors.

This was the sort of thinking that originated the cargo cult, and it has led to serious troubles for the administration in recent years. Sorcery is, in fact, still at the base of everything in native life. No Papuan culture has been discovered that worships anything resembling a god or even a group of gods. There are no priests or holy men in New Guinea society—only powerful sorcerers. In the native mind no man dies a natural death; all people die from the bad spirits often controlled by hostile sorcerers. This gives rise to the other troublesome aspect of native belief: the custom called payback—or revenge.

Don Hogg gave an example of how this works in practice from an actual case recently heard before the Supreme Court at Wewak. A young girl related to a tribesman named Dinenyeng had hanged herself in the village. Even though she had committed suicide, the natives knew that evil spirits had been invoked to force her to take her life. It became the responsibility of the girl's closest relatives to discover the perpetrator of this bad magic. "Many men took sticks from the kilimdara tree and set off to find the person who made the sorcery," Dinenyeng told the patrol officer investigating the case. The men were sure the sticks would draw them to the house of the guilty sorcerer. "Some people gave up because their sticks did not become heavy, but my stick became heavy when I reached the house of a woman named Foias, and I marked her house with twigs."

The tribesmen were already suspicious of Foias, who had been suspected of having caused other deaths by sorcery. Dinenyeng felt it was up to him to avenge the girl's death. Foias was working with her small daughter in the village gardens as he took his six-foot-long black palmwood bow and sent three special arrows into her. His bowstring snapped then, and he beat the woman to death with his heavy bow. Dinenyeng told this all to the investigating patrol officer without any feeling of guilt. To him it was not murder but payback. "It was my duty to do something about it because I was the dead girl's nearest relative."

Dinenyeng was convicted and served fewer than two years in prison. If the government attempted to inflict more serious penalties, there wouldn't be enough space to hold the prisoners. Besides, the government realizes that you cannot suddenly make a death penalty offense of something that has been an honored tradition for generations.

Often the convicted men come back from jail as highly respected men—heroes who by spending time in the white man's jail have learned something of the mysterious ways of the whites, perhaps even something of his sorcery.

Then one morning we got word that Tim Ward was in Port Moresby. Of all the people we had so far met, it was agreed that Tim knew more about the islands where we had been told Michael Rockefeller was being held than anyone in the world.

6

WARD TURNED out to be a sturdy, surprisingly young-looking fellow, with a square Irish-Australian face bearing features reminiscent of Tyrone Power's. He told us he had started his career in northern New Guinea and New Britain as a forestry officer, then became interested in the possibilities of the Trobriands and acquired a rudimentary guesthouse at Gusoeta on Kiriwina, which he had expanded from a few primitive rooms to a sort of bush motel with twenty-two rooms and a swimming pool.

"I'd move easy on that Rockefeller story," he said, after a few scotches had bridged the gap of strangeness between us.

I asked if he had been around when he disappeared.

"I flew one of the planes in the search."

"And are you satisfied that he was drowned at sea?"

Ward shrugged. "I wouldn't want to say. But there's a lot more to that story than has been made public."

Ward's reaction echoed a number we had got from other

people in the territory. Nobody would say anything specific but would only hint at untold scandals and fear that "stirring things up" might lead to some mysterious form of reprisal from the powerful Rockefeller clan. I found increasingly that the legendary Rockefeller wealth produced an almost superstitious feeling of fear, even this far away from the seat of their power.

But most people in the territory indicated that *something* had happened that hadn't been reported.

Some thought that Rockefeller might have caused his own death by offering high prices for the human heads he was trying to collect for his museum. Others thought that Rockefeller had been captured by a tribe of natives encouraged into headhunting raids by the rising market in skulls. Others hinted that Michael had angered tribesmen by staging battle scenes which resulted in the death of several natives and had been in deep disfavor with the Dutch government. Still others hinted that the young adventurer, fed up with the restrictive life as scion of the Rockefeller clan, had deliberately run off into the bush and was alive and hiding in a native village.

There were rumors even wilder than that.

While by no means sure our version of Rockefeller's fate was the correct one, I preferred to make no judgment until I got more substantial evidence.

Without giving away our story I tried to get some points of confirmation from Ward. Was it true that the Trobriand Islanders were fabulous long-distance sailors?

"Best seagoing people in these islands."

He seemed surprised to learn we wanted to charter his trading boat to visit the islands. I told him we were interested in the Trobriand culture and civilization in its primitive state.

"Well, you'll find them unspoiled, and I suppose primitive, though they've been visited on and off by Europeans for about eighty years. There really aren't many people out there—just tiny villages of a few hundred at most. Usually the only outsider they see these days is me and my trading boat. Even the government blokes don't get out that way much, and judging from things I've read about the islands in the early days, their way of life hasn't changed at all. They need very little of what we have to offer them— just a few things I bring on the trade boat—iron tools, cloth, tobacco, maybe soap. But if I don't show up for a year or so, they can get along perfectly well, as they always have in the past. On the other hand, there isn't much out there to tempt the Europeans into exploiting them. About all they have to export is some copra and maybe a few wood carvings and artifacts."

Had he ever heard of the island of Kanapu or Kanaboora?

Ward was puzzled at first, but when I gave the map coordinates, he seemed to recall some idea of the place.

"It seems to me that there is a tiny island out that way called that—and another a few miles away called Kanapa. But I'm sure there is no one living on them. They're barely more than a half mile long or so. Why do you ask?"

I decided to drop still another veil from our story.

"A chap I met in New York named Donahue said that these places were used as hideouts and rest stops by smugglers heading toward the Fijis."

Ward looked interested. "You may be on to something there. Certainly there're smugglers and pirates all through these waters, and they come through that way quite a lot because it's away from any ship lanes—too much shoal water and too many reefs. Those are dangerous waters for larger boats if they don't know the area very well, and very few people do."

"Ever hear of a planter out that way named Medwick?"

58

Ward shook his head, although like the government official, he found the name vaguely familiar.

What about the trade boat? Was it available for charter to those outer islands?

"Well, she's out right now trading in the islands to the east of Kiriwina—out around Kitava. Won't be back for a week or so, but you could have her then."

The charter price seemed reasonable—$40 a day with crew and food—so we made the arrangement to fly to Kiriwina on the once-a-week Patair flight a week from the following Thursday. Then, if the *Beverly Mary*—Ward's boat, named for his wife—was in port, we could set sail for Kanapu.

"Funny thing about that island Kitava," Ward said after a while. "There was a planter there something like this Medwick you describe. They called him King Cameron because he was the bloody-well-king of that island. Had a big shotgun and wouldn't let let anyone land without permission. They say he had as many as sixteen native wives. Nobody knew for sure because damned few people ever got to find out much about what happened out there."

"What happened to him?" I asked.

"He died a couple of years ago. I think he left the whole bloody plantation to the natives. Most of them are probably his children anyway. But they've let it all go to pot now."

That night we picked up our copy of the current *South Pacific Post*. In it was a story of more than passing interest to us, headed "NO PLEASURE CRUISE FOR THE PROFESSOR; he's off to study the territory's coral reef chain."

The story reported that Professor Rhodes Fairbridge of Columbia University was heading an expedition to study reef life in the Louisiade Archipelago—exactly the area in which we hoped to find Rockefeller!

The article carried disturbing details:

59

An initial party of about eight will board a 42 foot power cruiser Lindalee at Kiriwina Island.

The Lindalee will skirt the Louisiade reefs, the Conflict group, Trobriand Islands and the Tagula and Rossel Islands.

. . . The 800 mile reef has never been scientifically explored or described . . . the reef expedition has been financed by the Columbia University. . . .

Considering the scarcity of Americans in the territory and especially the rarity of visits to the Trobriands by outsiders, I couldn't help thinking the visit of Professor Fairbridge's expedition was, to say the least, a huge coincidence. Was it possible that our friend Donahue had gone to others with his Rockefeller report and that they too had sent out a group with a cover story of a scientific expedition to check on it?

7

EARLY THE next morning we loaded our gear into a Patair DC-3 which looked as though it had been left over from the war. Its interior appointments consisted of plain pipe seats bolted to a bare wood floor and cargo strapped into the rest. There were two other passengers—Australians, apparently planning to visit relatives at the island's Catholic mission. Donald Hogg came down to see us off, and as we were chatting, he mentioned that the bones of a white man had been found some years before near the place where Rockefeller disappeared but that a team of investigators, including some medical men, had concluded that they had apparently belonged to some prospector who had wandered into the area. No information was available on the presumed cause of death.

We flew out, passing low over the Owen Stanleys past wartime memories of the Kokoda trail and Buna and then over the clear-green bright sea dotted with hundreds of tiny, often unmapped and uninhabited islands. The Trobriands, well known to students from the works of anthropologists like Margaret Mead and Bronislaw Malinowski, are a group of twenty-two islands off eastern Papua. They have 14,000 people, 12,500 of them in Kiriwina. Of this probably only about 25 are white—Catholic missionaries, government people and Tim Ward's small staff. Kiriwina itself is a flat island with just a tiny coral ridge for elevation, shaped like a pork chop with most of the activity at the meaty end. It is about 20 miles long—14 miles wide at its widest, but narrowing down to necks of land only a few hundred yards wide. In the center is an all-weather roughly paved strip left over from World War II, when a small party of Americans briefly occupied the island.

The islands have a romantic image among New Guinea people. They are considered the closest thing in Melanesia to the traditional tropical paradise of Polynesia. The population is mostly light brown in color, in contrast with the darker coloring of the mainlanders and the coal black of some of the islands of the New Hebrides to the East. The girls are reputed to be the most beautiful and good-natured in the New Guinea area, and their traditional garb—a topless mini-skirt of grass—does much to add to their image.

We put down expertly on the barren overgrown World War II airfield, where a crowd of excited natives and three or four small trucks awaited us. The field boasted no tower, no buildings in fact. The airport was just a strip laid out on the coral. Cargo doors were swung open, and lean brown-skinned islanders quickly swarmed aboard to unload the eagerly awaited cargo from Moresby.

The guesthouse run by Tim Ward and his wife, Beverly, was a twenty-minute ride over dirt roads and a few crumbling remnants of wartime roads. The "hotel" turned out to be a long low building of wood, woven pandanus leaves and palm thatch, decorated with Trobriand Island carvings, shells and painted designs. It reminded me of the setting of a Somerset Maugham story.

Ward came out to direct the unloading of supplies. After exchanging warm greetings, I asked if he had any idea where the Fairbridge group was.

Tim waved vaguely seaward. "Out there somewhere. They managed to get a boat somehow, though how I don't know. Had to have terrific pull with the government to get an OK to charter that launch."

"Where did they say they were headed?"

"Out to the Sim-sims to look at the reef, though I can't guess what for. It's over toward your island, Kanapu, by the way."

I wondered whether it wouldn't be a good idea to reveal the whole story to Tim, since delicate diplomacy might be required in approaching Kanapu. Could we prevent the local people from hiding Rockefeller when they saw us? Donahue had spoken of danger. Should we have weapons or an escort? Ward suggested a chat in his private office after the supplies were unloaded.

"There's somebody here I've been talking to about your story, and he's interested to have a full report," he said as we settled into our rattan chairs. "I wonder if you could summarize that stuff about the smuggler."

"There's a bit more to it than I told you, Tim." And I sketched in the rest of the details—the Rockefeller angle which I hadn't hinted at in our first interview in Moresby.

Ward listened with keen interest, not interrupting until I was through.

When I had finished, he took a long pause, collecting his thoughts.

"Look," he said, "there's something very strange about all this. I could tell it when I chatted with you back in Moresby. I haven't ever been to this Kanapu Island, but I've anchored near it during some of my trading trips out that way on the *Beverly Mary*. It was usually dusk when we anchored, and several times we saw the lights of another ship, but when we hailed it and tried to approach, it slipped away."

"Who do you think it was?"

Ward shrugged. "Might be lots of people who didn't want to be seen, though there are damned few ships around this area. It's not on any shipping lane, and there are so many reefs and shoals that it's bloody dangerous for anybody who doesn't know the waters. Might have been smugglers. Might even have been a Chinese ship spying on our satellite experiments. A lot of the satellites orbit over here."

"What about Rockefeller?"

Ward looked thoughtful.

"I wouldn't say it was *impossible*, but I really don't think so. Your man Donahue was after something, or he had something in mind. The Rockefeller idea was just a decoy, I reckon."

"Why do you say that?"

"Well, in the first place, while it's true that these people are considered fantastic sailors—argonauts of the Western Pacific—they really don't sail *that* far. To go up to the Vogelkop—that's more than a thousand miles from here. These chaps normally sail mostly on a regular, practically ritual circle—it's called the Kula trading ring. It's been extensively written up—but to my knowledge they never sail out of this area. Also, they are not headhunters—never have been as far as I know. Nor cannibals either, though you wouldn't have to go far to find some who *have* been. Dobu Islanders were once cannibals, and they're almost as near to Kanapu as we are. Still, those days were over long ago in this territory.

"Also, your island is too small. I reckon it's less than a half mile long. There isn't any plantation on it. No room, though there are some copra palms. In that respect, there are a couple of islands with small villages which would be more likely. Your man has been around here all right. He knows the territory. It sounds as though he purposely jumbled up all the facts enough to be plausible to an outsider, but I wonder why."

I wished I knew. I asked about the possibility Rockefeller was being kept alive for magic purposes.

Tim shook his head.

"The magic's here all right, and nobody who's lived here long laughs at it. I've seen some very strange things myself. But I don't believe they would try to hold a European for that reason. Also these islands are small, and the local people aren't famous for their ability to keep secrets. I can't believe that there could be a white man living on any of these islands for all these years without rumors leaking out. Sure, there *have* been a couple of Japanese found holing up from time to time, but somebody almost always talks."

"Then you think the trip is useless?"

"Listen, Mac, I can only tell you what I think, as someone who knows these islands as well as any European. You've come a long way to look into this, and I can tell you there's *something* here, I don't know what."

Ward suggested I prepare a full report on Donahue's story, which he said he wanted to show to a "certain person."

I hesitated. The stakes were high. But I had already told

him about Rockefeller, so there was no point in holding back now. Laboriously I hand scrawled a five-page report on Donahue, giving every detail I could remember. Tim looked it over with keen interest when I handed it to him that night.

"I don't want to say anything yet, but I can already see two or three details in here that are very peculiar and significant."

Night life was far from glamorous on the island, consisting of little more than gathering for gossip or a bit of snooker pool in the bar of Tim Ward's lounge with eight or nine people representing a fairly large percentage of the white population of the island. Two men seemed to be long-term guests: a stocky middle-aged Yugoslav named Boris, with an unpronounceable last name, who was an old friend of the Wards', a businessman in Moresby who was taking an extended holiday on the island; and a young, totally bald archaeologist from Minneapolis named Brian Egloff, who was studying ancient pots of the islands under a grant from the University of Canberra. In addition, there was Bert, the barman and general assistant, a somewhat dour, stringy fortyish man with a gift for blasphemy, a couple of young Australians from New South Wales who were working as sort of unofficial Peace Corps volunteers with the nearby Catholic mission and a Welshman who was captain of a trading barge that ran between Kiriwina and Samarai, to the east.

"Hey, Brian," Bert asked, " 'ow many of these bloody snake catchers left here yesterday?" He was referring, I gathered, to members of the Fairbridge expedition.

Egloff, sprawled bare-legged in one of the native-made lounge chairs answered: "About five of them, I guess. All that's left here is the professor and his wife and Harold, the snake man." Harold I gathered was also an American and

65

had been introduced as the expedition's herpetologist. I got the feeling that the regular hangers-on at the Gusoeta Lodge were not favorably impressed. Feeling hot and thirsty, I mixed myself a tall whiskey with lots of ice and rejoined the group.

"'Ere," Bert said, as I settled myself onto a stool, "take it easy with the bloody ice!"

It turned out that my American taste for lots of ice in my drinks was a grave *faux pas*. The refrigerator's capacity was so limited that the cold cubes had to be rationed like diamonds.

Much of the gossip that night centered on the Fairbridge expedition, which was the big excitement of the week. The group, which consisted largely of young undergraduate volunteers, seemed to be under considerable local suspicion. Even Ward and Beverly, Tim's strikingly attractive blond wife, who joined the crowd in the lounge when they finished their administrative chores, seemed doubtful.

"The paper says that he has a grant of ten thousand dollars. I don't see how they could make it the way they are on that amount. One boat they have costs eighty dollars a day, I know that for a fact, and they seemed to have had plenty of pull in getting hold of it. She's a government craft and usually isn't let to outsiders.

"Flying all these people around here and there isn't cheap either," Boris said. "I heard they spent three hundred and fifty dollars for one charter."

As we talked, one of the party in question, the chap known only as "Harold, the snake catcher," ran through the bar holding a struggling two-foot goanna lizard, which he had just bought from one of the local youngsters. He waved at the group in the bar, unable to stop with his hands full of lizard.

"'E bloody tikes them up there and injects them to bloody death," said Bert, the bartender. "Bloody shame I call it. I bet 'e's collected more than a hundred of those little green file snakes. Buys 'em from the kids for a shilling apiece or something. Now what's 'e want them for? They ain't scientific specimens. They're common as dirt!"

8

THE NEXT DAY Tim informed us that the *Beverly Mary* was finally returned from its trading voyage to the east, and we went down to the dock to watch it unload. Included in the cargo was a wavy-edged giant clam almost three feet across, out of which Tim promised we would eat a chowder that night.

We were excited, of course, about the arrival of the trading ship and anxious to leave as soon as possible, but Tim thought the motor didn't sound right and wanted to overhaul her a bit before we took her out.

"Shouldn't be more than a couple of days," Tim said. "But come into my office. I think I have a few interesting points on that report you wrote.

"Look," he said, when we were settled. "It's still best I don't tell you who I discussed your report with, but anyway this man knows quite a bit about the intelligence situation in these parts. I think you'll be disappointed that he was more interested in the smuggling part of your story than the Rockefeller angle, but I won't say it is one hundred percent impossible that there might be *something* to it."

Stirred by a wartime memory, I asked whether his man had anything to do with the coast watchers. Just before the Japanese declared war, an organization of government officials and planters equipped with radios, each of which contained a secret crystal, were appointed to report sightings of enemy ships and aircraft and any "unusual movements." These men operated clandestinely throughout the war in the heart of enemy-occupied territory, often right under the enemy's nose, and were invaluable as sources of information on what was actually happening in the islands taken over by the Japanese. As a member of a cryptographic team at the Fifth Air Force message center in various parts of New Guinea I had frequent occasion to decode messages passed by these courageous men. On my return to Australia and New Guinea I had heard that the coast watchers had never been completely dissolved and that certain men in the islands still acted as intelligence informants to the Australian armed forces. It was my hunch that Tim's contact was one of these. He said nothing to change my idea. He just shrugged and said, "Let's not go into that sort of detail. What I *can* tell you is this. The *Lae,* the ship on which Sublieutenant Donaldson is serving—the man your man Donahue named in his story—is what they call a spook ship. It is an electronically equipped patrol ship with special missions involving radio reception and electronic surveillance. Its location is supposed to be secret. It is operating in these waters right now!"

This was impressive. It didn't seem likely Donahue could have simply made up a random alias and have it turn out to be the name of an actual Australian Navy officer operating in the exact waters he had named as harboring Michael Rockefeller.

"I wonder if this secret mission aspect is the reason that I never received any answers to the cables I sent to Donaldson and O'Hara?"

"Could be. Of course O'Hara is on the *Melbourne.* She's a big ship, and she's operating down south, so that trail is a blank one."

"Still, I wonder about O'Hara's past history of service. Maybe he was down this way on his last assignment."

"Could be," Tim agreed, "but that's not all. Jeffries and Lang—the chaps Donahue said were wanted on the murder charge with him—are the names of two patrol officers who are well known in the territory."

"Are they around where I can talk to them?"

"No, they're on leave in Australia. One of them is named Mel Lang, I think, and I can't find out the first name of Jeffries. Strange, isn't it? No question Donahue was up to something, but what?"

"As soon as you can get the *Beverly Mary* ready, we'll find out." But I said it halfheartedly. By now I was beginning to be afflicted by the lackadaisical island attitude toward time. If Rockefeller really was on the island, he'd still be there in a few days.

"Look," Tim said, "you wanted to know all about Rockefeller, whether he could have gotten ashore with all those crocs?"

"Right."

"Well, I'll let you decide for yourself. I've got to shake down the *Beverly* and might as well kill two birds with one stone and go after Fred and Charlie. They'll show you exactly what Rockefeller had to face swimming ashore."

"Fred and Charlie?"

"They're a couple of man-eating crocs that have been bothering people recently. Might as well clean them out. Want to come along?"

"Sure. But aren't *all* crocs man-eaters?"

Tim considered. "All of them *could* eat a man, and plenty of them *might,* but my experience is that mostly the man-eaters are certain definite rogues. The natives usually know just where they operate and even have nicknames for them." He pointed to a photo of himself and some islanders beside an enormous dead crocodile.

"That one's an eighteen-footer I killed about a year and a half ago. He had eaten a seventeen-year-old native girl. We found parts of her inside. It was horrible."

He reached into a drawer and pulled out a shiny bit of jewelry. "Here's an earring we found inside him."

I was now wondering about the saltwater crocodiles that abounded on the Asmat coast and remembering Peter Hastings' certainty that nobody could survive in the saurian-infested waters.

"Do you think Michael Rockefeller could have managed to swim ashore despite the crocodiles and sharks?"

Tim looked at me directly. "I *know* he did. Both sharks and crocs are plain unpredictable, but in nine cases out of ten—more really—they won't bother with a human."

Tim gave orders to ready the *Beverly Mary* for the following night. Crocodile hunting, it seemed, was largely a nocturnal proposition. They were located at night with powerful searchlights which reflect from the many-lidded saurian eyes.

"You just can't get close enough to them in the daytime. You've got to put the bullet in a tiny area right between the eyes; otherwise they'll slide backward and sink into the water, and you'll never find them. Besides a bad shot ruins the hide, and that can be pretty valuable."

Before I left, I asked Tim's opinion on one more matter relating to Rockefeller.

"Do you think it possible that a small village in the Simsims could actually conceal the presence of a white man all this time?"

"I doubt that very much," Tim answered quickly. "These people just aren't that good at keeping secrets. Word would have gotten out long ago."

"But you yourself admitted that almost nobody has visited those islands."

"True, but my trading boat gets to most of the islands a

70

few times a year at least. I think they would have heard about a stranger."

"But don't they keep a lot of their magic rites and beliefs secret?"

Tim nodded. "Yes, the sorcerers are pretty good at keeping secrets, I'll admit that. But it's a long time since 1961."

As he locked up the office, he had a parting thought. "You know, a certain number of Japanese *have* been turned up living in some of these islands many years after the peace without our knowledge. Rumors are that there still may be one or two left in the backcountry of the Admiralties. So I'll give you a very long-odds bet on finding your man.

"Here," he said, "let me lend you this." From a bookshelf he took down a well-thumbed copy of Malinowski's *Argonauts of the Western Pacific*. "Here's a passage I noticed last night after I looked at your report. I think it will interest you. It has to do with the Dobu Islands where they *did* have a tradition of cannibalism, in the past anyway. The area he speaks of isn't far from the Sim-sims where your man is supposed to be."

From Malinowski's book he read:

I met myself an old man in the island of Vakuta, who, as a boy, had been captured with a whole party by a village community of Dobu-speaking people on Normanby Island. The men and another small boy of the party were killed and eaten; but some women took pity on him and he was spared, to be brought up amongst them. There is another man, either alive or recently dead in Kavataria, who had a similar experience in Fergusson Island. Another man called Kaypoyla, from the small Island of Kuyawa in the Western Trobriands was stranded with his crew somewhere in the West of Fergusson Island. . . . His companions were killed and eaten. He was taken alive and kept to fatten for a proximate feast. His host, or rather the host of the feast in which he was going to supply the *pièce de résistance,* was away inland, to invite the guests. While the host's wife went for a moment behind the house, sweeping the ground, Kaypoyla jumped up and ran to the shore. Being chased by some other men from the settlement, he concealed himself in the branches of a big tree standing on the beach, and was not found by his pursuers. At night he came down, took a canoe or a raft, and paddled along the coast. . . .

Tim closed the book. "Ultimately the chap escaped," he said, "but I thought you might be interested in the bit about capturing and holding an outsider. Gives a little more strength to your man Donahue's story. But then Donahue could have read this same book, too, couldn't he?"

Back at the guest house we discovered that in our absence the members of the Fairbridge expedition had returned. The "snake man" was still busy buying green snakes from eager native boys at a shilling apiece, along with long, squirming goanna lizards. Mr. and Mrs. Fairbridge were in the pool where I joined them, glad to get out of the late-afternoon heat. Fairbridge was a tall, dignified, balding, fortyish man. His wife was trim, attractive, with graying hair, a good outdoors tan and a regal bearing.

His expedition, he said, was interested basically in the reef which extends through the Trobriand Islands. They had spent time diving and gathering specimens in the area of Kitava, and more recently in the Sim-sims. The reefs, Fairbridge informed me, were actually dead—that is, composed of dead coral, in contrast with the Great Barrier Reef off Australia—therefore did not boast a very rich marine life.

As offhandedly as I could, I asked Fairbridge if his group had visited the islands of Kanapu or Kanapa.

"They don't sound familiar to me. Rather small places, aren't they? I don't think we visited either of them."

Yet I couldn't help suspecting the coincidence in timing between my trip and the Fairbridges'. Donahue, busily peddling his Rockefeller story, naturally would have sought out someone representing Rockefeller's interests. This person in turn would have run a preliminary check on it as I had. If he found, too, that many points on Donahue's story checked, wouldn't it be possible for him to assign an expedition like this as the means for further investigation—an investigation that could be conducted without undue publicity or embarrassing attention?

But if the Fairbridges had found out anything, they weren't about to share the information with me.

After dinner, Tim asked me if I had found out anything about my island.

"No, they said that they hadn't actually landed on it."

"That's funny," Tim said. "I spoke with one of the girls on their boat. She said they *had* been on Kanapu!"

9

THE *Beverly Mary* was a trim, if vintage, 42-foot gasoline lugger. The main living space was a rear cargo deck with a boom over which a tarpaulin had been thrown to make a shaded patio. There was a small two-bunk cabin for the master and mate and another cabin forward for the crew; but as I learned, it was usually too hot to sleep in either, and everybody generally slept out on deck. Tim introduced me to Samuel, the captain, a sturdy and serious Fijian in his late forties, who, according to Tim, knew every reef and channel of the island seas. This was necessary as the

Beverly Mary drew more than four feet of water, and there were endless uncharted shoals and niggerheads waiting in the shallow waters of the Solomon Sea to claw out the bottom of an unsuspecting cruiser.

Aboard, in addition to Jim Anderson, Tim and me, were Boris, the lonely Yugoslav, and Brian Egloff, the shiny-headed anthropologist.

"There's a lot more crocs down there in the Asmat than around here. Not hunted out yet, though quite a few Chinese go in there taking out hides on the sly," Tim said as we chugged through the calm seas toward the reefs where "Fred" and "Charlie," the man-eaters, were believed to browse.

About two feet above the waterline Tim tied one of the hooks with its burden of rotting carrion.

As we chugged on, Tim explained that he intended to stop by a nearby plantation to borrow a shallow-draft launch for the night's croc hunting.

In the small boat which he finally acquired five Europeans, a skipper and two native boys made quite a crowd. "This isn't a crocodile hunt," Tim said sourly. "It's a bloody circus parade!"

By now it was dark, and we were sailing through a silver shining sea, in which porpoises broached and played beside us and shoals of tiny silvery fish jumped and splashed. Tim had prepared a hand-held searchlight attached to a 12-volt automobile battery by a 10- or 12-foot wire. After two hours or so he signaled the skipper to pull us in close to shore.

"Now keep it quiet from here on in, chaps. These fellers scare easy," he said.

Cruising slowly along the low-lying shoreline, he began to play the powerful light beam on the mangrove swamps where they touched the sea.

I could see that there would be absolutely no way to penetrate the mangrove swamp. The mangroves descended di-

74

rectly into the water like a forest of spider legs. The roots were too tangled and closely grown for any human to pass through and too tough to slash. Where the mangroves themselves grew, the sandy beach gave way to jellylike mud or heavy muck in which one would sink almost instantly to the knees.

After about a half hour of cruising, in deadly silence, Tim held up his hand, and the native skipper gradually brought the motor to a halt, careful not to cut it suddenly as the change in sound would be enough to frighten a croc even at a distance of a hundred yards.

"See him out there?" Tim whispered, pointing to a spot on the dim shoreline at which he was beaming his light. I couldn't see a thing.

"There! There! Right at the base of the mangroves. Looks like a big fellow from here!"

I still saw nothing. Signaling silence, Tim drew the dinghy we had towed behind us alongside and got in, careful not to bang his brawny .310 Johnson rifle on the metal sides. He had the light affixed now to the rifle barrel. I handed the auto battery to George, the islander who was to be Tim's helper, and Tim gestured to me to get in, too.

"Don't make any noise," he said.

As we paddled warily toward the shore, Tim kept the light constantly trained on the mesmerized croc. Finally I too saw them: two pink shining dots like twin bicycle reflectors. Still, it was hard to believe that behind that shine lay a 20- or 30-foot man-killer. Tim said, "He's frightened. The reflection is dimmer. He's closed three or four of his eyelids."

Now the dinghy was dragging its keel in less than nine inches of water. I got out to lighten the draft and dragged it through the shallow mud. Finally, Tim and George had to get out, too, all without letting the light stray from the croc's steady shining eyes. There was no sand or coral bot-

75

tom here, only foot-sucking muck. Despite the fact that Tim was carrying the rifle and light and George the battery, I found myself falling farther and farther behind as my 230-pound bulk pushed my feet deeper and deeper into the yielding slime. Soon my legs were getting so deep in the mud that I had to fall forward or backward into the water and pull myself out with my hands. I finally decided it would be easier to let my feet float behind and drag myself through the muck with my hands—much like a crocodile myself. Hearing my splash as I eased myself into the water, Tim momentarily turned his light on me and burst into a hissing muffled laugh. "You look like the bloody creature from the black lagoon!"

Now, swiftly turning the light back on the croc, he signaled for silence. As well as I could judge, we were by now less than 50 feet away, and I could see the eyes clearly, red, blazing, wide-set and angry-looking.

Moving with painful slowness, we got to within 12 feet. The croc's eyes looked to be more than a foot apart. I wondered how I would be able to move through the foot-gripping muck if he suddenly surged forward, but Tim had assured me that crocodiles seldom attacked under these circumstances. Suddenly Tim and his helper froze. There was a moment of absolute silence and then: Wham! The shockingly loud report of the .310 Johnson whined and reverberated over the water.

"Quick!" Tim shouted. "Grab 'im before he sinks!"

There was a sudden boiling turbulence in the water and a flash of yellow-white saw-edge teeth in the light of Tim's searchlight and then silence.

"He's gone," Tim said quietly. "We won't get him here. He's backed off in the mangroves." George cut a stick from one of the mangroves with his bush knife and poked around in the muck near the tangle of roots where the croc had disappeared. But it was clear that he had retreated forever into the impenetrable cover of the swamp.

We turned back to the dinghy and the launch, and I wondered how it would feel to be alone in the darkness in this great spread of oozing mud and mangrove swamp. The thought evoked despair and hopelessness. Is this what Michael had waded through?

The tide was getting lower and lower. Cruising back, we spotted two more sizable crocs glowing in the light, but Tim reckoned that it was useless to go after them with the tide dropping.

"How big do these fellows get?" I asked.

There's rumors of crocs in these waters up to forty-five feet," Tim said. "I've shot several myself over thirty." I thought at the time he was giving me tenderfoot talk—some Bunyanesque fabrication for the visitors—but I later learned that there have been verified kills of crocs up to 42 feet in India and that one 37 feet long had been killed in New Guinea waters.

We turned the *Beverly Mary* back toward Kiriwina and arrived just before noon. I was glad the trip was over, for now we were at last ready to take off in the *Beverly Mary* for Kanapu. It was already more than a month since I had left Kennedy Airport.

10

WE FINALLY weighed anchor for Kanapu, setting a course north along Kiriwina's coastline toward Tuma (the island of the dead) and then cutting due west toward the Sim-sims. Samuel, the Fiji skipper, indicated our route to me on the chart. A straight-line course would be impossible, he explained, because of shoals and reefs in the area.

Wherever we sailed there seemed to be low-lying tiny islands in view, often topped with graceful coconut palms. No other ships were visible, or likely to be, and no airplanes flew overhead. Even in this air-conscious territory we were off the normal path of traffic. At first, near Kiriwina we passed some of the typical Trobriand Island outrigger sailing canoes with their graceful triangular sails woven from pandanus leaves. It was in *waga* similar to these that the islanders took the long trading voyages which caused them to be labeled the Argonauts of the Western Pacific.

We sailed for hours through clear water, transparent and green down to a depth of 30 feet or more. Sometimes for an hour or two there was nothing visible but the empty sea turning green-blue at the horizon. Occasionally we could make out the dim outline of a tiny distant island. On the detail chart Samuel showed me I had indicated the location of Kanapu, our destination, and questioned him closely about it. But the taciturn Fijian simply shrugged and said, "Never see him, *Taubada* [on the north shore the respectful term for whites]. 'Im 'e something-noting, I tink."

Meaning that Samuel himself felt that the island was of no consequence and had never had occasion to go there.

As I watched the phosphorescent splash of water along the weather-beaten hull in the lengthening afternoon shadow, I thought about the Trobriand belief in magic and how it ruled every phase of their trips from island to island. From time to time I could fancy a foaming giant tentacle reaching out of the deeper reaches of the sea—the giant octopus *kwita* that, according to Trobriand myth, lies in wait for unwary canoes sailing the open sea. "It is not," says Malinowski describing the legend, "simply an ordinary large octopus, but a unique one, so gigantic that it would cover a whole village with its body; its arms are as thick as coconut palms stretching right across the sea. . . ."

Of course, says the legend, one seldom sees it, but one of the old men Malinowski spoke to told how he saw one once, coming from Dobu, to the south of the route we were now sailing. The old man said that he was in the center of a fleet of trading canoes, with other canoes to the right and left of him when "suddenly, from his canoe, they saw the giant *kwita* right in front of them. Paralyzed with fear, they fell silent, and the man himself, getting up on the platform (a decked-over section of the canoe between the dugout hull and the outrigger), by signs, warned the other canoes of their danger. At once they turned around, and the fleet divided into two, took big bends in their course and thus gave the octopus wide berth. For woe unto the canoe caught by the giant *kwita!* It would be held fast, unable to move for days, till the crew, dying of hunger and thirst, would decide to sacrifice one of the small boys of their number. Adorned with valuables, he would be thrown overboard, and then the *kwita,* satisfied, would let go its hold of the canoe and set it free." (Recently *Natural History* magazine reported that the remains of an octopus that would have had a 200-foot tentacle span were found off the Florida coast around the turn of the century.)

There are other beliefs too, held by local sailors. There are tales of malevolent cloudbursts and waterspouts. There are "living stones" that lie in wait for passing canoes, then actually pursue them and jump up and smash them to pieces. Some of these are said to be inhabited by witches; others are just "bad stones." But again a magic offering must be made. First a folded pandanus mat would be thrown overboard in an attempt to fool the bad spirits. But if this didn't work, a small boy, coated with coconut oil, decorated with valuable shells, armbands and necklaces,

79

would be thrown overboard to the evil stones. Sometimes by magic, a talented sorcerer could make the canoes actually fly over the danger spots.

Toward dusk a sliver of land began to emerge slowly on the horizon.

"Sim-Sim," Samuel said, pointing. "Maybe one hour, maybe more. We stop long dere tonight, *Taubada*."

It was almost dark when we reached our anchorage just off Sim-Sim Island, a volcanic outcropping with the fairly recent-looking crater cone clearly visible at one end. From the cone the land, lushly covered with coconut palm, sloped to a saddle and then rose to a small hill. On the beach near the saddle-shaped depression we could see the cluster of thatched houses that constituted the village. From the huts gleamed the lights of evening fires. In all, the island appeared to be less than a mile long, and I imagined it was even less in width. Yet it conformed somewhat to the island Donahue had described. In the distance I could dimly make out the forms of several dozen small outrigger canoes drawn up on the shore. I was anxious to go ashore and talk with the people, but Samuel insisted that we would not be able to come close until daylight.

As we gazed out toward the island, I became aware of a series of lightning flashes from the north, apparently striking somewhere in the distance since they were visible not as jagged streaks but only as flares of light on the horizon. At first I paid no attention, but I soon began to notice that these lights continued much longer than any heat lightning I had ever seen. They recurred at the rate of two a minute with almost measurable regularity. If the flashes *were* lightning, they must have been very far away as I could hear absolutely no thunder; with the anchor dropped and the motor stopped I would surely have been able to hear it at this point. All in all I watched and timed the flashes for most of the evening, and by the time we retired to our camp stretchers the flashes had been continuing for more than three and a half hours.

I asked Samuel about it, but he seemed uninterested, saying that it probably was only lightning. Yet I was puzzled at the frequency and long duration of the flashes and wondered if there might not be a volcanic eruption or some other cause. Certainly active volcanoes were not uncommon in the area.

"What is in that direction, Samuel?" I asked.

"Kanapu Island, *Taubada*," he answered.

As I dozed off, the lights were still flashing regularly on the horizon.

11

WE WERE awakened at six thirty by the sound of soft chattering and laughing, interspersed with the splash of canoe paddles. I looked over the side to see that at least a half dozen of the small outrigger canoes had come out to trade. The villagers handled the *wagas* with short paddles they maneuvered deftly with one hand. I fetched a supply of trade tobacco and paper, which I passed over the side as gifts. Every stick of tobacco had to be accompanied by a half sheet of newspaper for rolling cigarettes since there was no paper available in this litterless society. But the local people had only green coconuts to offer in trade.

Now that the sun was up I could see that we had actually anchored between two islands, the second one uninhabited, according to Samuel.

As soon as we had disposed of our morning tea, we went

ashore in the dinghy, with Yuwata, the interpreter, and Suli, the cabin boy.

The village, layered in the smoke of early cookfires, was silent except for the howling of dogs. Small boys quickly took us in hand and led us to the residence of the local chief, indistinguishable to my eye from the rest of the village huts.

The *luluai* turned out to be a surly-looking man with the broad-nosed features of an Australian aborigine, wearing a tattered T-shirt, a green peaked baseball hat as the symbol of his authority and an areca-leaf breechclout.

After greeting him and offering him tobacco and several American cigarettes, which he had apparently never seen before, I asked Yuwata to indicate that we wanted to make a further gift of Polaroid pictures. This obviously meant nothing to the old man, but when I took pictures of him and presented them, a reluctant smile of wonder passed his surly old face.

As we sat on the old chief's elevated wooden platform, I scanned the rest of the village for signs of—what? Could a white man have been hidden here? In one of the huts? Why not? Nobody would approach the island without being seen for at least an hour. Plenty of time to hide a prisoner somewhere in the bush. There was no way to approach the island by air. Trading ships (and the *Beverly Mary* was the only one in the area) came infrequently, sometimes less than once every few years. Even if a captive could get free, there was no way to attract the attention of the outside world until such a ship pulled in. There were no radios or other means of communication with the outside world. Of course, this was not the island designated by Donahue, but I could now see that a situation such as he described would be at least possible.

I told Yuwata to ask the old man if he had seen any *dim dims* (white people) in the area at any time.

Yuwata translated the question.

"He say nobody come here. Just *Taubada* Tim."

But I knew the old man was lying, because the Fairbridges had been there within the past week.

"Didn't a group of *dim dims* come here only a few days ago?"

Yuwata translated. The chief shrugged uncomfortably and grunted a reluctant answer.

"He say he forget those people. They here very short time."

Forget what probably was the most exciting event of the past several years? Impossible! But there was no point in calling the old man a liar.

But *why* had he lied?

I again looked at the surrounding huts and the circle of wondering faces of the villagers, who by now were gazing curiously at us. I thanked the chief ironically and gave him several more sticks of tobacco. He grinned slyly in acceptance and surprisingly answered "Thank you" in English.

Before leaving, I strolled around the village, passing out a few more strategic Polaroid snaps. But I got no more information from the villagers. Four *dim dims* had been there some days ago and had left after a stop of what seemed to be an hour or so. Other than that, they had seen no Europeans, except Tim Ward, for years. How many years? Nobody could remember. I felt certain that they were covering up, probably for smugglers whom they had helped with food and water and who in turn had warned them to say nothing of their visits. But as I looked around the few unadorned huts and at the crudely carved canoes and sitting stools and other household artifacts, it was apparent that this was a very poor village and an unsophisticated one compared to those of Kiriwina. Nowhere did I see the wealth of art and decoration I had seen on the main island. There were few signs of trade with the outside world except a few "walkabout" kerosene lanterns. Not even such leftover impedimenta of white civilization as tin cans and very little in the way of cloth. There were a number of steel knives and axes, however. The Stone Age, at least, was over. Nobody seemed inclined in any way to hide anything from me, and there was absolutely no sign of the knowledge of carving or weaving that Donahue claimed Rockefeller had passed on to the natives of the village where he was being held. Also, the tiny crude canoes of the village would hardly make it to the mainland, let alone sustain a months-long voyage of hundreds of miles. I was convinced that *this* wasn't Rockefeller's island at any rate. After a few hours we reboarded the *Beverly Mary* and headed again for Kanapu.

The island on the other side of us, Samuel explained, was uninhabited and visited only for copra gathering. It was tiny, and we could see that it contained no huts.

Around midday we passed near a small island that appeared uninhabited but had several thatched structures on it. I went ashore in the dinghy with three of the crew. The island was another copra stop. The huts were primitive unoccupied temporary shelters. The island was only a few hundred yards long. I told the crew through Yuwata to look for any signs of visits by white people—cigarette packs, matches, paper wrappers of any sort, tin cans, any bit of the litter that it is almost impossible for a European who has visited a place not to leave behind—even we were leaving bits of film wrapping, cigarette butts, empty boxes of wax vestas (the only matches that would light in that humid atmosphere). Jim and I also penetrated the limited interior of heavy mangrove growth, huge roots which on dry land here would have provided shelter for a man under their twisted trunks.

The heat was unbearable, at least 120 degrees. Both Jim and I were dripping quarts of salt perspiration. One of the

84

boys climbed agilely to the top of a palm and brought us a green coconut, which he split deftly with the aid of a stake which he sharpened and stuck into the ground. The milk was cool and slightly sweet.

As we turned to leave, convinced that the island held little of interest—not so much as a shod footprint other than our own—Yuwata came running up excitedly with a white object that one of the boys had found on one of the hut platforms. It was a bit of styrofoam about the size of a cigarette pack of the sort used to pack cameras or other delicate equipment. How had it gotten here? Probably floated ashore and been picked up by a curious copra cropper. It seemed to me to have little significance except that it was absolutely the only object which would indicate the existence of a world outside these islands.

I was so hot by then that I decided to swim out to the *Beverly Mary*, and removing only my shoes and hat, waded into the warm sea in my trousers and bush jacket and started swimming for the lugger anchored about 250 yards or so offshore. The sea was comforting but so warm that it was hardly refreshing.

I swam the 200 yards easily, impeded somewhat by the clothes I had decided to retain, and by the time I got close to the *Beverly Mary* I was winded but still in good shape. But when I was only 10 yards or so from the trading ship, I found that I was swimming hard without making any progress. It took awhile for me to realize that I was swimming against a sudden strong current. On the boat the crewboys stood smiling, ready to throw me a boarding rope, as I floundered futilely against the tide, unable to indicate the nature of my problem. Both Jim and Yuwata were still ashore with the dinghy. Momentarily I was seized by something near panic as I pictured myself succumbing to fatigue and sinking as the crew stood smiling on the deck, rope in hand, unable to understand my predicament. Finally, with a desperate surge of added energy, I managed to put myself in reach of the rope and pull myself to the boat. But I was too weak to pull myself up onto the deck and had to be hauled aboard ignominiously by the crew like some great flapping tortoise.

Jim and the rest of the crew appeared shortly afterward, and we heaved anchor, under weigh again for Kanapu. Why were we making so many stops? Partly because I knew we would probably not pass the same way again and did not want to miss any clues. And partly, perhaps from a growing sense that Tim was right—that there would be nothing at Kanapu. I suppose I was fending off anticlimax.

An hour after we left the previous island, identified to me by Samuel on the chart as Gabwina, we passed the hulk of a World War II Liberty ship, looming dramatically out of the sea, colored vivid red and white by rust and birdlime. We circled it in the dinghy, followed by swarms of fish that had apparently made a home of the vicinity of the decaying wreck. The bow was all that was visible, sloping out of the sea at better than a 40-degree angle. Slimy and corroded, the decks looked as though they would be dangerous to mount. In the forepeak I could see the shattered remnants of a 20-caliber gun, but little else of interest on the stripped decks.

Again the midday heat had become unbearable, and I could feel my skin roasting under its coating of ultraviolet ointment. The sea, as we pulled away from the wartime hulk, changed from transparent green to a brilliant royal blue. Climbing a few feet up in the rigging, I could see an island off our port bow. Kanapu!

As we plowed slowly through the sea toward it, I found myself tense and excited. But the closer we drew, the more I realized that this 12,000-mile voyage was not likely to produce spectacular results. As we approached, I could see that the island was no more than 500 yards long, covered with a beautiful fringe of coconut palm, but hardly large enough to answer Donahue's description.

The dinghy was paddled close to the beach, and we could see that Kanapu, too, had a number of thatched huts but no visible people.

Jumping from the dinghy to wade the last 20 yards or so through the shallows, we mounted a brilliant clean beach of yellow, coarse sand. Emerging from the sea parallel to our path was the five-foot-wide trail of a giant tortoise. Other than that, for as far as we could see, no footprint, not even a bit of jetsam—just clean bare beach, seaweed and stranded shells. Determined to miss nothing, Jim and I pushed into the tiny cluster of huts. They were deserted without a sign of habitation other than by the transient coconut gatherers. This island was even more narrow-waisted than Gabwina, and we quickly penetrated to the far side. I had the crew fan out, again looking for clues. Not so much for signs of the existence of Michael Rockefeller—because I now had to accept the fact that the story I had pursued so far was a myth, a confabulation, a pipe dream—but for some indication of *why* I had been told this fantastic story, why this tiny palm-fringed coral outcrop had been selected as the target of this elaborate hoax.

Even so, I circled the entire island, looking, like Crusoe, for the footprint of destiny. It was late afternoon, and a huge double rainbow arced across the sky. Neither Jim nor I spoke. At the far end of the island the dense vegetation gave way to sandy beach over which hundreds of gulls wheeled and screamed. On the beach were the remains of a primitive cookfire, forked sticks and a crossbars, probably used to roast a fish or tortoise. At the base of one of the sticks I found the only trace of outside civilization: several

87

streaks of pale-blue paint. Trobrianders don't have blue paint, but it hardly seemed to indicate that Rockefeller or anybody else had been here.

After an hour's desultory search we returned to the ship in the dinghy, leaving several of the boys to follow us with camera gear.

As we climbed aboard the *Beverly Mary*, I heard an excited shouting from the boys onshore and saw them waving their arms gleefully as they ran to the dinghy. Anxiously I watched as they piled full of excitement into the tiny craft and paddled with vigor toward the ship. As they pulled alongside, one of the boys excitedly held up a basket woven of palm leaves in the island fashion. In it were about three dozen tiny speckled gull's eggs. For the crew it was the triumphant end of a day's search.

III. Father Van Kessel

12

So NOW we knew for certain. Michael Rockefeller had not been kidnapped and taken to Kanapu. But just as certain was the realization that not one person I met in New Guinea believed the story that he had drowned at sea, though all seemed vague about what the actual story was.

Having come this far on a false trail, I couldn't help feeling that somewhere here in New Guinea I could pick up the thread of the *real* trail. There were clues, or at least hints, all around. Most of them tied in somehow with the enormous cultural gap that yawned between Michael Rockefeller of Harvard and Pocantico Hills and the dawn-age swamps and jungles of New Guinea, the ominous, yet fascinating contrasts that had lured Michael into returning to the Asmat.

By now I was convinced that veiled hints and clandestine tips would get me nowhere. The answer, I felt, lay in the jungle, with its beliefs in payback, cargo cult, ritual head-hunting that may have contributed to the fate of Michael Rockefeller. The only way really to understand them would be to absorb this way of life, to come as close as possible to *living* some of the situations Michael faced.

The obvious move, of course, would be to try for the Asmat coast where Rockefeller had disappeared in the first place. But this was no simple matter. The "act of free choice" was still on. We had no permission to enter West Irian except via Djakarta. Out letters from Joop Ave in New York theoretically would help us once we got to the capital, but from talks with other journalists and business-men I was sure that in the end I would not be permitted to make the trip.

There were two other possibilities. One was to enter West Irian illegally aboard a pearling lugger from Thurs-day Island. I felt there would be little risk if we were caught by the Indonesians: a fine perhaps, at worst a brief siege in custody. But now with the tense political situation it was anybody's guess.

The other possibility was to try to find Father Van Kes-sel, the Dutch missionary who had released the story that Rockefeller had reached shore and been attacked by can-nibals. Why had the newspapers played down his statement? And where was he? The newspaper clipping in-dicated only that he was operating a mission in the south-ern Philippines. Would I be able to find him—and would he talk or resort to the veiled silences and hints I had so often encountered?

This much I knew: To get into West Irian would take time, and once there, I would have to learn much about the Asmat ways before I could begin to probe this eight-year-old mystery.

I realized that what I had learned about the cargo cult in Moresby, for instance, only scratched the surface of this form of magic belief that has continued to plague the gov-ernments of New Guinea. Despite periodic announcements by administrators that all this nonsense has been put down, Papuans continued to believe that America would someday produce the valued cargo. Michael was a symbol of the rich-ness of America. Was there some tie between the cargo cult and his ultimate fate?

At the Davara Hotel, near Ela Beach in Moresby, I had

met Mick Healy, who had been involved in the most spectacular and one of the most troublesome uprisings of the cargo cult. In 1964 a tribe in New Hanover announced it would no longer pay its taxes; instead they were saving all their money to "buy" President Lyndon Johnson. By getting the "Number one man belong America," the natives of Kavieng and other villages in New Hanover were sure they would command enough magic to force all the white man's goods to be sent to their island. One native prophet predicted that the *Queen Mary* would arrive on June 16 and disgorge 600 black American troops who would "liberate us from the Australian oppressors."

The Australians became increasingly disturbed as the cult spread. In a short time more than 2,500 of the native population of 7,000 had become firm believers in the Messiah from the Pedernales.

Chief instigator of the uprising was Yali Singina, a former member of the Papuan infantry battalion who had become something of a hero during World War II, during which he attained the rank of sergeant—a fabulous accomplishment for a Papuan. He returned from the war a potential native leader whom the Australians hoped to use to head off the strong waves of cargo cultism that had arisen in the wake of the war. He was even taken on a trip to Australia to show how the "cargo" originated. But the Australians reckoned without the deep-seated native belief in sorcery. Yali was looking only for the magic key to the cargo, and on his return to his village of Sor on the Saidor coast of northern New Guinea he was hailed as the new leader who, by his close association with the whites, surely had learned the key to the cargo.

Yali *had* learned a great deal. He told his people that the whites were clean and industrious and kept their villages neat; why, Australian people even had tables in their homes covered with colorful tablecloths and decorated with pots of flowers! Soon patrol officers were gratified to see a cheerful new cleanliness in the villages influenced by Yali and astonished to observe the large number of native homes that featured rough-hewn tables with tablecloths and pots of bright flowers. At first, not realizing the cargo thinking behind it all, the Australians welcomed these new signs of native assimilation of the ways of whites. Yali became more powerful; he was given semi-official rank by the Australians and soon was appointing his own *saiteng* (sergeants), levying taxes, issuing a form of money of his own and drilling his army with dummy rifles. Some of his followers set up a primitive communications system by stringing vines through the trees to function as "telephone wires" and attached "radio transmitters" made of tin cans to the vines to resemble the mysterious boxes into which the whites were always talking and through which they obviously ordered their cargo.

At first Yali himself was not considered a proponent of all this cargo belief. But in time he was swept up in the fervor of his followers, who held a colorful ceremony in which he was crowned "King of New Guinea." In the eyes of government and mission people, the "coronation" was a wild and obscene demonstration in which women were passed from hand to hand (a generations-old custom). The missionaries began to grow concerned about Yali's popularity, zeal, independence and growing power, while Yali, who had originally inclined toward Christianity, now began to see the missionaries as one more barrier between his people and the cargo. His reign culminated in a trial, with all the earmarks of a frame-up, in which Yali was accused of having participated in the rape of women prisoners being held by his sergeants. He was sentenced to seven years, served his time, and returned quietly to his native village, with the clear understanding that he was not to foment any more new kingdoms.

Then in 1964 there was an election for Papua-New Guinea's first House of Assembly, and the cargo cult sprang up again. Prophets arose to spread the word that Yali would be elected to Parliament and drive out the whites. The great cargo ships would arrive from America the day he took his seat in the House of Assembly. Storehouses were built to hold motorcars the natives were sure were coming after election day. But while Yali received more votes than his opposing candidate, most of his votes were write-ins from other districts, and he was defeated. He lives still in the village of Sor, quietly, but like a fused bomb, still a threat in the eyes of the watchful Australians.

Even more troublesome was the Johnson cult.

On February 15, just before the election, Ian Spencer, a young patrol officer, entered a village on the north side of New Hanover Island with his polling team and found that a sign had been erected with a message scrawled on it in pidgin. It stated that the local people didn't want to vote for any Australian candidates, only "votim President Johnson bilong Amerika Tasol" (that's all).

A nineteen-year-old native named Bosmailik overheard some remark by Americans attached to an Air Force mission on New Hanover and, on the basis of his "inside information," declared himself a prophet and preached that if the people voted for President Johnson, the American chief would come and distribute cargo to everyone. As it happened, President Johnson *was* coming to Australia for a conference with the Prime Minister. It was probably the radio broadcasts to this effect in pidgin that started the first rumblings of Johnsonism.

The cult soon reached such proportions that Mick Healy, who was district commissioner of the area, felt obliged to mount an armed patrol to go to Bosmailik's village and explain that Johnson was not available for the job the natives had in mind.

93

Valiantly Healy harangued Bosmailik and his followers for several hours, but just as he was about to reembark in his boat, Bosmailik handed him a heavy sack containing $1,000 in silver collected by the natives to "buy" Johnson and asked if Healy would help close the transaction.

The cult quickly spread. Meanwhile, Bosmailik was pushing a new prophecy. A ship would arrive on April 10, he said, bringing President Johnson *and* the cargo.

Hoping to show up Bosmailik as a false prophet—a technique that had been effective in the past in breaking up local cults—Healy had the government spread the word: "Bosmailik is a liar. There will be no ship."

On April 9 Healy was amazed to get a courtesy message from the U.S. geodetic survey team operating in the area: "Will be landing party on New Hanover in 24 hours."

Hurriedly Healy got off a top-priority message: "By all means check with me before landing!"

Luckily Healy was able to arrange for a small party of the Americans in civilian clothes to land unobtrusively at a later date to take their readings without attracting the natives' attention.

"And did that end the cult?" I asked Healy.

"Not bloody likely. We had to call out native troops before we were finished there."

13

Two YEARS after the election an average of 200 cultists were being held in the local jail every day. Every time the Australians felt they were making headway in putting a stop to the cult, something else would happen.

There was the time an Australian patrol officer arrived at Taskul, one of the villages most active in the Johnson cult. One of the native porters had been to mission school and had learned the rudiments of reading. While unloading the officer's outboard motor, he was suddenly struck by the duplicity of the Australians, for there on the motor he could clearly read the letters J*O*H*N*S*O*N!

"Now, mastah," he said, "you see. Australians are always taking away President Johnson's presents to the people of Taskul!"

And what could the patrol officer say?

This strange, almost comical cult was strongest on New Guinea's northern coast, where, according to Donahue's story, the natives were holding Michael Rockefeller because he was "big bottle"—a powerful magic force. Certainly this sounded no more bizarre than the other cargo cult stories.

I asked where I could find modern evidence of the cult and was told the Madang area—the Rai coast from which Yali's cult had originated—seemed most promising. Only a short time ago there had been rumors of a "money-growing" cult at Sek. And not many years before, in the village of Bilbil, the natives had reportedly cut down all their crops and gone down to the sea to wait for the cargo. Local people said the belief was still fervent there, though played down by the missionaries, who, incidentally, were blamed for inadvertently encouraging cargo beliefs. When asked where the white man's goods originated, Fundamentalist missionaries would answer piously, "From God," which was exactly what the natives had thought all along. Many joined the Christian Church in order to learn the secret, only to quit in disgust when the goods were not forthcoming.

Jim and I flew to Madang in an Ansett Friendship Fok-
ker. The cargo cult, of course, tends to flourish principally
in areas with extensive exposure to white culture; Madang
is a town of about 8,500 people (including natives), fourth
largest in New Guinea. It was completely destroyed during
the war and has been rebuilt from the ground up; as the
busiest airfreight terminal in the territory and the second
busiest in the South Pacific, small wonder it should be regarded as a hotbed of cargo culture. It was in the Finisterre
Range of mountains behind Madang that Yali had earned
his sergeant's stripes during the war.

In the morning we paid a courtesy visit to Vince Smith,
local assistant district commissioner; the government likes
to know who is poking around in the territory and why, to
be sure the administration point of view is represented.
Cargo cult, he assured us politely, was a thing of the past,
and we would find no evidence of it in the area. The more
we talked, the more I realized that the government's opposition was directed not only to the pagan qualities of the cult,
but to the threat it represented of incipient anti-Australian
nationalism, since always it was the Australians who were
blamed for preventing the cargo from reaching the natives'
hands.

From Madang, it took more than an hour to reach the
plantation of Tom Huxley, a white-mustachioed planter—
one of those called B-4's in New Guinea because he had pio-
neered there "before" the war.

Huxley agreed that despite government denials, out-
breaks of cargo beliefs were frequent in his area to the
present day. In Rami, not far away, a local prophet had a vision that a flood would come soon, raising the Markham
River until it reached their mountain village, enabling big
ships containing the cargo to come right to the edge of
town. The Rami natives accordingly built an enormous
"wharf" up in the mountainous foothills of the Bismarck

96

range and sat down to wait patiently for the steamships to arrive.

We asked about the money-tree cult, but it seemed to have died out or at least was no longer evident in the area at that time. But back in Madang we came across Jack McCarthy, the wiry and abrasive correspondent for the *South Pacific Post*, who had actually gone with the local administration officer and a United Nations information director to the village in the mountains behind Alexishafen where the money trees were grown. He told us the story:

After a trek of several hours on horseback (horses are rare in New Guinea and are objects of cargo-cult worship by natives who regard them as huge pigs which can be ridden), they arrived in the village. They found an old man who readily admitted to being a believer in the money trees. Asked how he could believe such superstitious nonsense, he reached into his dilly bag and produced a tattered page from the *Pacific Islands Monthly*. It was an ad placed by the Earlwood Canterbury Permanent Building Society Limited of Campsie, Australia.

"Watch your money grow!" urged the ad, and illustrated its point with a drawing of a tree whose trunk consisted of shilling pieces and whose leaves were paper money.

"Look at this!" said the old man. "It is in your own language, and it shows what you white men can do with money. Why shouldn't we do it, too?"

At the end of the precipitous limestone ridge on which the village was built stood a newly built isolated hut. The building had no windows, and its sturdy wooden door was fastened with a long chain and a padlock. Seated in front of the house with a key hung around his neck was an old chap —guardian of the treasures within.

After a few words with the district official, the old guard reluctantly opened the door and allowed McCarthy and his friends inside. The place was dark—with light slanting dimly through the sago walls. The men were led along a dark narrow passage to an inside room, where they found rough-timbered shelves, a carved wooden head hanging on the wall, which also hung with a string of dog's teeth, the tusks of a boar and a woman's empty dusty *bilum* bag. Some dried and dead flowers drooped out of a beer bottle. The room was filled with a disgusting stench of mustiness and decay.

All available space in the inner sanctum was filled with tin receptacles—benzine tins, old cans and basins, each containing several silver shillings.

"They rattled, as we shook them," McCarthy remembered, "and I noticed a porcelain dish on the ground with more money and a child's sand bucket with two Australian coins in it.

"The old keeper who was our guide silently poked around in the dirt floor of the cargo temple and dug up several more coins out of the dirt which he very solemnly reburied."

The temple was chained up again, and the whites approached the leaders of the village.

"Why do you do this?" the UN man asked the wizened old chap who was apparently their leader.

"My father heard about this during the war," he recited the tale. "One of the soldiers told him that if you planted money in the ground it would grow, just like a tree. We never tried it until two years ago when a young man who had been a missionary teacher came and told us that this was true."

(Defectors from missions often passed themselves off as cargo prophets since not only could they read and write, but they also had had the chance to study the white man's magic at close hand.)

"The man told us," said the old man, "that the money

98

grows in many ways. If you put it in the bank for a long time, it grows a little.

"This was the same story that my father heard. The man told us to collect some money and that he would return. So all our people put in two dollars each, and when he came back, we had eight hundred dollars.

"He made us build this hut and collect empty drums and tins, and then he put some silver coins in each one and said some prayers. Before he left us, he said that in eight years the money would grow and we would be rich. Then he went off to the other villages and he promised to come back."

The rest of the men's council nodded in agreement.

"What happened to the eight hundred dollars?" McCarthy asked them.

"He took it with him," said the old man, "but he will come back soon. He told us so."

The three whites tried to explain the hopelessness of their belief and the impossibility of growing money in the ground, but the old man grew angry and pulled out the familiar advertisement.

"You tell us that this is wrong, but how do we know? Have you tried what this paper says? This is our money, and we can do as we wish with it. We have never tried this before. Perhaps we are wrong, but perhaps it will grow as the man told us. We can only try."

Another man took up the argument: "This is *our* business. Our women and children are in this too, and we must wait eight years."

The three whites continued to argue but without much effect. The natives, who looked undernourished and were covered with skin sores, listened carefully but then said, "You do things *your* way, and we'll do things *our* way."

"They went back to their darkened houses," McCarthy

recalled, "and as we mounted for the ride back, we could hear them mumbling on the strange ways of the white man. We left them there sitting watching their [magic] tins, faithfully believing that wealth would come and confident that the clever young man would return."

Looking through back issues of the *Pacific Islands Monthly* in the motel lounge, we saw that the ad for the money tree still appeared regularly. Apparently it was effective with the white population, too.

During my discussion with McCarthy several other locals had drifted into the thatched lounge of The Smuggler. As usual I steered the conversation to the subject of Michael Rockefeller, and I got the familiar store of rumors.

Then one of the local traders spoke up. He had heard there was someone up in Wewak, several hundred miles up the coast, who claimed to know the "real" story.

"Wewak is the airport where you can make connections to go out to the Sepik," Jim explained.

According to Anderson, people in New Guinea said that Michael had in fact first planned to go to the Sepik rather than the Asmat, since the Sepik area is the home of one of the world's great wood-carving cultures. But the great river valley resembled the Asmat in other ways, too. It was the center of a culture with a strong belief in headhunting rituals, and in remote areas it was said tribesmen still practiced cannibalism.

Within hours we had packed our gear and were at the airport, making the connection to Wewak, administrative center for the Sepik district, wartime Japanese stronghold and homeland of warrior tribesmen similar to those featured so prominently in the search for Michael Rockefeller.

14

WEWAK IS another jerry-built postwar collection of shacks, prefabricated houses and a few gimcrack modern buildings. It has a population of just under 9,000, with less than 1,000 Europeans. There is the usual collection of Chinese trade stores, plus the bigger general stores run by the trading companies.

We were driven to the Windjammer Hotel, the local accommodation, by Bruce Lawes. He was manager and owner of Sepik Airways, a tiny charter outfit which we planned to use for our flight to the village of Angoram, the principal starting point for Sepik River explorations.

Lawes was an enthusiastic collector and part-time dealer in Sepik art and in his own collection had some remarkable pieces showing the vivid and bizarre imagination of the Sepik carvers. He showed us what appeared to be two shell-decorated clay sculptures of native heads, but from his expression I could tell there was more to it than that.

Lawes took one of the sculptures, which were topped with kinky black hair, and turned it over. We were peering at the underjaw of a human skull.

"It took me ten years to find these," Lawes said. "I reckon they're worth more than a thousand apiece on the outside."

The skulls were prepared, Lawes explained, by first exposing them to the air until the flesh rotted completely off. Then the bare skulls were coated with clay and molded, he gathered, to look as much as possible like the original victim. The actual victim's hair, which had been removed earlier, was then reinstalled on top. The skulls were decorated with cowrie shells, which, placed horizontally, made realistic eyes, and painted in red, white and black, the three traditional colors of that area and of the Trobriands, too. The three colors were made of lime (white), burned coconut husks or other fibers (black) and macerated betel nut (red). Lawes estimated these prepared heads were more than twenty-five years old.

I asked if they did that sort of work anymore.

Lawes gave me an enigmatic smile. "Headhunting today is *tambu,* but it's a big territory and hard to police it all. It's a lot to expect for these fellows to give up a tradition they've known all their lives. They believe that you can't be properly married or own your own garden plot or take part in many of the manhood ceremonies or even wear men's clothing until you have taken the head of an enemy. It takes more than white man's regulations to convince them otherwise."

"Do they take only enemies' heads?"

"In terms of manhood rites, an enemy head is necessary —this usually means anyone from another village. But all sorts of skulls are—or were—preserved and worshiped. You often find ancestor skulls, not decorated like these but just bare, in native huts; they believe the spirit of the ancestor is pleased to have his skull venerated in the home. Nowadays, where government people go, the skulls are usually concealed. Still, if you ask around and they're sure you are neither a government man nor a missionary, you can usually find skulls in any of the villages."

As far as taking an enemy head was concerned, I learned, it had little to do with bravery—the head of a woman or even a small child would serve the purpose as well as any other. In most Sepik villages, until he had taken an enemy head, a man could not wear the genital covering of a flying fox skin considered appropriate to a grown man, but had to walk around completely naked and be mocked as a half-man by smirking women.

Besides the flying fox apron (a flying fox is a huge fruit bat common to the Sepik area), men had other ways to advertise their prowess at taking heads. The lime needed by betel nut chewers to neutralize the acid content of the nut is usually carried in highly decorated gourds or bamboo containers. A spatula of wood or of cassowary bone is used to dispense the lime, and these spatulas often have bunches of colored feathers hanging from them—each bunch denoting a separate killing and taking of a head.

Keith McCarthy noted on one occasion: "I saw one man sitting under the shadow of a *haus tambaran* [magic house typical of the Sepik area] and noted that his limestick had twenty-two bunches of feathers hanging from it. He was half-stupid with betel nut, his lips scarlet from the chewing, and his body had been freshly oiled so that it gleamed like ebony. His large, hooked nose was grotesque under a coating of white powder, but I saw that all in the village treated this moody killer with respect. Well they might, for he had been fortunate to get his record before the white man's laws stayed his success."

Certainly these white man's laws were applied stringently in the thirties, when Australian patrol officers first brought the government power to the district. Early in McCarthy's stay at Ambunti, an upper-river village, a party of men from the village of Komindimbit had been caught red-handed in a raid on a village up the Grasmeri River, a tributary of the Sepik. Nearly twenty people of the village— men, women and children—had been decapitated and their heads kept as trophies.

The government had no trouble finding and arresting the guilty men because the Sepik warrior is proud of his headhunting deeds. The tribesmen were transported 700 miles by boat to Rabaul, the nearest town where a court was sitting, and tried before their families, who evidently also had been transported to witness the proceedings. Seven of the men were found guilty and sentenced to hang. By the time they had made the long trip back to Ambunti, seven gallows had been erected to greet them.

In those early days the government hoped such harsh measures would convince the Papuans that taking heads was wrong. But a witness to the executions said that the prisoners lined up with their heads held high, and looked at the river for the last time, and then the leader stepped forth and spoke to the assembled crowd.

"I am to die," he said. "I am not afraid to go to meet my forefathers, for I am a man who has killed his enemies. The heads are in Komindimbit."

The death penalty was no more effective as a deterrent in the Sepik than it has been in more civilized areas.

Later these harsh punishments were ameliorated until today a native convicted of cannibalism or headhunting is jailed by the government for no more than two years. Often these men return to their villages as heroes, many of whom have gone on to become government-appointed headmen (*luluais* as they are called) of their villages.

There were a dozen or so local people sitting in the thatched patio of the Windjammer in Wewak that night. We fell into conversation with a couple—a teacher at the government school and an Australian Army captain stationed in Vanimo, down the coast—and in short order it developed that Carol, the teacher, knew someone who was supposed to have information about the actual fate of Michael Rockefeller. She agreed to take me to his quarters a few miles out of town.

We arrived after a short drive at a cluster of thatch and corrugated houses set in a quiet clearing in the forest. One of the houses was dimly lit, and through the intervening darkness I could hear the strains of a Vivaldi concerto. Carol knocked, and after a moment the door was opened by a wispy young man in bare feet, Bermuda shorts and a silk dressing gown. The young man, a school assistant named Don, seemed pleased at the unexpected call and invited us in to meet his house guest, Paul, an equally unlikely type, here in the rugged boondocks of New Guinea.

Carol briefly outlined my interest in the Rockefeller story, and Don was more than anxious to tell what he knew.

He launched into a long circumstantial story which he said had been told to him by the owner of a radio-phonograph shop in Port Said. According to the story, Rockefeller had passed through the Egyptian port city on his way to the South Pacific and had confided to the merchant that he was attracted to the Asmat area because of the freedom of its morality in regard to homosexual practices and had also hinted that he was eager to escape forever from the confines of civilization.

Thus, Don asserted, it was clear that Rockefeller had voluntarily escaped into the jungle to merge himself with the tropical tribesmen. He assured me that an article had appeared in the *Pacific Island Monthly* which supported this esoteric theory.

The story was so preposterous I didn't bother to question him too closely. Perfunctorily I pointed out it hardly seemed likely that if Rockefeller planned to run off into the bush, he would get himself capsized miles from land and then leap into a crocodile- and shark-infested sea and swim toward an unknown shore to make contact with his hosts.

My skepticism did little to shake Don and Paul, who probably are still spreading their version of the "real story" behind Michael's disappearance.

After a few days of inevitable delay by cloud cover, one morning we loaded our gear into Lawes' Cessna 206, and pilot Ian Cruickshank flew us at little more than treetop level toward Angoram, from which we would take a short hop to Ambunti, a trading post owned by a young Australian named Warren Hansen. Ambunti seemed the last outpost suitable for staging a trip upriver on the Sepik. "If you are looking for some of these headhunting blokes," Lawes had said, "it's up that way, where there aren't too many patrols, that you're likely to find them."

Cruickshank gave us a tree-cutting tour of the several hundred miles separating us from the river trading station. Flying up the winding river at points with our wheels almost in the muddy water, we skimmed over parties of canoeists, but they seemed accustomed to the sight of the low-flying Cessna and merely waved their paddles in a friendly fashion. Several of the canoes, I noted, were equipped with outboard motors. Other than a few power launches belonging to missions or government posts, these were the principal means of communications along the 800-mile-long river and its hundreds of tributaries. In some areas we passed native villages in the so-called grass country where the local people lived entirely in water or hip-deep mud, never seeing actual dry land in their lives. Their "farms" were supplied by the river, Cruickshank explained.

Pointing to a small grass island, he said, "See that? It isn't really a piece of land; it's just a lot of grass and earth which was undermined by the river currents and broken off. These big chunks float down the river, and the river people capture them as they go by and tow them to their villages to serve as their gardens. Sometimes a bunch of raiders from another village will cut the grass island loose and float it away, literally stealing the farm from its temporary owners."

I watched in awe as the piece of grass he pointed out passed under us, floating downstream to supply some land-hungry tribesmen with buoyant real estate.

Villages were frequent along this stretch of the middle

Sepik, and the people would come rushing from their houses as they heard us approaching upriver, waving at us with their paddles, bows and arrows or hands.

"These chaps are mostly friendly these days because a plane usually brings good things to them, although it's not so long ago that there was a good bit of violence along this way—even toward Europeans. Now they still have an occasional scrap among themselves, but in general they're peaceful. A lot of them have found out that their carved shields and other artwork are worth something to the Europeans and make a pretty good living selling their work to traders or paddling them down to Angoram, where they are bought for collectors."

In less than two hours we had arrived at Ambunti. Cruickshank taxied to a stop near a building, colorfully painted in Sepik designs, which served as the post office. We were quickly surrounded by eager blacks, who seemed to be unloading the long-awaited supplies even before we had stopped rolling. One of them offered to fetch "Mastah Warren" for us.

Hansen turned out to be a tanned, wiry, sharp-faced, boyish-looking chap in his late twenties. He had come to the Sepik as a clerk just over five years earlier and was now the owner of a chain of trade stores and a boat-chartering service reputedly worth more than a quarter of a million dollars.

Hansen owned a jet boat—a small launch operated by a powerful water jet which could speed against the current at better than 35 knots and, more important, could clear long stretches of water only inches deep, even pass over sandbars and gravel banks, because of its shallow draft and lack of a propeller.

Hansen agreed to charter his jetboat to us for $50 a day, including himself as pilot. I asked whether we might be able to get to one of the places where heads such as those we had seen at Bruce Lawes' place were actually being prepared today. He looked at me quizzically and answered in the peculiar bloody-sprinkled brogue which was his personal conversational style.

"I tell you bloody what? I'll look into the bloody what? villages and see if I can get anything bloody going."

"I don't want you to get them started *taking* heads."

"No bloody fear," Hansen said, waving a wiry bare brown arm assuringly. "We're just interested in bloody what? *art!*"

I remembered the rumors that Rockefeller had bought trouble by trying to buy decorated heads in the Asmat area and suddenly realized how this could come about without the slightest bad intention on the part of the collector.

My pleasure at the chance to make the Sepik jet boat patrol with Hansen was borne out later when he said he had been able to schedule a patrol meeting our demands and had even arranged with one village to let us actually witness the preparation of a human head, Sepik style.

This worried me.

"They're not going to actually take a head because of this, are they?"

"No bloody fear," Hansen assured us. "They'll just take one of their bloody what? ancestor's skulls and decorate that. They've all got a couple of skulls tucked away somewhere among the roof poles. Might be the head of somebody's granddad or old auntie."

I explained our interest in the magic beliefs underlying the headhunting and Hansen suggested that we visit the last of the big *haus tambarans* of the Sepik. This was at Kanganomon, a half day's journey downriver in the swift jet boat. While we were doing this, several of Warren's native employees would be traveling upriver in the double-dugout outboard-powered catamaran which Warren referred to as his river truck. The craft was a larger version of the one in which Michael Rockefeller made his last trip, but in this case it did not have to cope with tidal rip currents, only the powerful but slow currents of the Sepik. Also, it had two powerful outboards, instead of the single engine which had powered Michael's vessel.

"We'll take the bloody what? river truck and send it up the river with the bloody camping gear. Then we'll take the big bloody double canoes and send them up with big bloody drums of fuel, which they can leave at some of these bloody little villages along the way. Then we'll follow in the next day or so in the bloody what? jet boat," Hansen explained.

"The natives will be OK up there. I know them all, though I'm the only bloody white bloke most of them have seen. There's nobody on the river after my place. That's why I call the bloody company Las Kompani, it's pidgin for the last bloody company on the Sepik!"

The morning after our arrival we left at dawn for Kanganomon, four hours' cruise down the river by jet boat.

The Sepik village was basically a river port. As we swung into it from the wide muddy stream, we could see large floating logs which served as docks for the village's many canoes, some with fierce carved crocodile-head prows. The actual village was only a mile or so from the river, but in the brief walk we became covered almost head to foot by large brown mosquitoes.

"These here brown bombers ain't so bloody bad," Hansen said. "There's a lot of them, but their bite isn't too fierce. It's the little black buggers that come at night that give you the real trouble."

But I noticed that even the native carriers slapped and cursed at the insect swarms.

The *haus tambaran* is roughly the men's council house. It is also the town hall, the local church and the village social gathering spot rolled into one. *Haus tambarans* in the

Sepik area are famous for their elaborate and imaginative artwork and their soaring dimensions that form a lofty peaked roof raising itself often 100 feet or more into the air, supported on thick straight columns of jungle mahogany, each completely covered along its entire length with carving.

Building of *haus tambarans* has fallen off under the Australian administration, which had been in control of this area for many years before World War II. Not that the Australians didn't encourage art, but native ritual required certain practices in building the *haus tambarans:* In order to have the right sort of magic, each post—and the big houses can be 200 feet in length with twenty posts to a side —must be soaked in the blood of an enemy!

Under the watchful eyes of the Australian patrol officers, headhunting and bloody raids had almost ceased in recent years. *Haus tambaran* construction became a thing connected with "time-belong-before." A house might have been started with five or six poles erected. Then there would be a dormant period, then suddenly two or three more poles would be added, almost surely indicating an undetected raid on an enemy village.

We broke through the surrounding bush to find the Kanganomon house set in its huge clearing like a medieval cathedral. Inside, the ceiling soared like a Gothic nave, and the wooden columns, each about three feet in circumference, were completely covered with never-repeated deep-relief carvings of grotesque gargoylelike heads, crocodiles, lizards, dogs, birds, male and female genitalia in endless variety. Hanging from the crosspoles were more carvings, each again different from the next. On the pounded dirt floor were small stools carved in the form of dwarf human figures. Along the sides were huge slit drums in the form of elaborately carved crocodiles, many with their natural accompaniment of parasite birds carved as attachments. The masks and carvings hanging from the crossbeams turned and swayed eerily in the slight breeze which passed through the long building, adding to the bizarre haunting quality of the giant hall. This, Hansen explained, was the true "arse belong Sepik"—the heart of the great Sepik art, now fading under religious restrictions and commercial demands.

I stood in awe before the magnificent craft of the Sepik carvers, who along with the Asmat seen by Rockefeller, were the greatest wood-carving artisans of New Guinea.

We returned late that night to Ambunti, and the following morning loaded into the jet boat for the trip upriver to the May River and unexplored cannibal country.

15

MOST OF our gear, except for the camera equipment, had preceded us upriver. To lighten the load further, we decided to pick up interpreters and guides farther up the river.

"Will we need weapons?" I asked.

"Naw," said Hansen, bare-chested and in shorts for the trip. "We'll be all right with the regular gear."

"What's that?"

"Well, I got this sporterized what AR-15, and the shotgun for ducks, if we see any on the way upriver, and the Colt bloody .357 Magnum."

This seemed adequate to me, considering we were going to an area where we were supposed to be welcome as friends.

"Still, it doesn't pay to take bloody chances, does it?" Hansen commented as we set out on the 200-mile journey to the May River patrol post, last government control point, at the junction of the May and Sepik rivers. Beyond this was largely unexplored territory. Between Ambunti and the May River post there was nothing but river, swamps and native villages.

The ride upriver to the May River patrol post took from dawn until nightfall, with a stop halfway to refuel from the drums which had been left along the riverbank by Hansen's advance catamaran.

Hundreds of egrets, once nearly exterminated for their showy feathers, rose lazily from the 15-foot-tall reeds that lined the riverbank for miles and often raced casually with the jet upstream for several yards before settling again into the reeds. Occasionally we would pass small clusters of native huts along the shores and on the porches could see magnificently carved fighting shields. At infrequent intervals we passed groups of dugout canoes heading up or downstream on some local mission, and two or three times Hansen pointed out crocodiles slithering off into the muddy water.

The river, in color and composition, answered Mark Twain's description of the Mississippi—"too thin to plow and too thick to drink." In the middle, Hansen said, it was hundreds of feet deep. At frequent intervals it forked and split into smaller channels. Occasionally Hansen would veer suddenly into a yards-wide channel through the reeds, explaining that he was taking a shortcut. But no map on earth could have guided him on his way.

At dusk we turned off the Sepik for a brief run on the May River to the cluster of houses perched on a point above the river which represented the last habitation of government.

We set up base camp that night at the May River patrol post, where there are two or three huts belonging to the local officer, or *kiap*, including a crude jail with a corrugated tin roof. Warren owns a small trade store here and has built a house on 25-foot stilts; it overlooks the river just where the May joins the Sepik.

The next morning Warren showed us on the map where we were headed. The blue line of the May River continued for only a few miles, then dwindled into an uncertain dotted line and faded into nothingness.

"No boats have been up here where we're going," he explained, "though foot patrols have pushed through to Gwimi, the first village.

"You blokes will be about the fourth bloody white men these fellows have seen," Hansen said. "These people are still a bit wild. Reason the patrol had to push in there was the government had gotten complaints that the natives of Gwimi, where we're camping tonight, had killed and eaten the men of the next village—ten bloody kanakas— and taken all the bloody what? Women!"

I asked if he thought it was safe to camp there.

"Oh, yeah! They don't bother bloody white men, especially if they're armed. Only Europeans that get it usually are people who stir them up—like missionaries and patrol officers once in a while. Safer there than in your bloody New York, I reckon." (Rockefeller had been told something like that by Dutch authorities in the Asmat.)

"The *luluai* at Gwimi put in six years back in Wewak in jail for his part in massacring and eating that nearby village. Only got out this bloody year."

In the afternoon we headed upriver for Gwimi. The river got shallower and shallower, but the jet boat skimmed over gravel beds and rapids only inches deep, occasionally even scraping bottom with her fiber-glass hull, but without losing speed. Finally, after jouncing over several shallow patches, we found ourselves in a navigable area of the May River again.

At the junction of the May and the Muni rivers sat the village of Gwimi, perched on a steep mudbank. Standing on the shore to greet us were about thirty warriors carrying bows and arrows, wearing bones in their noses and no other clothing except skin-colored gourds on their penises. As we pulled into shore, the natives began to rattle their bows and twang the strings threateningly while shouting ferociously.

"Just bloody ignore that," Warren said. "It's their way of saying hello."

I was relieved to hear this. Later, I found out this tribe not only had eaten its neighboring village, but during the past four years had attacked and eaten three villages in the vicinity. Many of the men in the village were only recently back from a jail sentence for the most recent massacre a little more than a year before. Cannibalism in this area, at least, was often caused by sheer hunger. The few native animals—pigs, opossums, wallabies and tree kangaroos—are scarce, and surprisingly, only occasional catfish are to be found in the rivers—and crocodiles, of course. (When you eat a crocodile, it's said, your breath smells like carrion for days.)

We were offered the use of the *haus kiap*—a hut in the village, built at the instruction of the one government man who had reached this post—but we found it stuffy, overrun with mice, and filled with flies from the pigs which wallowed happily under the stilted floor. It was late, and we asked some of the men to put up our tent. As they started, clouds formed quickly in the sky, promising another one of the frequent drenching showers. Fires had been lit as soon as we arrived, so we quickly gobbled our dinner of *kau-kau*, roasted in the fire, and lubricated with canned Australian butter. For dessert there was tasty local pawpaw.

"They grow the best bloody *kau-kau* in the world up here," Hansen said, wolfing down the charred sweet potato. "You won't get kai like this in your Waldorf bloody Astoria!"

In minutes the expected downpour came, and we huddled in the tent for the rest of the night.

The next day we took off, now lightened of almost all our camping equipment and carrying nothing but our guns and camera gear.

"From just above here on, this is what? Unexplored territory," Hansen said. "We are off the bloody map."

Above us was one village which as yet had no name. It was populated by immigrants. These are Osulumani people who came from over the mountain from the south and have settled here only recently. Their village had never been visited. Hansen, in fact, had only recently heard of its existence from other natives.

The Osulumani village was only a few miles upstream, and the natives, who had heard our jet coming long before we pulled up to their mudbank, were lined up silently, bow and arrow in hand, waiting for our arrival. After having been initiated to the noisier welcome at Gwimi, this made me apprehensive, but Hansen reassured me.

"I understand these bloody people. Don't worry. It's all right. They're just a bit frightened."

Apparently he was right, because the local men rushed out to attach our lines to nearby logs and surrounded us in a jabbering crowd, examining our cameras, our clothing and even our sunglasses with curiosity. One native picked up an aluminum film can which we had discarded and returned shortly afterward wearing it in place of his penis gourd.

The river from this point on was new territory; it had never been navigated. Even Yako, our Gwimi guide, was excited, as he had never been to this area. It soon became apparent why. We were now in an almost continuous series of shoals, rapids and gravel banks which made the river impassable even for native canoes. I was thrilled each time we rounded a bend, expecting some sort of never-seen wonder to greet me. But Warren put me straight.

"There'll be no people up here," he explained. "There's a sort of bloody line at a certain parallel on the map, and if you trace it across the bloody range, you'll find that people just don't live above that."

Unfortunately he was right. After another half day's cruising we had to turn back for lack of fuel.

But I was still anxious to find the place where the original headhunting rites are practiced today. Warren had sent couriers to see if they could locate a village which would trust us enough to let us view the rites of the preparation of a human head. (Not the *taking* of the head. Just the artistic process of turning the head into the artifact we had first seen at Wewak.)

That night Hansen told us that we were in luck. His boy had found a village farther down the river—about a half day in the jet boat—where they might be preparing heads the next day. No questions were asked about where the heads came from.

At dawn we loaded in the jet boat and took off.

Hansen pledged us to secrecy, though we never could have found the area again even if we had been inclined to. The village we were visiting was spread, like so many others, for about a half mile along the river.

Most of the people seemed to be away, either traveling on the river in their canoes or tending to their gardens. A nucleus of elders, however, is always left to guard the village against strangers.

Two black, strong-looking men, wearing "arse-grass" and weird shell nosepieces which drooped down like the beak of a heron, were brought to greet us. We were led by a series of slippery local log bridges to the men's lodge, an open-sided hut which contained a large wooden slit drum in the shape of a crocodile, and had the usual broad, high benches on each side where the men of the village sat in the heat of the day and talked. On each side of the door was a primitive life-sized wooden figure. Sitting on the shelf were two dry, smoke-darkened skulls, one of them with a single tooth grinning inanely from its upper jaw. I was glad to observe that neither appeared to have been freshly taken.

In the tent also were the rest of the necessary supplies—a pile of black fluff, which I soon realized was human hair to be added to the bald skull; some reddish clay; sticks for painting decorations; coconut shells containing paint made from betel nuts (red), lime (white) and burned coconut husks (black); and small shiny giri-giri shells used to decorate the skulls and to simulate the eyes.

The two men, obviously leaders of the community, did not seem frightened or worried about our presence, once Hansen had assured him that our semimilitary safari outfits didn't mean we were government men.

The atmosphere was cheerful as a quilting bee, but I noticed that as a precaution or perhaps as a status symbol, Hansen had hung his Magnum on a post nearby.

We watched as the hollows and blank places of the skull grew features of red-gray clay under the skillful hands of the two men.

Giri-giri shells placed in the eye sockets bore an uncanny resemblance to living human eyes. Chewed sticks dipped in the tricolored paints were traced over the cheeks in spiral designs to resemble traditional war paint. A pig-tusk nose-bone was fitted through the clay septum. Gradually the heads assumed such reality I thought they would speak.

Were the sculptors following a conventionalized design? Or were they re-creating the features of the skull's original owner? This we could not find out, except that no two decorated skulls I ever saw had the same features. Also, while Sepik art is in general highly abstract and stylized, the faces on the prepared skulls were as natural as a human face. In the end, with their hair in place, they looked amazingly alive.

The preparation took about four hours, and we finally got back to camp long after dark. As we pulled to the shore, Warren's father, who had come up from Australia to help run the trade store, came out to greet us.

"Evening, boys! Out shopping for souvenirs?"

I grinned. Riding alongside the jet boat's inboard engines were several seven-foot shields I had bought that afternoon, plus a life-sized carved figure. Wrapped in pandanus leaves at the bottom of the boat were the two freshly decorated human heads.

16

DETRACTORS OF Michael Rockefeller had spread rumors since his disappearance that he had got into serious trouble by recording the activity of a warlike tribe in the Baliem Valley. There were recurring reports that Michael's party had stirred up warfare resulting in many native deaths.

Peter Barter of Trans Australian Airlines had offered to help me visit a similar—possibly *more* primitive—group in the Eastern Highlands. It was the Kukukukus—the "meanest men in the world"—whom I had seen terrorizing a group of Papuan tribesmen on my first visit to New Guinea in 1943. Barter said that his airline was constructing a new strip at a place called Marawaka, and that to date no more than a handful of whites had been there—no missionaries or anthropologists and only a few government and airline people.

Marawaka paralleled the conditions in the Baliem Valley in many ways. It was a land of warlike tribesmen and had been only recently contacted and not yet completely subdued. Marawaka is one of the newest settlements to be contacted.

The Kukukuku's odd-sounding name is regarded as anything but humorous by those who have been in touch with members of this large tribal group elsewhere. Keith McCarthy still carries scars in his belly and leg as souvenirs of his first visit to this warlike people. He comments: "The Kukukuku have a deserved reputation as the most bloodthirsty and vicious in New Guinea."

Kukukuku territory extends for miles through the Central Highlands, but not all their tribal areas have been reached and tamed by the government. It has many differences from the Dani culture Michael dealt with in the Baliem and is almost 600 miles away, but at least one thing the Kukukuku and Rockefeller's Dani tribesmen had in common: a deep cultural commitment to violence as a way of life.

The arrival of steel axes in these Stone Age communities eased some of the important functions of men in the community—building, carving, making weapons—while the woman's work—gardening and looking after the younger children—was hardly affected at all. As a result, the men had more time to devote to their elaborate battle rituals. When the government banned fighting and even the war dances which led up to the big battles, the men were left with very little to occupy their time. (This happened in Rockefeller's Baliem Valley, too.) In Marawaka, these activities had been effectively banned only within the past year.

Even after the Kukukuku had been contacted by Australian patrols, they continued their dedication to violence, not only in intertribal warfare but in casual relations with friends and relatives.

McCarthy saw an example of this sort of unreasoning hostility when Kukukukus visiting his camp got into a quarrel over the trade of some food.

"They began to yell at each other," McCarthy recalls. "Without warning, one whipped out a club and crushed in the other man's head with a blow. The killer hardly glanced at the body as he stepped over it to offer us his food —and the rest of the group appeared to be totally unconcerned as they continued their trading. I later saw it [the body] smoked, sitting on a platform holding a bunch of arrows in its hand."

Jumping-off place for Marawaka was the mile-high frontier town of Goroka, which we reached after a day-long ride along New Guinea's only highway, a road stretching from Lae into the highlands. During the trip we encountered two landslides, a forest fire and one frightening earthquake.

In Goroka, as in most frontier towns, the bar serves as a center for social and business information. And it was here in the bar of the Bird of Paradise Hotel that I got some firsthand knowledge of the Papuans' obsession with revenge, or payback. This was the motive most often mentioned by those who alleged Rockefeller was murdered.

A local businessman in the traditional local garb—knee socks, shorts and open-throated short-sleeved shirt—asked whether we had run into any trouble on the road. "The Asaros and the Chimbus are on the warpath, I hear."

I was sure that my Yankee leg was being pulled, and in a

way it was, since there was no real danger to whites. But it seemed that we had arrived during a period of strain between two local tribes. The Chimbus claimed that an Asaro Valley man had killed one of their tribesmen a week before and were now planning a payback raid. Two war parties had been organized, it was rumored.

As always with payback, it didn't matter so much whether the guilty party was found, as long as the score was evened up by a death on the enemy's side. Just the same, the Bundi tribesmen who had been involved in the killing had been taken into protective police custody that day, it was rumored, and police patrols were on the road planning to intercept the war parties. Tension had mounted to the point where local tribesmen, long accustomed to the peaceful "city" life of the Goroka area, were again walking around with their bows and arrows near at hand.

Payback is still a serious problem that more than once in recent years had resulted in major bloodshed and killings. Since the payback can be directed not only at the guilty offender (or rather the *presumed* guilty offender) but also at any of his clan or even his local language group, it is obvious that the targets of revenge are often completely innocent people. If payback is not exacted, New Guineans believe, the spirit of the victim will wander the earth, appealing to his relatives to avenge him so that he can go to his final rest.

These payback incidents are by no means confined to the remote and savage areas. Not long before, a worker at a Goilala plantation on the outskirts of Port Moresby had been killed when a tractor rolled over him. Though the incident was officially termed an accident, the brother of the dead man was not satisfied with the coroner's verdict. He learned the identity of the driver of the tractor, who for some reason was not available at the moment. So he decided that it would be just as fitting to kill the *brother* of the tractor driver, who happened to be a patient in the Port Moresby Hospital at the time. He went to the hospital, where he found the tractor driver's brother being wheeled from the X-ray room back to his ward, and without a word plunged a knife into him. After that he yielded to arrest with little or no resistance. As far as he was concerned, justice had been done, and the proper payback had been achieved.

Teitendau, an Obura fight leader from a village near Kainantu, nursed a payback grudge for years—a not uncommon situation. He was convinced that his brother, who according to Australian records, had died from natural causes, had in fact been the victim of a sorcery murder performed by a Chimbu.

Several years later the fight leader was with seven of his fellow clansmen when he ran into a party of Chimbu tribesmen who had come into Obura territory to trade for bird of paradise plumes. Teitendau and his fellow warriors fell on the five Chimbus and hacked them to death with their axes.

The Obura men were arrested and tried at Kainantu, the nearest government administrative outpost. As the accused were being led away under heavy police escort at the end of the third day of the court proceedings, two Chimbu warriors slipped into the area and cut Teitendau down with their axes. The murderers then presented themselves at the local police station, their axes still literally dripping with the blood of the Obura fight chief. They explained that they had doubts that full justice would be done, so they decided to arrange their own payback while the opportunity was at hand.

As a result of this new bloodshed, a full-scale tribal war nearly erupted in the area. The government had to send in a DC-3 with heavy police reinforcements, and when reports reached Kainantu that hundreds of Obura warriors were marching on the city, all the Chimbu plantation workers had to be evacuated on the same plane. The Oburas were finally placated by government officers and persuaded to return to their villages, and the trial of the dead Teitendau's seven accomplices continued under a heavy police guard. The Oburas were found guilty and given fairly light prison sentences; but one year later a party of Chimbus evened the score with another killing, and a few months later the Oburas retaliated with a payback killing of their own. It often seems that there is no end to payback.

The next day word spread through Goroka that government police had succeeded in intercepting the Chimbu revenge party and had persuaded them to accept pigs and other valuables in place of enemy life as payback. The Chimbus agreed—provided the government continued to try to find and punish the guilty man.

At 6 A.M. the following morning we were at the airstrip, since Marawaka tended to be socked in with cloud cover every afternoon.

Coming from a country where 60 miles is an hour's drive, it still was hard to realize how remote a place could be a mere hour's flight away in a Cessna. But Australian pioneer patrol officers have lived for years within 10 miles of the Marawaka people we were about to visit and had heard only rumors of their existence. Patrol Officer Jim Sinclair, whom I met in Goroka, had been one of the first to penetrate this country and to convince the fierce natives of the power of the government's rifles. He did this by visiting villages that had recently attacked and sometimes eaten members of other villages and informing them that the government wanted fighting to be *tambu* from now on. To show the power of the rifles, Sinclair had the Kukukukus plant a row of their heavy black-palm shields and fire at them first with their arrows. The natives were proud when one of the unbarbed, pit-pit cane arrows, tipped with black palm or bone, penetrated a heavy shield. But when the patrol officer lined up his police and had them fire their .303's at the shields, leaving them lacy with one-inch holes, the bushmen understood that the government was strong.

When Sinclair had patrolled near Marawaka in the fifties, he had been warned by the Imisis, themselves the terror of neighboring tribes, about the people near Marawaka. "They are bad people. They are no good true! The Butnari [another tribe] come and kill them. They are no good. They eat man. They kill the woman and pigs and bugger up the gardens. Oh, *Kiap,* it is the fashion of the wild men!"

At the Goroka strip we were already almost a mile high before takeoff. From there, the altimeter went up and up as we flew along the hump of the Bismarck Mountains alongside peaks topping 12,000 feet and over gorges, canyons and waterfalls which made walking in this territory a trek of weeks and even months.

The Marawaka strip lay on a steep downslope about 600 yards long, all grass. The mountains surrounding us were covered with mist.

"I'll have to just swoop in here, dump you, and turn around before that damn fog closes the place in," said Ian, the TAL charter pilot.

Minutes later we were unceremoniously unloaded on the tiny grassy strip surrounded by thatched huts and thatched Kukukuku warriors. The sight of the legendary mean men is impressive. They are small, almost pygmies, but powerfully built with deep chests and enormous thighs from climbing the steep mountains of their home territory. Each comes equipped with what seems to be a permanent burning scowl, which is so ingrained that their eyes are glaring even when their betel-stained teeth are grinning.

The Marawaka people wear a characteristic crisscross bandolier of yellow orchid stems running one way and white giri-giri shells running the other. Their noses are pierced at puberty, and each wears a cassowary bone or a boar's tusk in his nose—except for several men, obviously chiefs, who I noticed wore straight white or blue pointed objects which looked vaguely familiar. On close inspection, I realized that the nose pieces were ball-point pens! Later I found that they had seen the local patrol officers using them and had demanded them in trade.

Around his waist, each wore a girdle of cassowary bones into which almost all had stuck a long knife made from that same ostrichlike bird's thigh bones—except for a few suspiciously large ones which probably came from the tibias of fellow Kukukukus. Covering their genitals was a kind of sporran of grass that bulged out in front at least six inches. I was told that they never changed this garment until it rotted off. Hanging from their shoulders was what appeared to be a cloth cape but actually was a fabric made of beaten mulberry bark.

Each of the warriors carried a long black-palm bow and a sheaf of arrows. Several held crude fighting shields and the peculiar boomeranglike battle clubs seen only in this area. As we rapidly unloaded our cargo with the help of police who had run out to meet the plane, the warriors stood around us in a solid ring, whispering and staring at our red iron patrol boxes and our strange camera tripods, the like of which they had never seen. In the patrol boxes were several cases of cheap knives, a dozen or so trade tomahawks and cases of black-twist trade tobacco, all better than currency, which was unknown to them.

The patrol officer, Graeme Young, was the only other white man on the post, but the police assured us that the warriors, while they were "bush-kanaka true" (real wild men), would not harm us because they had learned that the white *kiap* in charge had guns that could damage severely and also good "cargo" like axes and knives and beads and cloth, which fortunately they wanted more than they did our lily-white bodies.

We explained to the young Australian administrator that we had come to see the Kukukukus on their home grounds —preferably some that had not become overcivilized.

"*None* of them are what you might call overcivilized," Graeme answered. "These people here have only seen about a half dozen white people in their lives. If you want to walk over those mountains for two or three days, you'll find some who may *never* have been contacted by a white man."

The next day, stripped down to a day's gear, carrying only a patrol box, camera equipment and food, we started on the trail into the bush.

The hamlets were laced together with trodden dirt paths, bounded in the villages with fences of pit-pit, a local sugar-cane which is one of the food staples. The gardens contained mostly *kau-kau* and taro. The women looked after them, poking about in the ground with primitive digging sticks, but running off in fright the minute we tried to approach them. Fear of strangers dominates the lives of these warlike people.

There is no such thing as a level path in the highlands, and the constant climbing and descending, crossing and re-crossing raging rivers on shaky log bridges were torture to our lungs and legs. Many of the villages perched like medieval fortresses on high cliffs that could only be reached by endlessly zigzagging up the sides on inches-narrow paths. Reaching the top of one of these fortresslike precipices, panting and puffing in the 10,000-foot altitude we had reached by this time, I had to be actually dragged the last few feet by sturdy Kukukuku carriers.

I remember thinking that if something should happen to me, I would have to be carried two days through bush, then wait a few days at Marawaka strip for the charter plane, then wait in Goroka to be flown to Moresby, where every other day I *might* make a connection with a flight which would link me to the Pan Am round-the-world circuit. And only two days after *that* I could be safe at home.

When we returned to Marawaka after a hike on these tortuous trails, the tiny valley where the airstrip perched was nearly full of warriors waving their spears and arrows, chanting, singing and making passes with clubs, spears and bows and arrows.

"It's the first they have had a chance to do a war dance since the government put a *tambu* on fighting," Jim explained, as we watched the increasingly violent tempo of the dance. We had returned at a moment when the patrol officer was off on other business. "I doubt if Graeme would permit this if he were here," Jim said. "They get too excited."

Not much later, down in the midst of the flailing crowd, shooting stills while Jim registered the scene on the Bolex from a hill above the strip, I saw what he meant. Sighting through the view finder, I found I was getting long tan blurs. Taking my eye from the view, I realized that the blurs were arrows! A Kukukuku ran past me with two arrows in his shield. Another appeared to be running right at me with his club but actually was aiming at one of his friends just behind me.

The dancing passion seemed endless, and it was afternoon before the tribesmen were exhausted. The "fighting" had been a form of war play. At the end of the battle, I was shocked to see two inert bodies on the field. A quick examination by one of the Papuan constables determined that the victims were merely stunned.

Still, I had come closer than I expected to seeing how easily even a mock war dance can get out of hand among people so recently involved in real and bloody battles. If the men had been killed, I probably would have been accused of inciting them to fatal warfare as Michael and his party in the Baliem Valley had been.

17

WE RETURNED to Moresby on April 20. It was by now more than nine weeks since I had started on what I had thought would be an assignment of less than a month. Though it was difficult not to become more and more caught up in the bizarre and primitive atmosphere of the New Guinea hinterlands, I had to face the fact that there was little more I could do from the Australian side of the border. There was pressure, too, from New York to wind up the assignment. A sheaf of cables in my mailbox at the hotel emphasized the fact that time was closing in.

Before we left, I had an opportunity to interview John Ryan, former correspondent of the Australian Broadcasting Company and now New Guinea correspondent for the *Pacific Islands Monthly*.

Ryan had been on the actual search party for Rockefeller back in 1961. Like most local people, he was firmly of the opinion that Rockefeller had not drowned but had reached the shore and had been killed there by natives, though the reasons for the slaying were not clear to him.

"Whatever it was, you can bet that those Dutch officials had something to do with hushing it up. A killing like that wouldn't look good on their record at a time they were trying to convince the world that they had successfully pacified the area and were more qualified to administer it

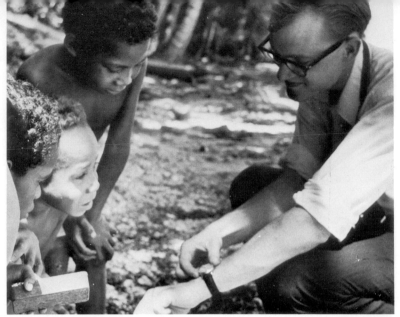

Michael Rockefeller tries to explain wonders of wristwatch to awed village youngsters.

Rockefeller tapes natives in Baliem Valley.

UPI

Rockefeller showed great curiosity over native ways and often was able to establish close relations with village young people.

Michael was an excellent canoeist and swimmer at the time of his disappearance.

UPI

Michael Rockefeller visited this village of Otsjanep on the Ewta River in New Guinea.

Corneles Van Kessel, Sacred Heart missionary, here in native paint at Otsjanep Village.

Tony Saulnier

Dr. René Wassing.

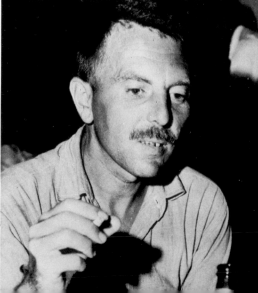

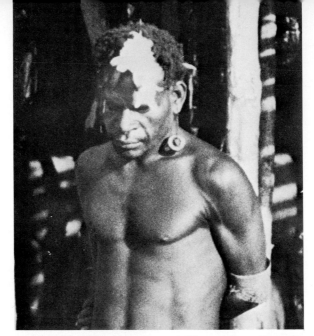

Ajam, fight chief of Otsjanep Village, whose kin were slain by a Dutch patrol and who almost surely was the man responsible for the fate of Michael Rockefeller.

Natives of Otsjanep Village work on revenge *bis* pole. Ajam is at extreme right. Photo taken by Tony Saulnier of *The Sky Above and the Mud Below* team.

Governor Nelson Rockefeller and Michael's twin sister, Mrs. Mary Strawbridge, arrive in Merauke to search for Michael. P. J. Plateel, governor of Dutch New Guinea, is at right.

UPI

District Commander F. R. J. Eibrink Jansen checks charts of search area.

UPI

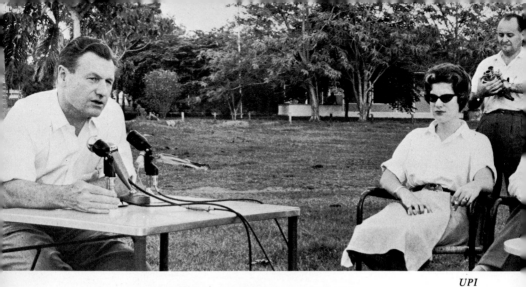

Nelson Rockefeller holds press conference to report on search.

Back in New York, Governor Rockefeller and Mrs. Strawbridge examine primitive art objects collected by Michael in New Guinea.

Author Milt Machlin goes ashore at Kanapu, remote island where Donahue said he last saw Rockefeller.

Author in Central Highlands with Kukukukus—described by anthropologists and explorers as "the meanest men in the world."

Anderson-Globe

Sepik River native starts decoration of human head.

Author examines partially completed head with giri-giri shells for eyes. Hair of victim and more shells for decoration are on banana leaf on ground.

PREPARATION OF HUMAN HEAD

Warren Hanson, trader and jetboat guide, with nearly completed decorated head.

Antique decorated head in Wewak area.

than the Indonesians, who were first starting their big drive to take over the territory."

"What about Father Van Kessel's report?" I asked.

"Seems like fair dinkum to me," Ryan said. "Van Kessel was certainly in a position to know. He was one of the last people to see Rockefeller, and he is one of the few people in the world who speak the local dialect. Also, he'd been in the area for many years. I think he was the first white to penetrate it. If anyone could get close to the natives, it would be him. But I must say he's the first one that seems to be willing to talk about what really happened."

Before I left the Pacific, I felt it was imperative that I talk with Van Kessel in person.

I booked a flight to the Philippines, where Van Kessel was last reported working, and the following afternoon took my leave of Anderson and a few local friends and prepared to head back for civilization.

At the airport next morning I was pleased to catch sight of the sturdy figure of Tim Ward, who was back in Moresby to conclude the business of selling out his Trobriand guest lodge to a syndicate of local Chinese businessmen.

"I picked up some interesting information about a week after you left," Ward said. "Chap named Albie Robbins who runs a trade store in Buniara said that on March 2 he was running his MVT to the mainland from Samarai when he spotted what he took to be a large white submarine, running fast enough to circle his slow-moving landing craft several times. The fact is that I myself had heard a report of a similar sub from the local assistant district commissioner about a year ago." Robbins swung his MVT into a tight turn to try to evade the big cigar-shaped underwater object, Ward said. The sub followed him easily but stayed behind him for only about 100 feet and then apparently left the area.

"I don't know how this ties in to your friend Donahue's tale, except that I'm convinced there is strange activity going on out there. I also heard something about those light flashes you saw in the Sim-Sims. A missionary's wife saw what she described as lights or flames which she reported in that area a month ago Monday. That's just after you had returned from the Sim-Sims. She must have seen the same lights. Her report was checked, but there were no reports of ships in distress in the area or of seismic activity. Her husband also saw the lights and thought it was a vessel on fire."

So, still pursued by the bizarre trail of Donahue's fancy, I mounted the plane for Manila.

In Manila, a city haunted by many memories of my war days, I set about tracing the Dutch missionary. I had written to Father Van Kessel through the Sacred Heart Mission but had had no reply. For once luck was with me. On the masthead of the Manila *Post* I saw the name of Tony Escoda, whom I had known since he was an orphaned child (his parents had been executed by the Japanese for their role in the resistance). Tony, in turn, led me to John Nance, a young newsman I had met several times in New York when he was first planning to go to the Orient. It was Nance who had broken the Van Kessel story.

Nance said that the Associated Press had sent him to see Father Van Kessel after Pierre Gaisseau, director of the Academy-Award winning film *The Sky Above and the Mud Below*, had issued a statement in Tokyo that Van Kessel was one of the few men who knew the true story of Rockefeller's disappearance. The story Van Kessel told was the one I had read in the New York *Post* before the start of my journey. Nance said that there was little to add to it, other than the fact that he had found Van Kessel to be an unconventional but charming man.

"Can I go down there and see him?" I asked.

"Afraid not," Nance said. "He's been sent back to Holland for a rest. Many of the Crozier Fathers were upset that he had attracted so much press attention with his statement. Some even said that he was a publicity seeker. But that wasn't true. We sought *him* out after Gaisseau mentioned his name, so he had nothing to do with initiating the story. Once I saw him, though, he seemed pleased to tell it because he felt it had been suppressed too long."

Nance was able to get me Van Kessel's address at the Sacred Heart Mission in Holland, and I made arrangements to return to New York via Amsterdam. In addition to Van Kessel, I hoped to be able to meet in Holland with Gerbrands and René Wassing.

So now the search for Michael Rockefeller, started by Donahue's wild statement in my office in New York, was to take me clear around the world.

I landed bleary-eyed at Schiphol Airport in Amsterdam, barely knowing what time or day it was. In my hand was clutched a penciled scrawl from John Nance: "Van Kessel, Driehuis Velsen (near Haarlem), Sacred Heart Mission is at Tilburg." Tired as I was, I was desperately anxious to make contact with Van Kessel. (For all I knew, he would be reassigned that very day to some exotic posting and I'd miss him again!)

I rented a car at the airport and in two hours had arrived in Velsen. A few minutes later I was knocking at the parish house door of the Velsen Catholic church.

"Father Van Kessel?" I asked the harried-looking housekeeper. The woman, who, unlike most of the Dutch, apparently spoke no English, pressed her fingers to her mouth and fled to the dark interior. I waited. In a few minutes a gray-haired curate emerged with his hands outstretched.

"Good afternoon, Father Van Kessel!"

It was a natural mistake, since I was dressed in my last

presentable suit and tie, both black—the garb adopted by many Catholic priests in Europe who no longer wear the clerical collar.

"*I'm* not Father Van Kessel," I said. "I'm *looking* for Father Van Kessel!"

I established the fact that I was trying to find the Sacred Heart Mission and was directed to its local quarters a few blocks away. I drove up to a massive stone house with huge golden oak doors and pushed the blue and white porcelain bell button. A lay brother answered.

"Father Van Kessel?" I asked again.

He held up his palm in a staying gesture and left me waiting at the door. Five minutes later the door opened and a slim, tanned, gray-haired man in a light-brown suit opened the heavy door. He had wavy graying hair and a thin sensitive face somewhat reminiscent of a younger Otto Kruger, the film star.

"I am Van Kessel," he said.

I breathed a sigh of relief. I couldn't have stood the thought of another disappointment. I looked down at the scrap of penciled address in my hand and couldn't help reflecting that New Guinea natives believed writing to be a form of magic—and wasn't it? With a few cryptic graphite scratches on a piece of paper I had been able to fly halfway around the world, push a bell, and find exactly the man I was looking for!

I introduced myself and gave him my card. Van Kessel regarded me with a quizzical but calm expression. "What can I do for you, Mr. Machlin?" he asked. His English was good, and only slightly accented.

"I would like to talk to you about the disappearance of Michael Rockefeller." He regarded me for a second or two, then nodded.

"Come in. We can talk better inside."

18

He ushered me into a large sunny conference room where a lay brother laid a cloth on a modern oak table and served us with coffee and buttered toast.

"I spoke with John Nance in Manila," I said at last, trying to lead into the discussion without setting off any alarms. After all, he had been chastened for his previous public statement. Was his recall to home headquarters after sixteen years in New Guinea and six in the Philippines some form of punishment for having spoken too freely? "He suggested that I could reach you here."

"Yes. That was quite a story he wrote."

"You liked it?"

Van Kessel shrugged. "I didn't like it. I didn't dislike it. It was the truth. It has very little to do with me any more."

"Would you be willing to tell it all to me in detail?"

"Why not? It is not a secret anymore."

"Was it ever a secret?"

"People just didn't talk about it," he said. "Everybody was afraid it would stir up trouble again. But it is the truth, and you cannot ever keep back the truth."

I decided to risk a frank approach. Certainly Van Kessel, for one, showed no sign of shrinking from the story.

"Father, would you be willing to tell me the full story on tape and to allow me to film the interview?"

"I will be available at eleven tomorrow, if you can do it then. After that I must be away for a while."

"I'll be here," I assured him.

The next morning in the flower-lined sunny courtyard of the mission Ftaher Van Kessel gave the interview which follows. It has been edited only for clarity and to eliminate redundancy:

FATHER VAN KESSEL INTERVIEW

MACHLIN: Father Van Kessel, you were one of the very first people to explore the Asmat coast, were you not?

VAN KESSEL: That's right.

MACHLIN: And you were in Dutch New Guinea at the time that Michael Rockefeller disappeared?

VAN KESSEL: I was there. I met him alive, and before the tragical incident. So I know him personally, also. And then he went for another trip into the mountains, in the former Dutch New Guinea, and then he came back to the Asmat coast.

MACHLIN: So you met him on his first trip?

VAN KESSEL: One of the first trips, *ja,* because he was in New Guinea for a couple of months.

MACHLIN: And then he went back—

VAN KESSEL: He went back for another trip, making movies in the mountains of New Guinea, and then he came back, and just on the trip back to me, I was waiting for him also, that tragical incident happened that he was drowned—

MACHLIN: Then he saw you at that time and asked you to help him arrange to film the actual artwork and the carvings of the—

VAN KESSEL: *Ja,* because I had to guide the travel and knew all the villages there, as interpreter, because every tribe in New Guinea, they have their own language.

MACHLIN: How many outside people do you think in the whole world can speak that Asmat dialect?

VAN KESSEL: About twenty, about twenty. Mostly missionaries and two doctors. There was a linguist who was studying the language, some government officials. Say, about twenty people who know very well this language.

MACHLIN: So that if the natives had something to say, there'd be only a limited number of people who could understand what they said?

VAN KESSEL: Sure, sure. And that is why I was very valuable, for example, to Rockefeller, to other visitors also, as a guide, as an interpreter, and so on.

MACHLIN: Well, then, what happened after he—how did he start on his last trip, and what happened then?

VAN KESSEL: They made a so-called catamaran, these two canoes tied together, including one or two outboard motors.

MACHLIN: There was only one outboard motor, because that was one of the problems—

VAN KESSEL: Oh, maybe, maybe. . . .

MACHLIN: One of the problems was that they needed two to buck the tides. . .

VAN KESSEL: Oh, well, I never heard the details. Anyhow, that is not so important. He started from the main post, the government post, from Agats, and then over the sea he went to my mission post in Basim, along the Casuarinen coast. And during the trip, because of rough sea—I think you can hear all the details from Mr. Wassing—something happened, and finally the whole catamaran was tipped over, and they were sitting on top of the canoes, and then, according to the report from Mr. Wassing, after more than twenty-four hours, sitting in the cold, without any drink or food, after one night, the first night, Michael jumped up from the raft, because very far away, according to me too far, he saw a small coastline, and he told Wassing "I'm a good swimmer, I'll try," and so he tied up two gasoline cans, kind of floaters, around his waist, and he jumped from the raft, and he started swimming.

MACHLIN: But Wassing objected to his trying—

VAN KESSEL: Sure he objected. He said, "You are crazy, they will find us because the canoe, the raft tipped over, anyhow was filled with water. The two natives. . . ."

MACHLIN: They jumped off earlier?

VAN KESSEL: They jumped off, and they reached the shore, to make time, to tell the first post, in this case it was Agats—

MACHLIN: And it was a result of this first report that help ultimately came?

VAN KESSEL: Sure. Because as I told you, he was on his way to see me, so I was waiting for him, and it was on a Sunday afternoon. I saw a big plane from the Dutch Navy, a Neptune plane, circling over the sea, so immediately I thought something happened, because I never saw a plane there. It was a very remote place. And not only passing over but circling in—and even a big searchlight. So I supposed that there must be something about Michael Rockefeller, and immediately I heard something from my small receiver.

MACHLIN: Wassing was quite an experienced man in that area?

VAN KESSEL: Not so. He was more in the office. No, he was not experienced there in this field.

MACHLIN: Why do you think Michael chose to ignore his advice?

VAN KESSEL: I can't imagine. His line was: "I'm a good swimmer and I'll try it."

MACHLIN: Of course, if he had gotten to shore . . . the mangrove swamps are so muddy and—

VAN KESSEL: Yeah, terrible, terrible.

MACHLIN: That even getting to shore you'd be in just as much trouble as if you were at sea, maybe even more so.

VAN KESSEL: Yeah, but don't forget that he was along the coast, before their trip, so he knew something about the circumstances. The shore is rather good—a little bit sandy, but the whole coast is practically only mud.

MACHLIN: Now, in that area, there are maybe eight or ten little villages, some near the coast and some up the little rivers . . . in other words, if he got on solid land or up one of the rivers, there'd be a chance there were canoes around—a chance that he'd be found.

VAN KESSEL: Everywhere, everywhere. There are local villages, and they're always out on the sea for fishing purposes.

MACHLIN: After the disappearance, you had a great invasion of foreign press and searchers?

VAN KESSEL: Sure. The first thing I did myself— I supposed

there was something wrong, and I heard it from the radio, and immediately the next morning, early in the morning, I went out in my canoe—the only means of transportation I had—to search along the coast, and even up to Piramapun to have a look, 'cause maybe he reached shore. That was the first thing. And then immediately the next day the first planes came in and the Navy ship and then you know, everybody—

MACHLIN: How long did the search go on?

VAN KESSEL: No more than ten days.

MACHLIN: For ten days? And Governor Rockefeller came down?

VAN KESSEL: He came also. I met him personally, and the twin sister of Michael—Mrs. Strawbridge if I'm not wrong.

MACHLIN: Yes. Then after ten days they felt that there was no hope of finding him?

VAN KESSEL: No hope, no hope. Especially because it was too far. In the meantime, they found Mr. Wassing, they saw him on the raft, and they picked him up by boat and he was OK. . . . Michael jumped off—where I don't know, because in the meantime another night he [Wassing] was drifting along the coast.

MACHLIN: He drifted for a whole night on that strong river current?

VAN KESSEL: Yes, and maybe more than fifty miles.

MACHLIN: And then the tide went the other way. So he possibly drifted back to the north. Was there any way to know where Michael was at the time?

VAN KESSEL: Well, it was impossible for Wassing to indicate exactly the spot where he jumped off, and it was important for the search, to find him. That makes a difference of two hundred miles. . . .

MACHLIN: So then the announcement was made that Michael Rockefeller was presumed drowned in the sea?

VAN KESSEL: Sure.

MACHLIN: And the search was called off?

VAN KESSEL: And the sea was full of sharks and crocodiles. It's a really dangerous sea. But it wasn't certain—he was drowned and he was eaten by the sharks or the crocodiles or—

MACHLIN: Then you were left again more or less alone—you returned to normal operations. There were no more newspaper people, no more searchers, no more airplanes?

VAN KESSEL: That's right, that's right. And helicopters, and so on.

MACHLIN: When did you hear something next about Michael Rockefeller?

VAN KESSEL: It was about one week after the last plane and the last helicopters and the last boat left, about one week after that. I heard some rumors in the neighboring villages. . . . I had my house in the next village, which of course was very close—nearly every day I saw the people also. They were my good friends. So after one week I heard some rumors, somebody telling that they found somebody, vaguely, and I was really interested. It could be possible that Michael arrived at [the village of] Otsjanep—not alive, that was practically impossible—but maybe they found the corpse or something. And so I was really anxious to know, to be informed a little bit more. So I started traveling just in that area, checking all those rumors, and it was just like a kind of puzzle, one rumor from that village and another rumor from another village, and there were a lot closely connected. So I was suspicious even about the possibilities of a killing. The first thing was, a small letter, a small note from a certain Dr. Dresser—one medical Protestant missionary from the TEAM [The Evangelical Alliance Mission] there in New Guinea—and I don't have that small letter anymore, but the contents were: "It is possible that Otsjaneps killed Michael Rockefeller."

MACHLIN: Yes. So he had heard rumors, also—

VAN KESSEL: Sure.

MACHLIN: And he put it in a letter?

VAN KESSEL: Sure, a small note to me, very small note.

MACHLIN: He had heard rumors from the same people or from other people?

VAN KESSEL: Other villages, other villages, because they are closely connected—

MACHLIN: The gossip was spreading through the villages?

VAN KESSEL: Yes, about sixty miles, the spreading of the story about Michael, they have all these contacts together. Funny thing, they never can keep silent about things, because you have to see the whole story in what you call in the way of black thinking. When you don't understand anything about primitive life, as I have after sixteen years there, you cannot understand it. . . .

MACHLIN: Is it true that they have a very special view toward death, that they tend to believe that people always die for some cause and always seek to pay back the person who caused the death?

VAN KESSEL: *Ja,* but you may not generalize, because the way of life of the different tribes in New Guinea is completely different. There are more than two hundred different tribes.

MACHLIN: No, but the institution of payback—

VAN KESSEL: You mean revenge?

MACHLIN: Yes, revenge killing.

VAN KESSEL: Ah, sure, that is true. I found that especially in that Otsjanep tribe, also, and even in the mountains.

MACHLIN: And not killings specifically directed against the person who caused them, but possibly a wife or child or anybody belonging to—

VAN KESSEL: Sure, sure.

MACHLIN: Then I think that this is an important fact, because wasn't there an incident some years prior to Michael's disappearance that caused them to have payback feelings toward—

VAN KESSEL: As I found out. This seems to be the reason . . . but I still didn't know exactly why [the tribesmen had killed Rockefeller]. But finally, I contacted Van Pey, a colleague of mine in a neighboring village. He knew a lot more than I did about that incident, and he gave me all the details also. It seems [from Van Pey's statement] that it was really the truth. That he had been killed and eaten by the people of Otsjanep.

MACHLIN: Did you get the full details?

VAN KESSEL: That is another thing. It seems to me more and more tragic for the father and mother and the twin sister of

Michael Rockefeller to hear about the tragic details. If they like to be informed, I can tell them, but it is better not to talk about that, I think. If somebody died . . . the wounds are healed already. It is nearly eight years ago, so I don't like to open again the wound.

MACHLIN: But actually attention has been focused on it [the Rockefeller story] again recently because of the "act of free choice" in West Irian. In fact, I think it has been published that he was found swimming. . . .

VAN KESSEL: At the time the whole thing was covered up, just a few official accounts that he was drowned. Just after the search there were some reports that he was killed by the natives, but these were immediately denied by the Dutch government. Immediately they said that it was impossible, and it was denied.

MACHLIN: Yes, but you heard these rumors that Michael had been killed, and you heard details?

VAN KESSEL: Yes, I found all the details. I even heard that relics were still in the village—eyeglasses and maybe even bones.

MACHLIN: And you reported all this to the government officials?

VAN KESSEL: I reported first to my superior, my bishop in New Guinea [Father Pitka], and I talked it over with one of the Dutch officials in Merauke.

MACHLIN: And did he take immediate action to find these relics?

VAN KESSEL: No. One of the terrible things is, I had to leave for vacation in Holland two months after I found out the whole truth. I was not able then—and it would even have been a little dangerous—to go right away to question the people involved in the killing, because they were scared.

MACHLIN: The villagers were afraid to be punished?

VAN KESSEL: Sure, sure. Actually I was informed by some of the Otsjanep people I talked to that when they found Michael alive, according to the story, the majority of the tribesmen were actually opposed to killing him.

MACHLIN: They found him alive—they were canoeing and they found him alive, still swimming in the water?

140

VAN KESSEL: *Ja.* Near the coast. But there was this fight chief Ajam—a fierce warrior. It had been one of his relatives that the Dutch had killed years before. About four years before, they had killed by accident some people of the village . . . a very sad incident, out of fear or whatever these Dutch people killed some natives. Anyhow, it is very deplorable.

MACHLIN: And Ajam, fight chief—

VAN KESSEL: This is what they told me. I was informed that when they did kill Rockefeller, it was a revenge, a payback for that.

MACHLIN: They told you frankly that it was a payback, that as far as they were concerned, he was any white person?

VAN KESSEL: Not the people of Otsjanep because they never really had made a straight confession to me. They were afraid. They tried to cover the whole story.

MACHLIN: So then Ajam, the fight chief, made the decision right on the spot that here was a chance for one payback killing for those four deaths four years before?

VAN KESSEL: *Ja,* no need to kill four people—one is enough for the payback.

MACHLIN: It was done immediately without torture or anything?

VAN KESSEL: They never torture, never. I know more than enough about the customs and the way of life. They never torture.

MACHLIN: So we can know at least that he didn't suffer any—

VAN KESSEL: No, no.

MACHLIN: And he wasn't held—

VAN KESSEL: No, I am absolutely sure about it. . . .

MACHLIN: Well, then, the tragic thing is that in a sense Michael's judgment was vindicated in that he *did* get to somebody that could have helped him, except under unfortunate circumstances.

VAN KESSEL: *Ja,* very unfortunate. If the shore was only two miles below that spot he was swimming right away in my hands, because I had my house there.

MACHLIN: It's interesting, because we had always assumed that he was mistaken in swimming to shore, but actually that wasn't a mistake. He *did* get to shore, and he *did* get to some people. His method worked, also.

VAN KESSEL: That is the most surprising thing in the whole story. His last words were "I am a good swimmer," according to Mr. Wassing, and he is really a good swimmer. The most surprising thing in the whole story is that he really reached the shore, because he jumped from the raft so far into the sea—

MACHLIN: Now, these people in the Asmat tribal areas still practice, I believe, ritual cannibalism?

VAN KESSEL: Sure, they do; they do, yes. Don't forget in fifty-six I was the first white man who appeared among the tribes, and they were really living in the Stone Age. Really Stone Age. They never saw iron or textiles. So you cannot be angry to that people. They have a kind of justice themselves. That is why, because innocent people were killed, out of a feeling of justice, they had to do something.

MACHLIN: Father Van Kessel, did you later discover some details that confirmed this story of the natives?

VAN KESSEL: Yeah. The most important detail is about the eyeglasses of Mike and his clothes, his underwear only. He was so wise to put off all his clothes except underwear. They told about spectacles, and that was practically the most confirming detail that it would be Michael Rockefeller. There is nobody else using spectacles except me.

MACHLIN: Do you think that those spectacles are probably in that village today?

VAN KESSEL: I don't know about "today," but at the time I was still there, they were, and I know exactly in the hands of the fellow—I forgot the name, because it is more than eight years ago now.

MACHLIN: And I heard tell that it's believed that his head and a knife, one of those typical knives that they make out of human thighbones, still exist.

VAN KESSEL: They always save the bones. They make daggers from the bones, and especially the skull. They are always after the skull. They have a kind of veneration for that. You may call it their religion, huh? It sounds strange, but it is more or less, for the primitive tribes, a religious ritual, the eating of the victim.

MACHLIN: What chance do you think that these relics—the eyeglasses, the bones, possibly even the undershorts—may still be in that village today or near it?

VAN KESSEL: I think not, I think not. After so many years.

MACHLIN: Ah, but the head is always kept for years and years. They never dispose of the head.

VAN KESSEL: That is right. But I am not informed what happened afterwards because I went to Holland, as I told you, two months after that, in January. I went to Holland and never came back to New Guinea.

MACHLIN: Michael himself was buying heads for the museum, wasn't he?

VAN KESSEL: Buying skulls—I suppose so . . . especially [for] scientific purposes or at least ethnographic purposes. They were after not only the wood carvings but even the skulls, because sometimes the skulls were very nicely decorated. So you may really call it ethnographical objects—

MACHLIN: Some people have said that it would have been almost impossible for Michael to have swum ashore because of the tremendous number of sharks and crocodiles in the area. What do you think of that?

VAN KESSEL: There are a lot of sharks and crocodiles, I saw many of them. But they are unpredictable. I was swimming also in that river, never alone—that is the best advice. You go into that kind of river where you know there are crocodiles—no, never go swimming alone. And the crocodiles and the sharks, they are not so aggressive, especially the crocodiles. . . . When you see them, you are coming close by in a boat or canoe, the first thing is they jump into the water and they run off.

MACHLIN: Now you were the first person to make this discovery, but didn't others afterwards find out the same thing you did from other sources?

VAN KESSEL: Sure, sure. You may call it public knowledge. Everybody knows in New Guinea. I myself, I was informed by my confreres, neighboring parish priest and the missionaries, they all know that. The whole question is this—the main point: the truth was, he reached the shore and he fell just into the hands of the village tribesmen who were still full of revenge feelings about those lost people.

MACHLIN: Well, why wouldn't they take their revenge on you, for instance? You were unarmed, you were in the village, and you were unarmed—why wouldn't they take their revenge on you?

VAN KESSEL: *Ja.* They answer it this way: You never should kill something close. I was the big man for them. I was like —you might call it a kind of king or something. I was the first one who brought them iron and knives and axes and tobacco and so on. They made a god of me. Now, you never will kill something close. I was only good to them.

MACHLIN: Father Van Kessel, in view of the fact that so many people who really understand and know New Guinea have heard the same story and confirmed it, why hasn't the story actually become accepted? Was there some reason that people didn't want this story to get out?

VAN KESSEL: Now you touch a rather delicate point. I saw that report—published immediately after, written by a Dutch officer—but immediately it was denied. So I felt the Dutch government was opposed against the truth, and I saw even the publication you showed me from the Associated Press, that I accused the Dutch government of suppressing the truth; that is a little bit too exaggerated. I never said it. It was not my idea. It was not my intention to accuse the Dutch government. . . . The whole thing was really a blunder of that lower official who killed the people; that is true. You have to face the truth. But why suppress the truth also?

MACHLIN: You could certainly say that the Dutch government was embarrassed and not anxious to have this new version of Michael's death come out?

VAN KESSEL: Yeah, that's right.

MACHLIN: Possibly because of the pressure by Indonesia, which was at that time trying to demonstrate that the Dutch were poor colonialists?

VAN KESSEL: Sure. I can imagine that. Then you can always abuse every incident. They . . . tell now, for example, that the Dutch government, they were killing in a colonialistic way all the natives, and that is absolutely nonsense. I can testify, I was sixteen years in New Guinea, that the Dutch government really did a good job. Why not confess a mistake? I am making mistakes also. Everybody will do that. This was a mistake. They took revenge, and they killed. They had to kill a white man. It just happened to be Michael Rockefeller. It is a pity, and it is a sad story; but it is the truth.

Van Kessel's statement brought out an important fact—that the rumors Michael had come ashore alive and been killed had started very soon after the disappearance. Again he stressed the point that the killing had not been directed at Michael but against the Dutch government in revenge for the killing of several tribesmen by a Dutch patrol officer.

Van Kessel was frank and to the point through most of the interview, but I noticed that he began to equivocate when it came to laying any of the blame on the doorstep of the Dutch government. The blame, as Van Kessel saw it, lay with the elusive patrol officer who killed the natives. But nobody seemed to know the actual details of that incident —who was this officer, when did the incident occur? Once again I had the impression that not only had Rockefeller's story been covered over, but that the unpleasant incident at Otsjanep had been expunged from history by the embarrassed authorities.

When the interview was over, Van Kessel escorted me to my car and gave me instructions for finding my way back to Amsterdam.

"Good-bye," he said. "It was good talking to you. I hope you are able to do something with my information. The story has been too long under cover."

I thanked him again and we shook hands.

19

I had hoped while in Holland to speak to Wassing, but he was away. Adrian Gerbrands was at the University of Leiden, however, and I made arrangements to see him on the following day. Gerbrands had been one of those closest to Rockefeller in the Asmat, and it had been he in fact who had first instructed Rockefeller in his study of the remarkable art of that area.

Adrian Gerbrands greeted me in his modern office adjoining the ancient University of Leiden. In addition to his work at the university, Gerbrands holds a post as director of the Rijksmuseum voor Volkenkunde—a folk art museum in Leiden. It was for this museum, as well as for the Museum of Primitive Art in New York, that Michael was collecting wood carvings at the time of his disappearance. Gerbrands wrote the introduction to the book published by the Museum of Primitive Art—*The Asmat of New Guinea: The Journal of Michael Clark Rockefeller*. He also helped prepare the captions for the many excellent photographs taken by Michael and others during his two expeditions to the Asmat.

I had read *The Asmat* prior to leaving New York, but not until hearing Father Van Kessel's full recital did I realize that certain portions of the book provided an ominous foreboding of what I was now coming to believe was the actual fate of Michael Rockefeller.

A great many, if not most, of the Asmat carvings incorporate headhunting symbols, and at some point in collecting artwork Michael seemed to note clear signs of continued interest in headhunting activity. In fact, when he was helping collect a "soulship" (*uranium*), a carving more than 12 feet long representing ancestors apparently on their way to the land of the dead, he noticed that the delivery of the carving to the mission post caused great agitation in the village where the carving originated.

Rockefeller quickly came to understand that they were preparing a ceremony called *emak tsjem*, one in which a feast house was constructed to be used in ceremonies preliminary to a headhunting raid.

The huge carved *bis* poles that were the primary goal of Rockefeller and Gerbrands had a grim significance. They were designed as revenge figures—not put in the house but outside before the *yeu* (men's residence). According to Asmat mythology, a man and a tree are synonymous.

In the introduction to the book *The Asmat*, Gerbrands is mentioned as one of those Rockefeller would have wished to thank. Among missionaries whose help the book acknowledges are Father Van Kessel, the Reverend W. Hekman of the Dutch Evangelical Alliance Mission, Father Superior Francis Pitka, Father John Smit and Father Delmar Hesch.

Gerbrands was courteous but cool. From the outset he made it clear that he would not allow himself to be filmed or recorded and would make no statements "on the record" about Rockefeller's disappearance.

It was obvious that he still had deep personal feelings about the story and a fervent loyalty to Michael, indeed to the whole Rockefeller clan.

When I brought up the question of Van Kessel's version of Michael's disappearance, he became quite emotional, once again demonstrating this phenomenon of triangular hostility I had noted elsewhere in New Guinea: the anthropologists and scientists, generally speaking, dislike and distrust the missionaries and the administration officials, each of whom, in turn, despises the other two.

Missionaries like Father Van Kessel, said Gerbrands, were ignorant of native matters and didn't really "live with" the natives as the anthropologists did. Some Protestant missionaries, Gerbrands said, didn't even go out among the people for services on Sundays but preached their sermons via recordings while they stayed at home.

Missionary reports on native affairs and culture were uninformed and unreliable, Gerbrands affirmed heatedly.

"Don't you think they've done any good at all?" I asked.

"They do little but interfere with the natural culture of the natives. Actually what right have they to impose their own values on these people in the name of so-called civilization?"

"Do you mean the Papuans should be encouraged to keep their customs even so far as warfare, headhunting and cannibalism?" I asked.

"Why not? This is their culture, not ours. It is a necessary part of their lives."

"But what about the victims? Perhaps they would be glad to see some of these customs stopped?"

"This is the problem of the local people. It is not up to us to interfere in the name of Christianity or so-called civilization."

"And what about the institution of payback?"

"This too is a necessary part of their culture and completely intermingled, so that depriving them of this custom affects their whole cultural system. This is one of the last places on earth where man can be studied in his truly primitive state, almost completely unaffected by the outside world."

"But," I pursued the point, "hasn't the presence of the missionaries helped minimize some of the earlier practices of headhunting and cannibalism?"

"Possibly. But I'm not sure that that is even good. They have done much to destroy the pure native way of life. It is *their* way. We should not interfere."

This was the root of one of the hostilities. The anthropologists were annoyed because wherever the missions and the government went, they modified exactly those customs and rites the anthropologists wanted to study. The goal of the anthropologist was to find a completely untouched culture, existing as it always had without the outside influence of the Western world. Wherever the others had come first, the primitive tribe was to some extent spoiled for study.

Still, I wondered how he could dispute the credentials of Father Van Kessel, who had spent sixteen years in the area and knew the Asmat dialect as well as any man in the world. Gerbrands himself, in fact, barely knew it at all.

"Do you think that someone like Father Van Kessel is capable of fabricating such a story entirely?" I asked.

Gerbrands nodded affirmatively.

"Since no positive evidence was found that Michael was drowned at sea," I asked, "why do you object to the story that he may have been found by the people of Otsjanep and killed in a payback rite?"

"Actually I'd prefer not to discuss the whole subject. It's past, and I would like to let it stay that way."

"But surely," I persisted, "if you don't agree with the story, you must have strong reasons."

"In the first place," Gerbrands said, "these people do not kill whites."

It was my turn to nod noncommittally.

"Second, these reports are just gossip from uninformed natives who like to chatter and boast. I don't believe they had any real knowledge of the matter."

"But some of the reports came from the villages actually involved, I'm told."

"These natives lie a lot in order to achieve status," Gerbrands replied.

"What about the missionaries? Many of them are reported to support the story."

"Missionaries are not entirely to be trusted in these situations."

"Do you have any more reasons for not believing the story?" I asked.

"Yes. I don't believe these people would risk punishment by killing whites."

"Do you have any other reasons for doubting the version of Michael's death reported by Van Kessel?" I asked.

"Yes. These natives kill for ritual purposes. They would not kill anybody whose name they didn't know, in order to use it in magic rites."

I couldn't help feeling he was trying to pull some academic wool over my eyes. I knew, as he knew, that heads were often taken for revenge purposes without knowing the exact identity of the owner—certainly without knowing his name. The important thing in payback was that the victim belong to the group or family from which revenge was to be exacted. As for their risking punishment by reverting to violence, from all indications to date they were willing to take that chance from time to time (and in fact several incidents *since* Rockefeller's death indicate that the violence is not over today). However, I felt it was pointless to reduce the discussion with Dr. Gerbrands to a dispute. He had his point of view. I couldn't help wondering, though, why he held his view so emotionally.

What I have summarized here is a conversation that took several hours. Much of it was devoted to discouraging any further investigation of the death of Rockefeller.

As I got up to leave, I noticed a large poster on Gerbrands' door: an overhead shot of Manhattan skyscrapers.

"You must be very fond of New York," I said, indicating the poster.

"I am," he said, "and besides I know the place from which it was taken very well—the heart of Rockefeller Center."

IV. Dias and Lapre

20

IN THE beginning the idea was that of Robert Gardner, Harvard anthropologist and founder of the Film Study Center for anthropological film research at Harvard's Peabody Museum.

Gardner, then thirty-five years old, blond, six three, strong and slender, was a romantic figure on the Harvard campus. Five years earlier he had become the first director of the Film Study Center at the university's Peabody Museum. He had already made a dramatic and important film on the Bushmen of the Kalahari in Africa and was casting about for a group of primitive people who would illustrate conditions in an agricultural culture—one of the three types of culture recognized by sociologists, along with the hunting and gathering society, of which the Kalahari people were an example, and the pastoral society, on which Gardner was later to report in Ethiopia.

In an interview at the Peabody Museum, Gardner described to me the genesis of the expedition which was to result in Rockefeller's tragic disappearance.

A friend, Harold Coolidge of the Natural Resources Council, told Gardner of a conversation he had had with a botanist recently returned from the Baliem Valley in Netherlands New Guinea. It sounded to Gardner as if the people of that valley might be suitable subjects for the study of primitive and virtually uncorrupted agricultural society. Gardner's interest was further sparked after a meeting with Dr. Victor De Bruyn, then director of the Bureau of Native Affairs for Netherlands New Guinea.

"De Bruyn knew western New Guinea well," Gardner says. "He had studied it as an archaeologist and anthropologist, and he had lived in the interior as an Allied intelligence agent during the war."

De Bruyn also felt that the Baliem Valley could make an important contribution to our knowledge of mankind and thought the Dutch government would lend enthusiastic support to such an expedition.

"He wanted the Peabody Museum to do research there," Gardner told me, "and he felt confident that the pacification program that his government had started in that area ten years earlier had by no means seriously changed the way of life of these tribesmen."

The Grand Valley of the Baliem River, target of the proposed study, had been discovered by Richard Archbold during zoological and botanical explorations of the New Guinea highlands in 1938. It achieved romantic fame as a real-life "Shangri-la" when an American nurse and two companions who had survived a World War II plane crash in the area were rescued in an elaborate glider operation and told of the little-known existence of this primitive people living outside the range of the civilized world.

The valley, 40 miles long and 10 miles wide, is estimated to contain as many as 100,000 people, and the only whites at the time of Gardner's projected expedition were a handful of workers at the government post in Wamena and a few missionaries who had established airstrips in some parts of the valley.

Gardner, more and more convinced that the Baliem Valley offered a magnificent opportunity to film primitive man, discussed the possibility of the project with some of his students. One of them was a young pre-med named Sam Putnam, who thought he would like to accompany such an expedition and felt that as an expert photographer he could make an important contribution. Putnam also said he had a roommate who was very interested in primitive art and life and would probably be interested in accompanying the group after graduation—Michael Rockefeller.

During his undergraduate years Michael had been an excellent student (he ultimately was graduated *cum laude*) but had shown a tendency to restlessness and a hunger for excitement which would ultimately lead him to Gardner's expedition. He had various methods of sublimating his restlessness. Once he was picked up for racing at 80 miles an hour along the Maine Turnpike, and again he was arrested for speeding on a Connecticut parkway. During the summer Michael hardly lived the life of a millionaire's son. One summer he worked in a Puerto Rican supermarket. 'Another year he worked as a ranch hand on his father's spread in Venezuela. Except for poor eyesight, Michael was an excellent specimen physically, six feet one and a superb swimmer.

Rockefeller, a senior majoring in English, was, like so many students at that turning point in life, uncertain what he wanted to do after graduation. He had already shown some interest in primitive art and been thinking vaguely of doing research in South America, but when he heard about the New Guinea trip, he became very excited about joining.

Though many might like to do so, few were in a position to make it possible. The project would take many months. Those participating had to be willing to give up considerable time without pay, to pay their own expenses and to bring useful skills to the project.

Gardner felt that young Putnam and Rockefeller would be assets to the expedition. During the several months before the project could get under way, Rockefeller could complete his six months' military obligation. By now the idea was really taking hold; De Bruyn assured them that the Dutch government would give full cooperation and even some financial assistance. In the end, the Dutch government contributed more than half the cost of the expedition, including not only the valuable services of its New Guinea experts but also some $25,000 cash out of its meager budget for the territory.

"Actually the Dutch already knew that they would soon have to get out of the area," Gardner told me. "There were pressures not only from Indonesia and independence movements, but also from the Dutch people themselves, many of whom regarded the huge primitive area as a large and useless financial burden."

Actual sponsor of the expedition was the Peabody Museum, with some additional support from scholarly grants. None of this, however, represented Rockefeller money, according to Gardner, except indirectly in the sense that Michael was a trustee of the Rockefeller-supported Museum of Primitive Art.

Michael was already a talented and expert photographer, but on an expedition of this sort he would have to contribute some other skill, so he took up the study of sound recording for the film Gardner planned to make.

Others recruited for the project were Karl Heider, then a doctoral candidate in anthropology at Harvard and a close friend of Gardner's, Peter Matthiessen, the naturalist and novelist, Elliot Elisofon, the *Life* photographer who was a research assistant at the Peabody Museum, and Jan Broekhuyse, a doctoral candidate in sociology and anthropology who had actually been a patrol officer in the Grand Valley and had some knowledge of the Dani people and languages.

Not all these people, or several others who worked on the expedition from time to time, were able to give full time to the project. Elisofon could spare only a month; Matthiessen was limited to several months. In the end the permanent cadre of Americans was built around Gardner, Heider and Rockefeller, since even Sam Putnam would be unable to arrive until the end of his first year in medical school.

Michael, who was stationed at Fort Devens, Massachusetts, during his military service, was able to visit Cambridge frequently to consult with Gardner on the forthcoming project. Elisofon briefed him thoroughly on the cameras and equipment he would need, since Michael would be largely responsible for still photography in Elisofon's absence. Some of the equipment was brought to Elisofon's 120-acre spread on Vinalhaven Island of Penobscot Bay in Maine for testing. Just to keep in condition, Michael swam back and forth across icy Crockett Cove every morning.

"Michael was enthusiastic and really threw himself into the work from the start," Gardner commented.

In January, 1961, Gardner went to New Guinea to make preliminary arrangements for the expedition. While some parts of the valley had been partially pacified, there were still large areas that were basically uncontrolled, and it was these areas that intrigued Gardner. "I had often wondered about the differences between ordinary and ritual warfare," Gardner comments in the foreword to his book on the expedition, *Gardens of War*. Now Gardner was to be confronted with a people who thought war was other than a necessary evil and who practiced what anthropologists call ritual warfare. "Ritual" in this case meant a repeated and indispensable activity necessary to the survival of the culture, and warfare that was sacred rather than profane. "I wondered if greater understanding about violence in men could be achieved if it was studied in a metaphysical context completely different from our own," Gardner wrote. He particularly wanted to study these New Guinea natives who "had been killing each other for as long as we have known that they lived there."

21

Jan Broekhuyse, who already had been in the area six months learning the language and scouting the territory, accompanied Gardner on his first trip. The prospect of reconnoitering the Dani territory for a truly primitive tribe may have seemed daunting to Gardner; from his research at the New York headquarters of the Christian and Missionary Alliance, which sponsored many of the missionaries in the area, Gardner got "the unmistakable impression that the Dani were deceitful and barbaric pagans, driven by the devil to loot and kill as they fancied."

Gardner had even seen a photo, taken by the original team that discovered the valley, of Dani shooting arrows at the expedition's plane as it swooped low to land.

Gardner took the warnings with a slight grain of salt, chalking them off to the traditional coolness between anthropologist and missionary. The area selected as most likely for the expedition was called Kurelu (which meant "wise egret"), after a famed fighting leader with unusually light skin and craftiness.

The people of the Kurelu had never admitted the missionaries, though some other Dani tribes had been at least partly "Christianized" by the Fundamentalist American missionaries. Even there, their success was attributed by

Gardner more to the missionaries' lavish use of trade goods and medicine than to any genuine belief.

When writing of his impressions of these missionaries, Gardner tempered his opinions, but not much: "There are many men of God in New Guinea," he wrote, "who live and behave in harmony with their Christian precepts and who are a solace to any soul who comes within their ken. Others, though, constitute one of the profoundest risks confronting pagan man's entry into the contemporary world, a risk that those of the Kurelu had so far miraculously elected to avoid."

The Kurelus, Gardner decided, were about as uncorrupted as any people an anthropologist was likely to encounter. Early in March he and Broekhuyse started up the Baliem River in an outboard-powered motorboat lent them by the Dutch government station a few miles downriver. Accompanying them was only a native policeman named Abututi, who would serve as interpreter.

As district officer Jan had visited several parts of the valley in the past and had even once met Kurelu himself. The meeting had not been cordial. Jan had encountered the chief after a wearying day's march on the trail.

"Jan was too exhausted to test the strength of his authority in the face of Kurelu's displeasure at finding a *waro,* or reptile, as whites are known in the Dani, patrolling his territory," Gardner recalls in telling of the meeting.

Jan felt that Dani belligerence was somewhat exaggerated in the stories told by panic-stricken missionaries. Several of them had been roughly handled, but none ever killed in the Baliem. But then a certain kind of violence was the rule, not the exception, in the Dani way of life.

"So with an exchange of greetings, probably the traditional *Eyak nyak halabok* [Hey, friend, I eat your feces], they parted, neither expecting nor hoping to meet again," Gardner reports.

That seemingly rude greeting probably symbolizes as much as anything else the difference in values between these people and the "civilized" world.

In any event, Broekhuyse did return to the Kurelu, bringing with him still another "reptile" in Gardner. Early in March they awoke in a camp perched on a limestone ridge pointing eastward into the Baliem Valley. The valley is named for the river which winds down 9,000 feet from the mountains of the central ridge through the plains into the swamps and ultimately empties itself into the Arafura Sea along the Asmat coast—the same Arafura Sea into which Michael Rockefeller was to be swept in his swamped catamaran nine months later.

Across the broad valley floor Gardner could make out a series of native gardens and irrigation ditches sloping up the mountain which bordered one end of the sweeping plain. In the foreground stretched forests and villages fringed with green banana trees. Rising columns of smoke gave evidence that the population was awake and preparing a morning meal.

"How peaceful the valley looked that first morning," Gardner recalls. "It was impossible to believe the terrified reports I had read . . . a few months earlier."

But a careful perusal of the pastoral scene brought Gardner up short, for through his binoculars he saw unmistakable signs of hostility—a series of tall watchtowers of lashed poles at intervals of 400 yards along some apparent frontier stretched as far as the eye could see.

It was clear to Gardner that these people were not just farmers but warriors.

Gardner decided to go with Broekhuyse and Abututi to the land beyond the watchtowers—Kurelu's domain. Though the group was traveling light, there were still more supplies in their boat than they could carry, so they were obliged to try to recruit some carriers from the nearest village. It took a full morning of talking before Abututi could convince three of the more adventurous local youths to accompany the strange expedition, since the local people felt that if they ventured into that land across the valley, they would surely be killed. At that it took the offer of an "irresistible number" of cowrie shells, which Gardner had had the foresight to bring along for trading in this moneyless society.

By now even the most remote Dani tribes had at least heard of white people, but their impressions were not generally favorable. They believed the whites came to steal their pigs, to take their women or perhaps to set fire to their holy objects in exchange for a better way of life. Not only that, the whites would try to stop their tribal dancing and, above all, the warfare which was such an important part of their lives. So Gardner and Broekhuyse had no reason to expect a warm welcome from the Kurelus.

But Gardner was unafraid. He was confident that the reputed hostility of the Dani would not be visited on his little group:

First, we were completely independent; we were neither missionaries nor agents of the government. [I remembered Hanson making this point about our own group when we had filmed the Sepik headhunters.] We had no message, either spiritual or mundane to impart, and no advice to give or demands to make. In fact we wished to disturb the lives of the Dani as little as possible. Secondly, we were accompanied by Abututi, a Dani himself, whose belief in our sincerity, and whose total familiarity with the behavior and values of those with whom we hoped to live meant that our chances of explaining the purposes of our visit were extremely good. Thirdly, I had carried all the way from Newton Upper Falls, Massachusetts, a perfect specimen of *Cymbium diadema,* an object [shell] prized above almost all others by the Dani who cut them into irregular saucers to wear as necklaces and exchange for pigs or other wealth.

The small party set out across the valley at midday, proceeding across the sunny mile-high valley, passing gardens, crossing ditches on perilously narrow mud-covered poles, past dead fires set by warrior sentinels earlier in the morning.

It occurred to Gardner that with his eyes riveted on the difficult terrain, unable to scan ahead for enemy traps or ambushes, his assurance to the reluctant carriers that he would protect them must have seemed less than convincing. Later he learned that the Dani had been watching every step of his progress since the previous day.

"Nothing is more conspicuous in this landscape than the shape, color and locomotion of fully clothed white men."

Before they reached the distant settlement, it was necessary to cross the no-man's-land that separated the two mutually hostile communities; it was composed of abandoned gardens, swamps and clusters of a short bush called *pabi,* which means both excrement and the enemy. "It was a land through which indeed no one would go unless to do violence to those beyond," Gardner comments.

Finally, the small group reached the slopes controlled by Kurelu and his allies. The confrontation took place in a large area the size of a football field, used, it was learned later, to celebrate a victory dance each time an enemy man, woman or child was killed.

They walked into the clearing in total silence, but suddenly several men erupted from the bush and began to run alongside them toward a spur of higher ground ahead. They had apparently been shadowing the group all along and had now revealed themselves, since it was apparent that the group had Kurelu territory as their destination. Once past the screen of grass the expedition found a crowd of fifty or so men silently waiting their arrival.

With as much assurance as they could muster, Gardner and his group approached the cluster of three or four older men awaiting them on the knoll, none of them the famed chief himself. Gardner was still sure that if he could make his aims clear, all would be well. He started his conversation with an alert middle-aged tribesman who gave his name as Wali. After a period of greeting, squatting and smoking in the fashion that seems traditional in these encounters, Gardner indicated to Abututi that he should explain that the white men had come from a place many days' walk away because they had heard that the people of Kurelu were the finest farmers and the best warriors in the area.

Because of this, Abututi was to explain, the white men wanted to "sit down" with the people of Kurelu for a long time and learn from them.

The request was a large one, Wali was to be told, and it was important he didn't think they were poor people without wives, pigs or crops of their own. Therefore, they had brought shells which they would exchange for the privilege of staying with the Kurelu.

Abututi explained all this, and the canny leader Wali seemed to understand quite well.

His people, he indicated, would be glad to have the white men stay. They would even supply food and houses for them. But first he would like to see some of these shells the white man had brought.

Gardner had carefully wrapped the *Cymbium diadema* in a small separate box, which he now fetched from his pack.

"With Wali watching intently I opened the box, but the shell had been only partly revealed when he pushed the wrapping back over it and asked that it be closed immediately. For a dreadful moment I wondered if my stratagem in procuring the shell had been in vain. But then I realized by the unmistakable look of cupidity on Wali's face that he wanted no one else to see what he already considered his."

The three carriers from the enemy tribe had been huddling in fear near the feet of Abututi, who carried the rifle, which they hoped would protect them from being slaughtered by their neighbors (in fact, the gun was not loaded). As darkness approached, the three faded into the night and took off for home, so frightened that they didn't even wait for their payment of cowrie shells.

Gardner went to sleep assured that he had found the destination for the Harvard Peabody expedition. He would send for Heider and Rockefeller as soon as they got back to the government post.

22

BEFORE LEAVING the Kurelu, Gardner spent a week establishing a base camp on a ridge in a grove of araucaria trees at a place called Homuak. The site was selected because of its excellent water supply and because the area was not already inhabited by natives and was large enough to sustain a field station of eight tents or so without intruding on the life of the tribesmen, as would have been the case if the group had elected actually to live in Wali's village, a three-minute walk from camp.

While waiting for Heider and Rockefeller, Gardner and Broekhuyse discovered the art of the Asmat people who lived on the southern coast where the Baliem eventually emptied itself after joining the Eilanden River. The pair spent the last two weeks of March paddling around the fascinating and unexplored villages of the Asmat, including Otsjanep, where Gardner was vastly impressed with the weirdly baroque carving of the local *bis* poles. While in the Asmat, Gardner also met and became friendly with one of the important experts on Asmat art, Adrian Gerbrands.

At the end of March Heider and Rockefeller arrived at Biak in northern Dutch New Guinea, and ultimately the group arranged for the last of the supplies to be flown by a chartered DC-3 into Wamena, from which point it was packed into the Baliem Valley.

At Wamena they had contact with some of the local officials who had been told that the government regarded the expedition as a very important project and that the group were to be given as free a hand as possible.

This advice from higher headquarters was necessary, since neither the local missionaries nor many local officials were pleased to hear the group was going into the warlike Kurelu. The area had been seemingly pacified by a small government patrol post in 1958 and 1959 but ultimately had reverted to its ritual warfare and the government post had been withdrawn. In 1960 a Franciscan father had made a brief attempt to "civilize" the Dani of that area, also without success.

As the Harvard Peabody group passed through Wamena, they left seeds of hostility which later were to cause them a certain annoyance.

At the camp Michael was enthusiastic and excited. His astonished exclamation of "It's *unbelievable!*" became almost a password. The basic expedition group, all well over six feet and fair-skinned, must have been equally astonishing to their Dani hosts, who averaged five feet three in height.

Certainly Michael didn't shirk work. One day, Heider recalls, he made an entire day's march on a primitive trail to photograph the process of salt gathering by the Dani women at the so-called salt well, where sheaves of pounded fibers were soaked in brine to be carried back later to the village and processed by burning into the salt cakes which were the Dani's only source of this important mineral.

But when Michael got to the brine pool, there were no women there to be photographed.

"That's OK," Michael said cheerfully. "We'll go back tomorrow."

And so on the following day, he went with Sam Putnam, who had arrived in June as soon as summer vacation started at Harvard Medical School. The two youths spent another entire day on the trail to get photographs of this one rite— photographs which later appeared in several of the books that resulted from the expedition.

If Michael had any problem, it was that he tended to be a bit headstrong and impetuous, often following his own counsel and ignoring advice of more experienced men like Gardner. But he was aware of this fault—one which was to prove fatal to him in the end.

His first efforts at photography were less than sensational —at least as far as he himself was concerned. By summer the group had been augmented by several more people: Peter Matthiessen had arrived, and in May Eliot Elisofon joined the group as still photographer.

A jungle-wise veteran, Elisofon had brought some jam with him to relieve the monotonous and generally sweet-free camp diet. Delightedly Michael proceeded to smear several native bananas with the sticky stuff and devour them greedily.

"He was totally unaffected and natural and suffered perhaps from the family complex of feeling that he had to work even harder than the rest to prove himself," Elisofon told me in his New York apartment, packed with a lifetime collection of primitive art picked up on assignments around the world.

Once in a relaxed moment in camp Elisofon challenged Michael to balance a long Dani throwing stick on his nose, first demonstrating himself how it could be done. Michael was trying to achieve the difficult equilibrium as the Kurelu men looked on fascinated, when Heider appeared on the scene.

"Stop that immediately!" he said. "What do you mean teaching these people new motor skills?" Michael stopped but doubled up with laughter.

It was, in fact, impossible to live with the Dani without somewhat changing their lives, a problem which deeply concerned Gardner and Heider. Despite the fact that there were hundreds of pigs in the villages, for instance, no one in the party was allowed to buy one to ameliorate the dull diet of Spam, bully beef and canned foods for fear this would harm the Dani culture and economy.

But the impact of the group on this Stone Age society was nevertheless enormous. So many aspects of the white man's life were baffling to the Dani. Why did they wear so much stuff covering their bodies, concealing the body's appearance? Where were their penis gourds? Did they in fact have any penises? Where were their women? Where were their pigs? (A good many of the wars were fought over stolen pigs or stolen or raped women.) Despite the seeming neutrality of these strange men, the Dani were careful never to leave them alone for any length of time with any of the female members of the tribe.

"Actually," Elisofon says wryly, "they weren't really that attractive to us. I doubt there was any danger."

Of course, the panoply of Western goods also fascinated the tribesmen. Matches intrigued these people who had always made fire with a friction fire-bow. So did the bright

Coleman lantern used in the tents at night. It was not unusual for a tribesman to push his way unceremoniously into a tent and, ignoring the occupants, go up and stare mesmerized at the lantern until, suddenly catching sight of his own grotesquely distorted reflection in the shiny reflector, he would emit a scream and run howling from the tent. Partly in an attempt to minimize their different appearance from the Dani, all the members grew beards like the Dani.

Meanwhile, Michael was sharpening his skills as sound man and photographer. Often at night while the others were reading or relaxing he would take his Nagra recorder and walk to one of the nearby settlements to record songs or even the ordinary sounds of village life.

He was learning new things about photography, too, largely that taking pictures for a scientific expedition in the field was not the same as taking pictures of one's friends and family in the states.

Michael's first examination of his early work threw him into a deep depression. "In retrospect," he wrote in his diary, "my approach to photographing the extraordinary life we found among the Ndani [Dani] was quite naive." He blamed himself particularly for not having taken greater advantage of the experiences offered by Bob Gardner and Peter Matthiessen, who were accomplished photographers. "I now know that an eye sensitive to the aesthetics by itself assures little. . . ."

But Michael apparently learned a great deal during those months, because his photographs, as they subsequently appeared in Gardner's book *Dead Birds,* in his own posthumous book with Gerbrands, *The Asmat,* in Matthiessen's book, *Under the Mountain Wall,* and in Heider's scholarly work *The Dugum Dani,* were artistic and professional.

Toward the end of May Elisofon was called back to work at *Life* magazine. He was disappointed because in his entire stay there had been no serious battle or skirmish for him to photograph. Heider and Gardner cite this as further proof that they were not paying the natives to make war.

"If we had been, we certainly would have had them stage one while Elisofon was there, wouldn't we?" Heider said. In point of fact a major skirmish did erupt just as Elisofon's plane was taking off, leaving it to Michael to take the still photographs.

"I had complete confidence in him as a photographer," Elisofon said. "I was in fact amazed at how proficient he had become in so short a time. He was no dilettante. He was a competent professional."

Michael also learned a great deal about a grim side of life that few modern men can comprehend. The ritual warfare Gardner had hoped to study was flourishing after the brief "pacification" in 1958 and 1959.

In just over five months the Kurelus were involved in nine battles and nine raids, considerable fighting by any standard. In these conflicts some eight men and boys were killed and dozens wounded.

As the battles raged, Michael, Gardner and the rest of the group moved in and out of the combat areas securing a close-up reportage of the fighting. Though they all risked being wounded or even accidentally killed, Heider assured me that the members of the expedition were in no danger from deliberate hostility because they were regarded as neutrals and had no part in the quarrels which instigated the troubles.

Heider managed to make the two- to four-hour walk, depending on the wetness of the trail, every ten days or so to Wamena to pick up supplies and mail. On one of these trips he ran into one of the Dutch Protestant missionaries, who offered to drop in and visit the group some time.

"This was the last thing we would have wanted," Heider told me. "The missionaries were, of course, known to be opposed to the fighting. If the missionary showed up, we would be associated in the Dani mind with the previous attempts by missionaries to pacify them, and our position as neutrals would be hopelessly compromised. It was essential that we not be identified with the church or with the government."

As gracefully as he could, Heider declined the offer. It was this missionary who later complained to government officials that the Harvard Peabody group was stirring up war in the Baliem Valley. As a result, an investigator was ultimately sent to the valley from the government in Hollandia, and Gardner himself went to the capital to explain. Certainly some of the local officials at Wamena were miffed at the group's lack of rapport and contact with them. The expedition had spent only a minimum of time at headquarters before heading into the field; according to Heider, this may have been a diplomatic error.

"Although our relations with the Dani were excellent, during the first months our activities were misunderstood by some government and mission personnel. We had assumed that anthropology in general and the goals of our expedition in particular were familiar to the Europeans in the Grand Valley," he said.

"Actually," Heider told me in his study at Brown University recently, "they really hadn't been clued in by Hollandia, just told to give us fullest cooperation. We had arrived at the Grand Valley preceded by a lot more rumors than information. But they wouldn't have had any importance if they hadn't been picked up and magnified after Michael's disappearance.

"We sought out the most untouched part of the Grand Valley—that is, with warfare still going on—and did not identify ourselves with either the government or the missions. Our desire for neutrality between the forces of change and the Dani was misinterpreted, and we were suspected of encouraging warfare to make a film. We had not encouraged warfare, but neither had we tried to end it. A political storm blew up that reached even The Hague. We were investigated and exonerated, but it was some months before our relations with government and missionary personnel became really cordial."

The anthropologist's position in any event is untenable, Heider says:

"In order to understand war and ritual, he must be a neutral observer. But in a situation like the Grand Valley in 1961, when most Europeans and Americans were working to change the Dani way of life, it was difficult to explain this neutrality to either the Danis or the outsiders. No matter what we said, or did not say, our mere interest in the activity which other outsiders were trying to suppress seemed to give support to the Danis and to work against the activities of change."

It was essentially these circumstances which led to headlines such as ROCKEFELLER GROUP CLASHED WITH DUTCH and others which were reported at the time of Michael's disappearance. These were somehow linked in people's minds with the Asmat, though the Baliem Valley was hundreds of miles away. By the time these stories had been rewritten, a distorted sort of rumor emerged: Rockefeller had been killed because his group had started wars in which numbers of natives were killed.

The rumors from the Baliem, combined with statements by certain less than friendly Dutch officials, were perpetuated and even extended in press reports at the time of Michael's disappearance. *Time* magazine quoted a part of the official Dutch report which, according to Heider, exonerated the group. According to *Time*, the report stated: "It was known to the authorities that the leader of the expedition [Gardner] was very keen on filming tribal warfare. In the first two months there were about seven deaths and a dozen or more wounded around a village called Kurelu." This

Time cited as an indication that the group had stirred up trouble. Out of context it is hard to evaluate the quote from the report.

But regardless of what the report may or may not have said, it was clear the Danis needed no one to stir up wars for them.

After the departure of the Harvard Peabody expedition in August, 1961, a Dutch police post was put up in the territory immediately adjoining Kurelu's. Peace apparently reigned for five years, and again the government put out word that the area had been pacified. Then on June 4, 1966, a battle occurred which, according to Heider, "could only be called a massacre." More than one hundred men, women and children were left dying and dozens of compounds razed by fire. In a counterattack in the following days another twenty or so people were killed. The only effect of the "civilization" of the police post was that steel bush knives, more deadly than any previous Dani weapons, had been added to the arsenal of the tribesmen.

23

WHICH BATTLES Michael saw and recorded is no longer certain, but his photographs show he had plenty of opportunity to learn the aspects of life and death in a primitive world. He took many photographs of actual battles in progress, wounded men and the weird death ceremonies in which the deceased is propped up in a chair and decorated with shell finery and other valuables before being cremated.

Of interest in passing is the fact that the Danis, like the Kukukukus I visited in 1969, dismembered fingers to remember the dead. Among the Kukukukus I had observed young widows wearing necklaces made up of their spouse's fingers. But among the Danis it is the widows and daughters of the dead man who must yield their fingers. Several joints are hacked off following each death of a relative, and since the Danis are so warlike, many of the women—even most— wind up with little better than stumps for hands.

Michael photographed this gruesome ceremony.

The excitement of these primitive contacts obviously suited the restless Rockefeller. He was constantly in action, rowing, swimming, hiking. He became adept at recording the songs and dances of the Kurelus; he grew a beard and started an Indian wrestling competition among members of the expedition and ultimately became the champion. More and more he felt inclined to make anthropology his life-work.

In late June, inspired by Gardner's accounts of the Asmat art, Michael decided to go to the coast. The expedition was scheduled to finish in August, but Michael had little taste for going back to America so soon.

Sam Putnam and Rockefeller were given introductions to Gerbrands and joined him at his base in Amanamki. At this time they also met the crew-cut, mustached thirty-four-year-old René Wassing, an anthropologist attached to the Dutch Bureau of Native Affairs in Hollandia.

By an exciting coincidence the pair arrived just in time to witness an important ceremony commemorating the construction of a new *yeu,* or bachelor's house. On their very first night they were able to witness and photograph the drumming and other portions of the ceremony, including those involving the *an* tray in which grub offerings are made to symbolize human brains—a significance of which Michael was at the time unaware: The natives believe that they can gain a person's power or knowledge by eating the brains in a special ritual. The *an* tray is used at the time of headhunting raids to collect the brains of the enemy; with the pointed end of a stone ax, a hole about an inch in diameter is made in the temple of the enemy's skull. The brains are removed with a bamboo spatula and collected in the *an* tray. To the Asmat warrior a tray full of brains and a tray full of grubs had an appealing similarity.

The ceremony also involved the placement of fireplace carved poles. These differed from the usual *bis* poles in that those placed around the fireplace are basically memorial in purpose, whereas those placed outside the *yeu* house are revenge figures. They were displayed usually just before a headhunting raid.

On the following day, for photographic purposes Michael requested and paid for a reenactment of some of the ceremonies which had gone on before his arrival, and then arranged for a major canoe display near Gerbrands' base village of Amanamki.

Michael enthusiastically photographed the canoe regatta, including shots of the blowing of a headhunting horn and simulated shots of people throwing lime at a simulated enemy.

In the afternoon ten men from the village of Omadesep some miles upriver brought art objects for Gerbrands to buy. While they were there, they asked the anthropologist's help in settling a dispute with Omadesep's neighboring village, Otsjanep. It was decided that the group would go there by canoe and find out what the problem was.

Two days later they started downstream for Omadesep, which was in a section called the Casuarinen coast. For some reason Michael was trying to hold down his picture taking, perhaps in order to observe better what was going on around him. "However, when one is beset with one marvellous sight after another, what can one do?" Michael wrote. He shot roll after roll of color film, even as he realized that Gerbrands had only one roll of film left until further supplies arrived from Holland. But the urge to record these bizarre and moving scenes overwhelmed any sense of guilt he may have felt.

Michael never lost interest in the many and varied views along the river and the endless sound of wild birds which followed them downstream.

They spent that night in a rest hut belonging to the people of Omadesep. Supper that night consisted of cold rice, cold herring and cold tea, since the more satisfactory canned goods and supplies were completely inaccessible because of the darkness and the endless impassable mud on which the canoes had been left by the receding tide. The next day, in fact, the explorers had to be dragged sledlike to the river, sitting in the canoes.

Three hours of paddling brought them to Omadesep, where they were met and escorted by a flotilla of four war canoes. But Michael was disappointed to find that the village was far from untouched by civilization. A Roman Catholic mission school was already functioning. The art, too, at first seemed shoddy and second-rate—mostly new stuff carved for the pleasure of the white man and his trade goods. But after a long wait and some requests from Michael for drums and shields not carved specifically for sale, interesting objects began to emerge. This excited Michael, who wanted to buy as much as he could for the Museum of Primitive Art. In fact, he got so involved in the trading that he was only persuaded with some asperity by Gerbrands to stop for lunch.

In the afternoon Michael negotiated for the purchase of several huge *bis* poles and again photographed a ceremony in connection with them. These *bis* poles had been carved about a year before the ceremony. After the ceremony they cease to have magic value and are thrown away in the jungle to rot.

The *bis* poles are executed by master carvers who specialize in this work. The relatives of the dead persons to be represented on the pole provide him with food and lodging, which are his only pay for carving the huge revenge poles. Usually, as in this case, several poles are carved for a *bis* ceremony, the number depending on how many ancestors have to be avenged and on how prepared the community feels it is to take the necessary action. The *bis* pole is actually a pledge to the ghost of the ancestor that his death will be avenged. The pledge is made during the ceremony before all the other members of the tribe and involves much boasting, so that any warrior who backs out of his promise would be sorely humiliated. Few do.

The final pole ritual consists of a mock battle between the men and women of the group, in which the women attack the men. This is meant to expel from the village the ghosts of the ancestors carved in the poles.

That night, the Omadesep people explained their trouble to the white men. For many years they had been in intermittent conflict with the fierce tribesmen of Otsjanep. Now the Omadesep chiefs hoped that, with the white men to act as go-betweens, they might approach the leaders of Otsjanep and arrange a peace treaty. If they had attempted to go on their own, it is certain that they would have been killed before they could explain their purpose.

So the next day the Gerbrands-Rockefeller group took off for the Faretsj River, where the Otsjaneps maintained a temporary village. A number of dugout canoes filled with Omadesep warriors accompanied them. Gradually the river narrowed as the small fleet proceeded up the winding Faretsj River past overhanging and fallen trees which blocked their passage—a position no doubt chosen by the Otsjaneps for precisely this strategic advantage. These fierce warriors traditionally protect their communities by felling trees across the rivers leading to their villages.

Suddenly they rounded a bend, and there was the Otsjanep outpost, its huts built high in the trees for protection against enemy attack. As they paddled cautiously up to the village, Tamtji, the Omadesep guide and go-between, shouted reassuring phrases to announce the coming of the white men. Because of the bad blood between the villages, there was a considerable doubt about their reception. But after a while they received a welcoming shout from one of the Otsjanep chiefs, who suddenly appeared on a nearby fallen log.

Michael was impressed by the untouched quality of this village. It was wilder and more remote than any he had seen before. The Omadesep people used the occasion to show their friendly intentions toward the Otsjaneps, though from Michael's writings it is doubtful that he or even Gerbrands realized the depth of the hostility between these groups.

A tree house was provided for Rockefeller and his friends to spend the night. In the early evening two "wild men," as Michael called them, were brought in to view the strange white men, who cheerfully posed for their awestruck examination.

"As I write this," Michael noted, "villagers are singing in our tree house: *weo we toma weo—tare jabarino.* Probably some song to commemorate the event of our visit."

On July 1 Rockefeller and his group proceeded via winding marsh waterways to the main village of Otsjanep.

The Otsjanep warriors accompanied Michael but with a certain reluctance, since it meant leaving their wives unprotected in the temporary village on the riverbank. Despite the supposed truce between the two tribes, the suspicious Otsjanep tribesmen were clearly worried that the men of Omadesep might return to molest their women while they were away on the river voyage.

Meanwhile, the Otsjanep people had apparently heard rumors about the staging of *bis* pole ceremonies for the whites at Amanamki and Omadesep and felt that they should also hold a display. The huge poles were set up on a special scaffolding built for them the following morning. These apparently were the same poles that had been carved the year before for Pierre Gaisseau and *The Sky Above and the Mud Below* film team.

After the display Rockefeller and Gerbrands made arrangements to buy the poles for their museums. They also bought shields, which Rockefeller chose for the Museum of Primitive Art with the advice of Gerbrands. A down payment in axes, knives and tobacco was made. Since the objects were so large, the Rockefeller-Gerbrands group could not bring them in their boats, so they arranged to have the Otsjanep people take them in canoes to Agats, where the balance would be paid. This would take several days because the villagers' larger canoes had been left behind in the outpost settlement. The arrangement was made to meet at a well-known point on the beach of the estuary of the South Eilanden River and from that point proceed together to Agats.

Rockefeller and his group got to the rendezvous on time, but there was no one there to meet them. They waited several more days, but "for some reason or another," Michael reported, no one showed up.

The theory of the Amanamki paddlers was that despite their peace festival, the Otsjanep tribesmen suspected a possible trick from the Omadesep people and were unwilling to leave their villages unprotected.

24

EN ROUTE to the rendezvous point the Rockefeller group decided to stop at Biwar, a village on the west side of the South Eilanden River, to examine and possibly purchase some unusual carved paddles and canoes. At the time of their trip the tide was high in the Eilanden estuary and the weather tranquil, so the paddlers decided that instead of following the narrow, winding Faretsj River, they would take a sea route, which would be much shorter and save considerable time. The sometimes-dangerous swells of the Arafura Sea would be avoided by staying close to the mangrove-lined shore.

In order to get to Biwar, however, the canoes had to cross the mouth of the Eilanden, which at this point is several miles wide.

This is what Michael wrote about the route:

> Strong monsoons sometimes sweep the heavy swell from the Arafura Sea into the estuary, making the crossing a rather hazardous undertaking in an Asmat dugout canoe which is not a seagoing craft because it lacks anything like a forecastle to break the waves. Though there was a kind of a swell when we arrived at the estuary, our Asmat paddlers, after having measured the sky and waves with expert eyes, decided that the crossing could be made. We reached the other bank without much difficulty. . . .

Accordingly, Michael may have felt that the repeated warnings about the dangers of these waters were exaggerated.

The party next paddled to the village of Atjametsj, where they collected some carved figures and shields. Of particular interest to Michael were the elaborately carved canoe paddles involving stylistic representation of multiple heads.

The heads served an ironic function which was duly noted by Michael. They represented relatives whose heads had been taken by the enemy and whose deaths had still not been avenged. In this fashion the descendant of the victim could never forget his duty to avenge the killing. The carving of the accusing ancestor's face was located just above the point where the canoeist's fingers gripped the paddle. As a result, the paddler worked always under the demanding stare of his unavenged kin. The other motifs telling the story of the ancestral debt were also carved in such a way that the paddler always had them in view.

This last venture effectively marked the end of Michael's first Asmat exploration. According to his later notes, the trip had been equal to his "wildest dreams."

Yet he also sensed something tragic in what was happening to the Asmat people. He had observed uncomfortably how eager many of the tribesmen were to leave their own cultural patterns and follow those of the whites. Even the most tattered shorts or shirts of the whites were valued over the colorful decorated near nakedness of Asmat tradition. He worried about the impact of the economic and cultural invasion sure to come in the name of civilization: "The West thinks in terms of bringing advance and opportunity to such a place," wrote the millionaire's son. "In actuality we bring a cultural bankruptcy which will last for many years, and what is more, poverty. Poverty after all is a relative thing."

Fortunately, Michael noted, on his trip these spoiling influences were not so much in evidence. Instead he had seen "imposing remnants of a marvelous past."

Not so imposing from a Christian or Western point of view, he of course realized. "For the Asmats," he wrote, "were a ferocious headhunting people constantly engaged in inter-village war and raids of varying degrees of deadliness." But the sculpture he deemed some of the greatest ever to emerge from a primitive culture.

En route to Merauke aboard the government launch *Tasman*, Michael met a Dutch official who suggested that the ideal vessel for him to use on his return was a catamaran such as that being used by one of the Dutch patrol officers. Michael made a mental note of this for his possible return to the Asmat.

A few days later he and Sam were back in the Baliem Valley with their exciting stories from the coast.

In August the expedition came to an end, with Gardner having to return to other work and Putnam returning to medical school. Heider decided to stay on in Kurelu, but he accompanied the remainder of the group to Wamena, where they would catch a plane for Hollandia and pick up a scheduled flight for the United States.

There was a party at the guesthouse in the administrative headquarters in Wamena that night to celebrate the end of a remarkable and successful expedition. All the remaining Americans attended—Gardner, Rockefeller, Putnam and Heider.

At the time Peter Hastings was in the compound and invited to join the group. He found them, he said later, pleasant and easy to talk to, but "strangely reserved about their experiences in the valleys near the Baliem."

It is probable that most of the group were still sensitive about the accusations made against them, of which they had been so recently cleared, and perhaps apprehensive that further unfavorable reports might leak out.

In any event Hastings said that he put down the group's reticence to fatigue and professional reserve.

But Michael was extremely curious about Hastings, about why he had shown up in the Baliem exactly as the Harvard Peabody group was leaving. Hastings said that he tried to convince Rockefeller and Gardner that it was pure coincidence, but neither seemed satisfied with his answer. The Americans left early to return to their camp for the night, and when they were gone, Hastings questioned the district officer.

The Dutch official told Hastings that he had consented to the expedition's work in the valley only because of high pressure from Washington and The Hague. As far as he was concerned, going into the uncontrolled areas was not a proper act and tended to stir the natives into the clashes which followed.

"You must see our point," the district officer said. "We send in white men to establish authority and say that there must be no more pig stealing, bride stealing or murder. Then a group of white men appear and encourage the very things we are trying to put a stop to. We are very angry about it."

Michael and Gardner gave Hastings their side of the matter later. According to Hastings, they denied that any deaths had occurred during their stay. When I asked Gardner and Heider about Hastings, they didn't remember his visit at all. Nevertheless, Hastings said that he later talked to Heider separately, and Heider remembered once being approached by a Kurelu tribesman who asked him what he thought of wars. Heider's answer, according to Hastings, was that the group neither approved nor disapproved of war.

"But there *was* a war," Hastings persisted.

According to Hastings, Heider refused to answer.

(Yet there was no doubt that there was war, and plenty of it, in the final reports of all participants. It can only be conjectured that the Harvard Peabody group was being discreet or that Hastings in some way misinterpreted or didn't understand their answers.)

"I saw quite a lot of Mike in the next few days," Hastings remembers. "He was an energetic, abrupt young man with a real passion, I thought, not only for his work, but for primitive peoples. He kept questioning me closely about the possibilities of field work in the headwaters of the Sepik in Australian New Guinea." (Apparently Rockefeller was not yet absolutely certain that he would return to the Asmat.)

"When I told him that various people had worked the field, he seemed disappointed. He said he would stick to his original decision to go to the Asmat. . . . He talked a little of his family and of his father, Governor Rockefeller, of whom he was very fond. He insisted that I should stay with the family if I ever found myself in New York again."

It was not clear whether Michael at this point was planning to go back to the States, since all his arrangements were made to return to the Asmat. But about this time he received mail from home with bad news. He confided to Heider that he had been informed that his father was planning to get a divorce.

"He was very upset about this and decided that he would have to go home and see the family before going on with his work, even if it was just for a week or so," Heider told me.

In Hollandia, waiting for their plane connection, the three returning Americans, Gardner, Putnam and Rockefeller, again encountered Hastings. They had meals together several times, and during one of them Michael asked Hastings if he would like to join him in the Asmat.

Hastings admits that he had already had enough of the primitive life in the Baliem Valley and not so regretfully declined.

"The last time we met was the night before I left for Biak," Hastings recalls. "We decided to see *Ten North*

Frederick in the flea-bitten little cinema in Hollandia. After the theater Mike and I had a couple of drinks together back at the hotel."

"Frankly," Michael told Hastings, "we are all very worried over what you are going to write about the fuss we had in the Baliem. There's been quite a row over it in Holland, and I'm afraid it'll get out in the States."

"I told him that if I wrote anything at all about it, I would write both sides," Hastings said. "He asked me again if I would go with him, and I said it didn't seem possible, and he agreed. Then we shook hands, wished each other luck, and went to our rooms. I left Hollandia next morning. I never saw him again."

25

IN NEW YORK Michael apparently talked with his family for a few days about the impending family crisis and, deciding that there was nothing he could do, made ready to return to New Guinea. But first he went back to Cambridge to view the photos taken on the Baliem Valley expedition and to talk with Gardner. While there, he told Gardner that after the second Asmat expedition he hoped to return to Harvard as a graduate student in anthropology. The experiences he had had in New Guinea had determined what he felt would be his future way of life.

Gardner was busy editing the film of *Dead Birds*, which was later to win a Robert Flaherty Award. Together he and Michael looked over the photographs prepared to that time.

"It was clear that Michael was pleased with what he saw, and he asked if he might assume the major responsibility for putting together the photographic book," Gardner says. Since he knew that Michael would be in Cambridge for his anthropological studies and would be near the photo collection for at least three years, the offer seemed highly appropriate and sensible to the anthropologist. So it was decided, and Michael took off immediately for New Guinea. In all he spent only about a week in the States, but his hasty departure and return fed the rumor mills which seemed at all times ready to grind out gossip about the son of Rockefeller. This time the stories had Michael ordered to leave the country as a result of the inquiry into the Baliem Valley activities and allowed back only because of vigorous intervention by his father. All members of the expedition categorically deny this, and the bulk of evidence seems to indicate that the rumors were surmise, based on Michael's amazingly fast turnaround trip to America. Since nobody at the time knew the reason (his father's divorce plans), the trip was attributed to troubles with the Dutch government.

Michael arrived at Hollandia after an exhausting voyage just in time for his rendezvous with René Wassing, who was to be his principal companion on this expedition. René had arranged for them to fly out the next morning at 8:40 to Merauke so that they could catch a 6 P.M. boat—the first in two months—to the Asmat. The swiftness of all these transitions left Michael's head in a whirl.

His plan was to spend ten weeks collecting further artifacts in the Asmat, revisiting some of the villages he had seen with Gerbrands and traveling to some he had not seen before.

Unfortunately the bulk of his notes and most of the photographs from this second expedition were lost at sea, but enough remains to get a vivid image of the scene.

In the course of his work Michael received help from

many of the local missionaries, including Father Van Kessel and Father Gerald Zegwaard of the Catholic Crozier Mission, Father Smit and Father Hekman. He also received the assistance of Father Superior Francis Pitka and Father Delmar Hesch of the American Roman Catholic Mission, among others. It is interesting to note that of these, three had publicly expressed the opinion that Michael was murdered by Otsjanep tribesmen—and these were knowledgeable men.

Father Zegwaard, the Dutch priest who was the first missionary to explore the Asmat, was one of the best informed, especially about native myths. He told Michael the Asmat myth of creation which reveals the importance of wood and wood carving in the Asmat concept of the universe.

According to the legend collected by Father Zegwaard, the great creator of Asmat mythology was Fumeripits. It was he who built the first *yeu* house by drawing an outline of it on one of the rare sandy spots of the Asmat coast. Suddenly the drawing in the sand metamorphosed into an actual hut, made of wood with palm thatch for walls and a row of entrances facing the river, just as *yeu* houses are made today. But there were no people in it.

Fumeripits set about creating human beings by carving them from the nearby mangrove trees, until he had a full population for the *yeu* house. But they were just wooden figures without life. Fumeripits then made a drum by hollowing out a log with carving and fire and fixing a lizard skin over each end as a drumhead. With this he summoned the stiff wooden figures to life until they rose up and began dancing to the rhythms of the drum. This was the start of life, and since then, the Asmat natives have regarded the mangrove tree as a symbol of man, with its roots as the feet, its trunk as the torso, its branches as arms and its fruit symbolizing the head. This is why the cockatoo and the opossum and other fruit eaters are regarded as symbols of head-hunting.

Ultimately Fumeripits created six *yeu* houses and populated them with humans carved from the trees. But his work was interrupted when a giant crocodile tried to destroy all his newly built houses and the people in them. A battle ensued between Fumeripits and the crocodile which lasted for five days. Each day the crocodile succeeded in destroying one of the houses, but each day Fumeripits wounded him more severely. On the sixth day he succeeded in killing the crocodile before he managed to destroy the last domicile of mankind. Fumeripits then cut the crocodile into pieces which he threw in different directions. It was from these pieces that the races of mankind, brown, black and white, were born.

The legend expresses an essential concept of Asmat belief: To create life, one must kill.

Zegwaard was an important source of native lore to Gerbrands, too. It was Zegwaard who explained to Gerbrands the significance played in headhunting ritual by the sago tree, which is regarded as a symbol of womanhood.

A fine-looking, tall, mature tree is selected when a sago tree is felled for ceremonial purposes. It is dressed in a woman's skirt, to emphasize its womanlike characteristics, but masculine symbols are added to show it contains both male and female qualities.

"The ritual of cutting down a sago tree incorporates many references to the slaying of a human being during a headhunting raid," Gerbrands writes.

Before a headhunting raid, the men give a recital before the tree of their past achievements. This is supposed to act magically to terrorize the enemy at a distance in advance of the attack. Of course, it also serves to reinforce the fighting spirit of the warriors preparing for the raid.

When the tree is felled, the men attack it with fierce yells as though it were the enemy itself. Holes are then cut in the trunk of the tree and left open for six weeks so that the capricorn beetle, whose larval worms are highly prized delicacies with magic significance, can lay her eggs in the tree. Meanwhile, a special palm-shaped leaf from the center crown of the tree has been selected, and during the interval of waiting it is formed into a ceremonial tray, or *an*. When the waiting period is over, the Asmats attack the sago with much shouting and yelling and remove the mature grubs, filling the *an* tray with them and grubs from other trees. The tray is then carried back to the *yeu* house, where it is accorded the same reception given to the body of a dead enemy.

Wassing and Michael managed to acquire two 18-horsepower outboard motors for this trip and with them were able to range much farther up the multitudinous rivers and inlets of the Casuarinen coast than was previously possible. Also, they were able to carry more trade goods and consequently return with more artifacts. The use of the motors meant that they could travel with only two native helpers, Simon and Leo, who served as interpreters.

But on the final occasion only one motor was available.

There are several versions of how Michael came to acquire the catamaran in which he ultimately traveled the Asmat. Probably the most reliable version comes from C. J. McKenzie, who got his information from Rob Eibrink Jansen, the Dutch resident at Merauke. Jansen told the Australian reporter that he had sold Rockefeller the craft, which was based on a similar one used by a local patrol officer, and even commented that he had not been paid for it at the time it was lost at sea.

The catamaran had a bamboo deckhouse for shelter; but

unlike the patrol officer's catamaran, which had a thatched roof, this one was of tin, which may have added a certain topheavy quality to the makeshift craft.

Jansen says he warned Michael of a number of things. The catamaran would need the full power of at least two 18-horsepower motors if it should leave the sheltered waters of the coastal rivers. It must never be overloaded. If he ever thought of crossing the mouth of the Eilanden River, he must never try to do so between noon and midafternoon. This would be dangerous—almost suicidal—because of the currents at that time of month. Some estimates said that the tidal bore could be as high as 20 feet and could rip scores of miles up and down the river. Crossing on Saturdays was particularly dangerous because radios along the coast which might help him in an emergency were turned off at midday. If by some chance he should be swept out to sea by the tide, Jansen warned him, all he had to do was sit pat and the tide would change and bring him back to the shore.

Jansen told McKenzie that Michael ultimately ignored every one of his warnings.

In any event the one-motored catamaran functioned well in the beginning of the trip, even though heavily loaded with axes and other trade goods.

Michael was thrilled with the important objects he was finding. A preserved note dated October 4 indicates Michael's fascination not only with the primitive art he was collecting, but also with the bizarre culture that had produced it. ". . . as remarkable as the art," Michael wrote, "is the fact that the culture which produced it is still intact; some remote areas are still headhunting; and only five years ago, almost the whole area was headhunting."

In a letter home he described the conditions which were such a radical change from his earlier way of life. Within a few days after leaving in a jet from New York, he wrote, he was sitting in a hut on stilts, without light, furniture or running water, scribbling by the light of a single kerosene lamp.

"Our living since our arrival," he wrote, "has been out of a Marx brothers movie. The Papuan houseboy who was supposed to bring in the wood and to tend the fires for our meals showed his face briefly the first morning and vanished into the jungle ever since. I'm not sure what shocked him—perhaps my 6:30 A.M. appearance."

As a result, Michael wrote, he was forced to attempt the fire, with only the help of Wassing, with the logs the native had already brought. When they finally managed to ignite it, the fire burned so strongly that it charred a hole right through the floor of the hut. In fact, neither Michael nor Wassing was strongly versed in the bushcraft so important for survival in New Guinea.

Michael's experience in the Baliem had not really prepared him for life in the riverine Asmat, and Wassing had little more experience than he. It has been suggested by many experts that in retrospect, it seemed careless, to say the least, for Dutch authorities to have sent Michael out without at least one experienced patrol officer.

"Nights," Michael wrote, with the humor of a schoolboy writing from camp, "are really the most fun.

". . . a rhythm created by the patter of mouse feet over the walls and ceiling with crickets chirping and frogs burping in counterpoint. The roosters here are affected by a curious neurosis which causes them to crow at midnight. Last night we had an earthquake to rock us to sleep."

On October 25 Michael and René paid a return visit to Amanamki where he had visited Gerbrands several months before. They were recognized and given an enthusiastic welcome, possibly because they had come to pick up and pay for some of the *bis* poles on which they had put down payments in the summer.

Michael found the work exhausting but inspiring. He

began to daydream about the mammoth exhibition which he would be able to mount with the large quantities of art objects he had been able to purchase. "Nothing approaching this has ever been granted a single primitive people," he wrote, "you can imagine what fun I am having dreaming these wild dreams and creating earth-shattering hypotheses about the nature of Asmat art."

One object particularly inspired interested comment: a carved head with a pointed protuberance which represented the stone ax used to make a hole in the skull of a trophy head in order to remove the brains.

At Tjemor village on the upper Undir River he encountered a mysterious figure carved by a local artist to represent the artist's father. He had never seen anything quite like it and tried assiduously to get a description of its purpose or function. The figure had been placed in front of the carver's house with a rattan line attached to it. Dangling from the line were a number of feather-decorated sticks. To the left of the figure was a string to which a number of pierced shells had been attached.

When Michael and René inquired about the strange objects, they encountered an apprehensive evasiveness. The people would only tell Michael that the object was in some way "bad." As soon as the two whites turned away, the figure, the shells and the feathered sticks were spirited away. Michael suspected that the figure may have been created to announce an impending headhunting raid, with the figures serving a similar function to that of the *bis* pole elsewhere.

On November 13 Michael wrote a letter in which he says he traveled for some time with two of the Catholic fathers (one of them Father Smit) who had been in the area "since the demise of headhunting three to four years ago." It may have been during this period he collected some of the few actual heads which appear in his collections decorated with cowrie shells, fiber, seeds and sago palm leaves.

Altogether there are four of these shown in his Asmat book, plus a curious wooden imitation trophy head "made to sell to whites" from Otsjanep.

On November 15 he wrote that he had just returned from a fifteen-day voyage in the catamaran to the northwest corner of the Asmat during which he and Wassing had visited some thirteen villages.

"The only difference between Mark Twain and me," he wrote, "is that his characters used poles all the time, while we use an outboard engine most of the time and poles part of the time. . . ."

Not infrequently Michael and René, after allowing themselves to become stranded on a mudbank, had to get out and push their awkward craft through the heavy sucking mud. The boat itself they named the *Chinapsitch* after the most talented woodcarver they had found in their travels. Sometimes they called the boat the *Fo-Fo* after the pet hornbill they had bought in the village of Amanamki.

Language presented a problem, and they could communicate through their Asmat houseboy, who interpreted the local Asmat dialect into Malay, which René in turn interpreted into English for Michael's benefit.

It was during this period that Michael also availed himself of a chance to have a long talk with Father Zegwaard, with whom he had previously chatted on the boat from Merauke to Agats.

There were two more letters after that, both dated November 16. In one Rockefeller wrote, ironically: "I assure you that I by no means enjoy the prospects of Christmas in Agats." In the second he described the process of recuperating from the long grueling trip to the northwest Asmat. Much of the time was spent in cataloguing, transporting, packing, marking and organizing the many artifacts they had acquired. Apart from that, the exhausted pair took advantage of the respite by sleeping late under their protective netting in the mornings. They got a welcome relief from their monotonous field diet of Spam and Australian corned beef and rice every day at 1 P.M., when the hospitable sisters of the mission arranged a feast in seven pots to be delivered by a messenger to the government rest house. Each pot, Michael noted with lip-smacking delight, contained some "unusual goody."

That was his last letter. The plan now was for Wassing and Rockefeller to return to Atsj, a large village of about 1,500 people which lay about 35 miles away. It was up the South Eilanden River, a few miles away from Amanamki; they would visit Father Van Kessel at Basim en route.

Though a route was available via the inland waterways to Atsj, avoiding the dangerous river estuaries, apparently Michael and Wassing decided they would save time by cutting across the mouth of the South Eilanden.

The departure was set for Saturday, November 18.

On the following day the catamaran was swept away and capsized by the tidal bore of the North Eilanden River. Michael Rockefeller was presumed drowned at sea or eaten by marine predators, according to the story given out by Dutch authorities.

But the official story always has been clouded by a fog of vague, sometimes conflicting stories which I found became less vague the closer I got to the scene of the action. Woven through all these stories was the thread of suppression: I had been warned that the story was better left untold, that digging too deeply would lead only to trouble.

With Van Kessel's tape I had a fairly full account of Michael's end, one that I believed was probably true. Gerbrands, who represented the view of authority, had not been able to change my mind on that. But there were still haunting gaps and loose threads to Van Kessel's tale. Now that I was back in New York I had ideas about how I would go about clearing up these enigmas.

26

BEFORE PUBLISHING a story on my New Guinea experiences, I sent advance copies to Governor Rockefeller and to his former wife, Mary Rockefeller, even though I was fairly sure my findings would not be news to them. But I wanted to provide them with the opportunity of making any additions or corrections should they be so inclined.

From Mrs. Rockefeller I received a friendly but disinterested reply, thanking me for sending the article and stating that it had been turned over to Stephen Rockefeller, who handles such details for the family.

From the governor I received a brief note:

> DEAR MR. MACHLIN:
> In the absence from the State of Governor Nelson A. Rockefeller, I am acknowledging your letter of August 1st regarding Michael Rockefeller and your trip to New Guinea. The fact is that when the governor completed his search, he considered the matter closed.
> > Sincerely,
> > STEVEN V. DAVID
> > Rockefeller Family and Associates

The answer did not surprise me. I had always felt that the governor would prefer the matter be dropped; as for veiled hints that pressure would be put on me to discontinue my research, I discounted that idea—attributing it to the almost superstitious fear of the might of the Rockefellers, and I still do. No pressure has ever been put on me or anybody else.

I came across a startling report filed in the Sydney *Herald* by Keith Willey. An Army newspaper in Indonesia, *Berita Yudha,* reported that one of its medical officers in the Asmat area had actually got a confession from one of the men involved in the killing of Rockefeller!

There had been a severe cholera epidemic in the area, and the medical officer, knowing the natives believed all illness to be caused by magic, told them that the disease might have been caused by the hovering unavenged spirit of Michael Rockefeller. Under such coercion the natives admitted that members of their tribe had killed and eaten Rockefeller.

But despite diligent inquiries made through the Indonesian embassy and others, I was unable to track down the actual story.

I wondered if Ajam, the fight leader, and his colleagues still lived in Otsjanep—after all, less than ten years had passed since Rockefeller's disappearance. If he had been murdered, it was reasonable to assume that some of the actual killers were still alive. Now that the "act of free choice" had been settled overwhelmingly in favor of retaining the Indonesian government, perhaps it might be possible to visit the Asmat and research the story on the spot. So when I learned that a researcher named John Campbell had been granted a permit to visit the exact area in which Rockefeller was lost, it seemed a fantastic opportunity to clear up the questions that still bothered me. I asked if he would accept an assignment to go to Otsjanep, and Campbell (this is not his real name) agreed—but only if he and his participation remained our secret. Campbell, who had a reputation for accuracy and diligence, was concerned that this might constitute a conflict with his regular assignment. I briefed him on my findings, and he was intrigued; but he drew the line at the murder theory—perhaps just out of a reluctance to accept such a bizarre climax to Rockefeller's life.

"I am not necessarily asking you to find proof that Rockefeller was murdered," I said. "I am asking you to find out, as best you can, what actually happened. If the murder theory turns out to be false and a different one is proven true, that will be valuable news too."

In April, 1970, Campbell took off for New Guinea.

One of the first people I had consulted on my return was Count Hervé De Maigret, who had been a radio technician for the film *The Sky Above and the Mud Below*. Some of its scenes had been shot in Otsjanep only a year before Rockefeller's presumed end there.

Hervé was very interested in my transcript of Van Kessel's tape, especially since he said he was certain that Tony Saulnier, the still photographer with the French film team, later killed in a tragic plane crash, had actually photographed Van Kessel, who had been of help to them in the village.

From his shelf Hervé pulled the book of photographs of the French film expedition published by Saulnier. It is called *Headhunters of Papua* and contains, as Hervé said, several excellent photographs of Father Van Kessel at work among the Asmat natives. I didn't recognize him because of his full beard.

But more important, Herve pointed out to me an actual photograph of Ajam—the man accused of having led the killing raid!

That the French team had the specific photos I needed was not the coincidence it might seem. They had been drawn to the village by the same lures that attracted Rockefeller—the best *bis* pole carvings of the Asmat. As for photographing Ajam, this too was natural since he was one of the two or three most important men in the village. Leadership in Asmat villages is based on accomplishments and seniority and is not as a rule hereditary. One of the top men in the village is the fight chief, who is the most accomplished and canny warrior, as well as generally the most successful, as measured in number of heads taken.

Ajam had a fierce intelligent face with the prominent nose which tends to distinguish Papuans from other dark races. In the photo he was supervising the construction of a *bis* pole. His only garment was a white cockatoo feather.

To be absolutely sure of Ajam's identity, I confirmed the identification with Pierre Gaisseau, whom I met some weeks later, and by telephone with Gerard Delloye, producer of the film.

"I can make the identification easily," said Delloye. "You see, Ajam was my adopted tribal father!"

"And do you believe that he could have murdered Rockefeller?" I asked.

"I believe Ajam was Rockefeller's killer," Delloye replied. "Ajam was a strong man with a streak of violence. To me the story seems logical. We of the film crew knew of it long before it was made public, but did not want to be accused of sensationalism or publicity seeking in regard to our film. We were very much aware of the still smoldering resentment of the tribe toward the Dutch over the recent killing of their clansmen."

A Dutch officer named Beltgens had been assigned to guard the team, along with a squad of armed native police. The French team reported seeing heads cut only a short time before their arrival. According to Saulnier's book, Beltgens was constantly on the alert against possible danger.

"He knew the Asmats and in his opinion these peaceful villagers would not hesitate for a moment if they had a chance of extending their skull collection at our expense."

Saulnier discovered that the cargo cult was also a powerful

196

influence even in as remote a place as the Asmat. Beltgens told him of a recent patrol during which he found an imitation radio aerial rigged up by one of the chiefs to simulate the white man's aerials. The chief maintained that the aerial put him in contact with the tribe's ancestors. The chief told him that his ancestors had said that the Papuans would shortly rise up and oust the white man and take possession of all his cargo. This would take place, said the chief, against a terrible disturbance—a red sky and terrible storms. (The similarity of some cargo myths told in tribes hundreds of miles apart is noteworthy in view of their lack of communication.)

Now the time had come, the chief announced, when the spirits had actually begun to send the white man's cargo!

"Where?" asked the excited tribesmen.

"There, behind the tree," said the chief, whereupon the tribe hurled themselves on the site indicated and began to dig frantically with their sticks and spears. Sure enough, a dozen tins of bully beef appeared—just possibly planted by the wily chief.

When the film team arrived at Otsjanep itself, Beltgens told them a grim story. Only six months before, the village had been visited by two men from a village on the Ewta River. The two men never left Otsjanep, Beltgens said. They were killed and eaten. "So we had better be on guard," Saulnier wrote; "the whole region was secretly ready for a sacred revenge."

While the team was finishing its work in Basim, Father Van Kessel's village, a pair of messengers arrived from Otsjanep for the moviemakers.

"The priest told us that the messengers from Otsjanep had come not only to fetch us, but to lodge a complaint against the inhabitants of Basim," Saulnier reported. "They had seen spies from Basim prowling around their village. Only six months earlier 114 members of several

Otsjanep tribes had gone on a journey of exploration to prospect and barter along the coast, and, if the opportunity presented, hunt a few heads. Only fourteen returned. And as they did not agree and were not from the same tribe, only five survived in the end. Could it be the peaceful inhabitants of Basim, our present hosts, who had killed and eaten them?"

Van Kessel told them that all the men of the village tribes hunted heads regularly; it was the basis of what might be called Asmat civilization.

In Saulnier's book on the Asmat village I found passages which showed a chilling prescience.

For example, the incident creating the payback situation that resulted in Michael's death involved a Dutch patrol officer who panicked and shot several tribesmen.

I discovered that a similar incident had almost occurred to the French team, which was impressed by the exciting and savage welcome given them by the tribesmen (somewhat like my own greeting by the Kukukukus) .

"In fact," Saulnier wrote, "the police boys who knew the local people better than we did were considerably frightened by the sight of the tribe approaching in full war dress. They reached for their rifles; but everything went off well. The Asmats were only coming to welcome us."

Shortly before the French team completed filming the carving and construction of a *bis* pole, Beltgens became worried. He said it made him uneasy to remain too long among a tribe whose secret life they did not really understand, and he thought he saw a few veiled threats. Beltgens was so disturbed he insisted that they depart the following day, even though the filming of the sculpture was not yet completed.

The French were furious; but Beltgens had the authority to force the issue, and the team returned to its base camp in Cook Bay. Later they vented their anger again and asked

198

why they couldn't return to Otsjanep and finish shooting the *bis* pole ceremony.

Beltgens refused categorically.

"We would have risked the worst if we had stayed there a day longer," the Dutchman said. His chief reason for concern: the totems whose carvings the French had so enjoyed studying represented members of the tribe recently killed by police machine pistols. Beltgens and his native squad chief were convinced that completion of the *bis* pole might be a signal for revenge.

All this, remember, was written one year before Rockefeller appeared on the scene!

A week later I received from Jim Anderson a story which had even greater bearing on the Rockefeller murder theory. Two American missionaries, Stan Dale and Phil Masters, had been killed and eaten by primitive West Irian tribesmen in 1968, *seven years after the disappearance of Rockefeller!*

This repeated the pattern I had observed earlier. The government or the missionaries or the social scientists would deny that headhunting, cannibalism, or cargo cult still existed—only to have a flagrant example turn up long after the custom in question had supposedly died out. When I wrote of the cargo cult near Wewak in 1970, Stuart Inder criticized me by saying that the sect had been stamped out years ago. Yet a serious outbreak occurred in that very area *a year after I left*. As for headhunting and cannibalism in the Sepik, authorities solemnly assured me that it was a thing of the distant past, and yet I had met people who had been punished by the government for cannibalism within a year of my arrival, and I had actually witnessed the preparation of human heads, an art allegedly long forgotten.

The incident at Ninia in which the two American missionaries were killed is a case in point. There seems to be a willingness to believe that what the missionaries or government *want* to be true *is* true, a "blind spot" phenomenon clearly illustrated by the diary kept by Dale, one of the murdered missionaries.

In an early entry dealing with the people of the four valleys east of the mission base at Ninia, Dale says:

"The people of the Heluk Valley have burnt their fetishes. . . . Within that simple statement lies a triumph and a tragedy. From the time we first began preaching the Gospel at Ninia we knew that ultimately we should have to deal with the matter of the fetishes. They are associated with magical powers which dominate the lives of the people in a deeply intrenched Satanic system. . . ."

As long as the natives retained their fetishes, Dale wrote, it would be "quite impossible to be wholly committed to Christ."

Dale saw it as an important part of his mission to make the natives destroy these magic objects as a defense against their backsliding into pagan ways.

One group, Dale wrote, had not destroyed their fetishes even though they had professed Christianity. Ultimately Dale, disturbed by this seeming tendency to cling to old beliefs, asked the converts to burn their fetishes immediately. The village leader promised he would do so the following day. In the morning still more local people came and said that they would burn their fetishes, too, and the whole idea was taken up with apparent enthusiasm in the area.

"With excited whoops," Dale wrote, "they went racing up the mountain to their villages, diving into the men's clubhouses and dragging the bags of fetishes out of their dark corners."

Even the old wise men, casters of spells, carried their fetishes to the mission station to be burned. Now Dale felt he was making real progress in Christianizing the indigenous population.

For two or three hours a group of excited youths of the tribe ran from place to place gathering fetishes and throwing them in the heap to be burned.

"Then they sang hymns of praise, giving thanks to God for their release from these things which had for so long kept them in bondage," Dale wrote. "A match was set to the pile, and as the flames leaped upward, they broke out again in spontaneous songs of joy."

At least that is Dale's interpretation.

The following day some of the new "Christians" from Ninia went to a string of villages on a ridge to the west and persuaded the villagers to burn their fetishes also.

This Dale probably saw as a high point in his Christianizing of the local people.

But there were warning rumbles of discontent he should have noticed. "Some men from Ninia called to us across the valley that the people from Palingama, another of our preaching posts, were coming over to make trouble," Dale wrote two days after the orgy of fetish burning.

With the blind courage of his intense faith, Dale went immediately to the troubled area with a few of his Christian converts to explain to the people why it was necessary to burn the fetishes. As they approached the area, Dale's native companions noticed apprehensively that they were being trailed by men carrying bows and quivers of fighting arrows.

Dale told the others to wait and went ahead alone to investigate. "I saw a few men with bows," he wrote, "but they disappeared as I got nearer."

Dale went ahead with his plan. He gathered people in the center of the village and explained why they should free themselves from the power of the fetishes as the people in Ninia and the other villages had done.

There seemed to be some agreement, and Dale's Ninia Christians began gathering up the magic objects.

But resistance was growing now. A large group of hostile men had gathered across the river from the village and started to chant and shout.

"I could see that they were starting to work themselves into a fury," Dale wrote. "I strolled down to the river bank with the intention of discouraging them.

"Suddenly the whole crowd of them came charging down to the river and began shooting arrows at me."

But the river, fortunately, was too wide at that point, and the arrows fell short.

Dale's Christianized supporters came running to his defense, but cloaked in his vision of Christ-given immunity, Dale told them to desist and decided to circle through the bush alone, "intending to come up behind our assailants and get quite close to them so that I could reason with them."

By the time he had completed this maneuver the hostile natives were gone. Dale might have safely returned to argue another day when things were calmer, but he elected to follow them and try to persuade them that Christianity was the right way. Dodging several arrows which were shot at him, he managed to overtake some of the stragglers and remonstrate with them.

In retrospect it is astonishing he wasn't killed on the spot. But he was allowed to leave with an unpunctured skin and returned to Palingama, where he burned a huge pile of fetishes.

A week later, acting on a report that the people in the Heluk Valley wanted to hear the Gospel, he dispatched two of his recently converted Christians to preach to them. But in a grim finish recalling the black humor of the old joke "send more missionaries," the two Christian emissaries were ambushed, killed and eaten.

Shocked and bewildered, Dale radioed for police help to go in with him and recover the remains of his converts. But when he arrived finally with a district officer and four police-men, it was obvious that they were walking into another ambush. The district officer and the policemen refused to proceed any farther.

"This was the crucial moment," Dale wrote. "I knew that it would be extremely dangerous to go on without them, but burdened and heartbroken over the fate of the two young men, I felt that I could not face the Christians at Ninia again without doing all that was in my power to re-cover their remains."

So he continued on the trail alone. "At first, I walked slowly, for every bush could conceal an enemy, but then the Lord gave me an assurance of His protection and I stepped out more briskly."

By then, apparently shamed by his raw courage, two of the policemen returned to support him. But all they could find at first were the trampled yam beds where the can-nibals had danced a celebration of their feast of Christians. A heavy fog was settling in, so Dale decided to make camp in a local hut with one of the policemen, while the other and some boys who had joined them continued the search. As Dale began preparing an evening meal, the enemy tribesmen struck.

"I had moved away from the fire in the center of the hut and was getting something from a pack near the door, when I felt a violent stab in my right side. A five-foot arrow was imbedded deeply in me," Dale's diary states.

"I snatched it out with one swift straight pull . . . hear-ing as I did an expression of satisfaction from outside. As I scrambled away from the door, another arrow pierced my right thigh. We were surrounded. The enemy could pour arrows into the hut from every direction, and the bright fire made us clearly visible to the attackers."

The ambush and shower of arrows had taken a matter of seconds, and as Dale hurried to douse the fire and the policeman struggled to unholster his pistol, three more arrows hit the missionary in the left thigh, right forearm and left side.

The attackers, seeing the missionary apparently fatally impaled, began their death chant, but at this point Dale's policeman managed to get his pistol into action and shot one of the attackers dead. At the same moment the other policeman arrived with his revolver and joined in the fire. The combined power of the two weapons terrorized the tribesmen, and they fled.

Dale, seriously wounded and in agony, wanted only to be allowed to rest awhile to recuperate from his wounds. But the Ninia boys, wise in matters concerning arrow wounds, told him that by morning he would be too stiff to walk and in even greater agony. The only choice was to walk all night.

Somehow Dale, perhaps bolstered by his naïve but deeply felt faith, managed to make the trip, suffering, he wrote, "great waves of pain . . . the air seemed to be wheezing in and out of me." Twice he begged the boys to leave him on the trail to die. But ultimately, Dale wrote, he clung to the promise of the Bible: "I shall not die, but live and declare the works of the Lord."

Apparently the Lord *was* with him, for he miraculously reached Liligam, where he was carried by litter and finally picked up by an MAF plane and taken back to Ninia. He recovered in a nearby hospital.

Five months later he had again made his way into a village of hostile tribesmen. This time he was accompanied by another American missionary, Phil Masters. This time neither of them came out. A helicopter from a geological camp sent to investigate was told that the party had been ambushed. One native boy escaped.

He said that at the junction of two rivers the group had heard the brush rustling in the bush—a signal that the ambushers no longer care if the victims know they are there. Moments later a horde of screaming natives burst from the bush, firing a hail of deadly arrows. The native carrier had managed to break through the line and flee to safety. Nothing else was known.

The helicopter pilot flew to the site of the ambush with Indonesian police armed with submachine guns. They found nothing but spent arrows, ripped-up clothing belonging to the missionaries and yellow clay blotched with enormous quantities of human blood, so thick that one of the Indonesian police slipped on it and fell.

Later the police managed to collect and bring back some more grim and conclusive clues—bones and skulls identified as the Americans, and a jawbone with teeth with fillings. Added to this pathetic heap returned for burial was a man's fatigue shirt, crusty with dried blood and sieved with arrow holes.

The tribesmen involved were the Yalis, from whom the stone axes used in the Asmat were obtained at the end of a long trade chain. They lived near the east end of the Grand Valley—where Michael Rockefeller and his friends had traveled on their first expedition—seven years before.

27

IN JUNE, 1970, my faith in John Campbell paid off. I received a batch of film, notes and tapes which gave a vivid and convincing picture of Michael's last days. Campbell had succeeded in taping interviews with several of the missionaries who had previously refused to comment on the disappearance—people who had actually been on the scene at the time of Rockefeller's disappearance. He had even managed to locate and speak with the elusive Dr. Dresser, mentioned several times as someone who knew the real story but refused to tell it.

To follow the story properly, we should begin with a letter written to his superior by the late Father Francis Pitka, head of the Crozier Mission in Agats. This letter was found and recorded at Agats by Campbell:

DEAR FATHER PROVINCIAL:

By the time you read this letter, Father Provincial, the first six months in which the Crozier fathers have been more or less on the run in New Guinea will have passed. In that half year many things have happened in the Asmat area. We have learned much I hope from these experiences. Shortly after you left New Guinea to return to the United States, the tragic events centering about Michael Rockefeller took place. I have had very many inquiries and letters concerning participation of the Crozier fathers in the search for Michael. As a consequence I think I shall write principally about the search as we observed it and took part in it here in Agats. It was on a Saturday morning, November 18, that Rockefeller and his companion, René Wassing, set out on a catamaran. They were accompanied by Leo and Simon, two native men from Shurum. As usual, Rockefeller and Wassing were disposed to spend much time at the mission house while they were in Agats. On Friday evening before their departure Michael had talked with me quite a while. He had given me several checks to pay us and others for woodcarvings that he had purchased. Just that morning he had been examining some carvings that had been stored under the rafters of the mission house. As a matter of fact, I might very well have gotten a lifetime remembrance for carvings. Mike had climbed up over the ceiling to hand me down the pieces of carving from there. As he was handing down a shield it slipped from his grasp. My hands were extended upward to grasp it and somehow the shield had eluded my hands and the lower edge of the shield had banged me in the face just below the left eye. For several days I nursed a sore cheekbone and I felt fortunate that the bruise was so slight. It appeared as if I would have a slight injury to remember Mike by during his planned absence of a month on a trip to the Casuarinen coast. Since the party would be gone for a month, they were carrying a heavy load of supplies and gear. Too heavy a load. The catamaran burdened with the weight of their equipment was slow to respond to the ups and downs required of a boat while traveling through really choppy waters. We learned later that this was the cause of the tragedy. As the catamaran entered the waters outside the mouth of the North Eilanden River it ran into the very choppiness Father Hesch had described to us in his earlier letters. You may remember, Father Provincial, it was Father Hesch's description of those dangerous waters, especially at times when there is a very strong outflowing current against inblowing wind from off the sea, that induced us to seek to secure larger boats. It takes very little wind to raise up troublesome waves against a fast current. It was over choppy waters that the catamaran had to cross, in order to continue down the coast to the mouth of the South Eilanden River. As we later found out the catamaran did not make it. That Saturday night at almost midnight I was awakened by continued pounding on the Mission House doors. My first feeling was one of foreboding. It was only a week earlier that I had been awakened by similar pounding at the Mission House door and we had learned that the mission sawmill was on fire. On the front porch I found a group of men who were excitedly trying to tell us about the boat. At first it seemed as if one of the mission boats was adrift on the sea. The men referred only to "Tuan's boat." Here in this part of the world any white man is called a Tuan; but the situation became clear and we decided it was Tuan

Rockefeller and Tuan Wassing's boat. Then we got more of the story. The catamaran, failing to rise quickly enough on the waves, had submerged under them. The outboard motor had been swamped. Being of wood construction, the boat had not sunk but continued to float on the surface of the sea. After several hours of drifting there had been no prospect of a boat coming to their rescue. Leo and Simon made an attempt to swim to shore. The Asmat people around here swim like fish since they spend so much of their lives on and in the water but this was almost too much. Leo and Simon were in the water for almost five hours. Leo had to carry on his back the almost exhausted Simon the last stretch to the shore. They then plunged through the mud along the coast to the village of Per and when they reached the village afterward catechist Leo had gotten together a group of native rowers. Shortly after midnight they had reached Agats and gone immediately to the HPB [Dutch administrative headquarters] to report the tragedy. Leo and Simon had last seen Rockefeller and Wassing sitting atop the zinc sheet roof of the almost-submerged catamaran. Catechist Leo and his rowers came to the Mission House to arouse us and tell us of the mishap. By this time it was already very early Sunday morning. Since Father Miller was to leave at dawn to go to Ewer for Sunday mass and I was scheduled to offer a 7 A.M. mass in Sjuru and a 5:30 P.M. mass in Agats, neither of us was free to accompany the HPB and he set out at 2 A.M. Leo and Simon accompanied him back to the area of the mishap. No success. On Sunday afternoon planes from Biak began to scan the seacoast from Agats to Cook Bay. They would wing up the coast as far as Agats and then bank around over us to head back down the coast again to Cook Bay. After a few passes up and down the coast the planes shortly discovered the catamaran and reported on the radio that one survivor was to be seen sitting atop the bottom of the canoes, for the catamaran had capsized by this time. It seemed that Rockefeller and Wassing had put so much of their goods on top of the zinc roof that the whole thing had collapsed, capsized in the swell of the sea. The lone survivor had been sighted just before dark. A boat from Cook Bay had tried to reach the survivor but because of the darkness and lack of proper equipment to search the sea at night it was impossible to effect a pickup of the survivor at night. There was naturally much speculation as to which of the two was the survivor. The next morning Mr. Wassing was rescued from his precarious perch on the up-turned boat. He was not in bad condition after his harrowing experience. It was learned from Wassing that he and Rockefeller had no way of knowing that Leo and Simon had reached shore. On Sunday morning after an afternoon and a night adrift Rockefeller decided that something had to be done. There were no boats in sight and probably none were coming. Mike lashed two empty gasoline jerricans to his body and began the long swim toward the shore. Since the planes could detect no evidence of Rockefeller on the sea or on the coast there was a possibility that he had somehow made it safely to shore. A radio message came to Agats that the planes were to organize a search along the shore line where Rockefeller might yet be found alive. It was November 20. Immediately after the receipt of the message Brother Paul took in our Maapi boat an officer and four policemen and searched from Agats along the seacoast to the village of Omadesep. At high tide it is possible to go over the mudbank and stay quite close along the shore with the boat while the police and the natives from the villages tramped through the mud along the shore line to look for any bit of evidence that would indicate that Mike had been there. . . Here they met Father Van Kessel, MSC, the missionary to the Casuarinen coast area, coming with a party from the opposite direction.

Father Van Kessel boarded the Maapi boat from the canoe in which he had been traveling and the search party went down the coast to Cook Bay which was now the headquarters of the land, sea and air search. From Cook Bay

Father Paul took a party of searchers to Basim on the Fajit River near Awp where they again encountered another group of searchers without a trace of Michael, so Brother Paul returned to Agats. On the following day with more fuel, supplies and gear aboard Brother Paul set out again with another search party to check the coastline and visit the villages beginning from Agats to where the mishap had occurred. Still no trace of Michael. By this time it was generally agreed that the entire coastline had been thoroughly searched and that little could be gained by going over the same area again. All small boats and canoes traveling along the coastline continued to keep a watch on the shore for any new evidence but all in vain. Brother Paul returned to Agats. The search had been concentrated on the area between the mouth of the North Eilanden River and Cook Bay because that was the direction of the flow of water. Mr. Wassing had been picked up about 16 miles out at sea from Cook Bay and Michael could have had meager success swimming against the current. He would have had to go along with the current by swimming toward the landward side of the current and hope to get into the most rapidly moving water and thence work his way to shore. Thus if he was to reach shore at all it would have to be between the North Eilanden River and Cook Bay. That, Father Provincial, is the story of the search from Agats. Planes from Biak and other places searched the seas from Agats down the coast. Finally a continuation of the search was considered futile. Governor Nelson Rockefeller had returned to the United States, bigger ships returned to Merauke and smaller craft like our Maapi returned to their posts and the search was concluded. There comes a time when the judgment concerning the futility of further search had to be made. It was apparent that Michael had not reached shore and that he was a victim of the dangerous seas with which he tried to give battle in an effort to reach shore. Personally I had not been an actual member of the searching party nor had the other fathers and brothers except Brother Paul. He had kept the boat going all through the search; in the meantime he got very little sleep and even less food. For he had taken only a small quantity of supplies along and little had been available during the search. We realized that we could personally be of little assistance in actual searching, for no nonnative could proceed over and through the knee-deep mud along the shore . . . ; the natives alone can meet that situation. The police directed the searching party and we provided one of the boats to convey the police and others empowered to direct these searching parties. If we had had a second seagoing type of boat we could have doubled our participation by accompanying a search party and thus helping to cover more of the coastline at the same time. We did all that we could to help find Mike alive as we would have done for anyone else. We understand that it is not at all impossible that when we least expect it one or more of us crashes in a disabled boat and is carried out to sea. We surely would want others to do everything possible to find us and bring us back. This tragedy of Mike has driven home another lesson in sea safety. In case of a mishap don't leave a drifting boat and try to swim to shore. That seems to be a basic principle of water safety; that principle holds true also in New Guinea. If Mike had stayed on the catamaran he would be in New York now. In a letter from Mr. Wassing we have received his personal thanks. I'm sure he will permit you to reprint his fine letter.

Netherlands New Guinea, March 17, 1962.

Statements made to me by Wassing and others culled from an interview he gave to a Dutch newspaper *Algemeen Dagblat* give a detailed picture from the point of view of the victims:

Wassing's description of the incident:

"We left Agats around nine in the morning to sail across the open sea to Amanamki; we took with us the two Asmat boys Simon and Leo. The water was high, but it seemed quiet. We arrived at Per and stopped to inspect a carved canoe which Michael had commissioned earlier and planned to take to America with him. Michael made a partial payment of two axes and four pieces of tobacco for the canoe.

"As we prepared to leave, Simon urged us to hurry because the waves on the river were becoming dangerously high. We managed to get out by noon and sailed again until we reached the mouth of the South Eilanden River. It was still low tide; but the current was now running out to the sea again, and it was a powerful one. We headed into the sea until two fifteen in the afternoon. Then something terrible happened. A following wave came over the stern and side of the boat, stopping the engine and swamping the hulls. We sank visibly in the water, and the current continued to push us out to sea. Simon and Leo were afraid and said that they would like to swim for shore. We gave our permission, of course. They each took a jerrican, emptied the gasoline out of it and jumped into the sea using the cans as life buoys. As they left us, I asked them to try to get help from someone on shore. They promised they would, and it turns out that they did."

That message of the swamping of the boat was received and acted on in a fantastically short time, and the Dutch government acted quickly to get all possible air and naval elements to the scene. Three Neptune search planes combed the area. Twelve naval vessels, all that were available, searched the myriad rivers and estuaries. Radio messages were dispatched from Hollandia to the Dutch embassy in Washington, where a pink slip emerged from the code room with a message for Governor Rockefeller. This was telephoned immediately to the Dutch ambassador at his Virginia farm. But Rockefeller had been hounded by the press for weeks over his announced divorce and was trying to remain incommunicado. As a result, he didn't get the message from the ambassador until the following afternoon.

That evening Elliot Elisofon was having a cocktail party in his New York apartment. Hugh Moffat, news editor of *Life,* phoned and said he had heard a radio flash that Michael Rockefeller was missing. But for the moment, Elisofon says, he pooh-poohed the idea. However, a few minutes later Robert Gardner called and confirmed the report. Excusing himself, Elisofon, accustomed to being sent to outlandish and primitive places without much notice, went to his room where he kept two suitcases, one packed with Arctic survival gear and the other with jungle gear.

From the privacy of his room he telephoned Rockefeller, whom he knew well from their days of preparing an exhibit of primitive African art together. He offered his help in organizing Rockefeller's search expedition and handling the press. He insisted, however, that he would go only as a friend and not as a journalist. He felt too close to the Rockefellers, and to Michael in particular, to want to capitalize in any way on his inside situation. He then called Moffat back and said, "I'm going to New Guinea with Nelson Rockefeller to look for Michael. Is that all right with you?"

Moffat said it was fine with him. Then Elisofon asked, "Even if I don't have a camera hanging around my neck? I don't want to do this as an assignment."

Moffat sighed and answered, "Use your judgment, Elliot. You have my OK to go."

Elliot made a reservation on the governor's scheduled flight to Hawaii, pulled his tropical suitcase from the closet, and went out into the swirl of the cocktail party to take his wife, Joan, aside and tell her quietly, "I'll be gone for a while. I don't know how long. I'm going to New Guinea to look for Michael."

And then he was off to Idlewild Airport.

At the airport he met Rockefeller, looking tense and depressed but in reasonable control, and Michael's twin sister, Mary Strawbridge, who was in a state of near shock. Fortunately Elisofon's kit included a small supply of Miltowns, which he used to soothe the distraught girl. Accompanying Rockefeller were his press secretary and his bodyguard, a state police lieutenant.

The group was forced to stop overnight in Hawaii to arrange for a chartered jet to fly them to Hollandia, the nearest jet strip location to the Asmat. Elisofon used the time to equip the group with whatever tropical gear was available in Honolulu—mosquito nets, insect repellent, antimalaria pills, large flashlights and batteries—and lots more Miltown for Mary. A Boeing 707 jet was chartered to fly the group to Biak. Elisofon's authority and knowledge of conditions the group would face must have been a comfort to the governor, who found himself not only in a tragic personal situation but in a delicate position politically. He realized that any publicity during the search would be interpreted in many public sectors as an attempt to sentimentalize and soften his image following the recent unpleasant publicity on the divorce. He was determined to seek as little personal publicity as possible. It was Elisofon, rather than the press secretary, who coped with most of the increasingly aggressive press when they finally reached the Asmat in a DC-3 chartered in Biak, which then flew them to Dutch administrative headquarters in Merauke. There the governor was met by J. P. Plateel, the Dutch governor for Netherlands New Guinea.

But all this had taken time. While messages and planes were flying to and from the Asmat, the Rockefeller catamaran had been drifting out into the Arafura Sea.

"We realized that our situation was precarious," Wassing recalls, "but we weren't panicked. We had hopes that Simon and Leo would be able to find help before our situation worsened. But we were soaking wet and very cold as the sun began to go down in the afternoon. Also we seemed to be drifting farther and farther out to sea. The waves, too, were getting larger. We tried to get out of the way of these seas washing over the canoe hulls, but a sudden large roller came along and completely capsized the catamaran. [One version has it that the boat capsized while they were trying to wrench pieces of tin from the cabin roof to use as paddles.] We were lucky we weren't separated from the craft right then." Boating people have speculated that the use of a tin roof instead of a thatched one had added to the top-heaviness of the catamaran, increasing the chances that it would capsize.

Now they were in an infinitely worse position. Wassing could hardly swim at all and clung desperately to the hull. Whatever water, food or other supplies they might have had and whatever shelter the cabin might have provided were now gone. Also, Michael began to wonder, what actual chance was there of Simon and Leo's reaching shore, and if so, would they get help in time to save them?

"We tried to paddle with pieces of wood," Wassing says, "but it was useless. We just had to treat the overturned hulls as a raft and drift where the current was taking us, farther and farther out to sea."

Dusk came and then nightfall, and with it more damp and chilling winds. Somehow the stranded pair survived the seemingly endless hours until dawn. By the first shafts of morning light, at about 5 A.M., they were able to make out what appeared to be land. Desperately they tried again to paddle toward it with pieces of wood broken off the catamaran. But they had no effect on the outward drift.

"I felt then that the situation was urgent," Wassing recalls.

It was at this point that Michael proposed swimming for shore. In all probability had Wassing been able to swim they both could have jumped in at the same time as Simon

215

and Leo. Possibly it was a sense of loyalty that kept Michael aboard, and possibly a sense of seamanship—the knowledge that in case of a marine disaster the standard advice is to stay with the boat.

But the situation at this point might have appeared different in Michael's eyes. To the south there was no land for hundreds of miles. Without help soon there was a chance that they would not survive until help came, and they had no way of knowing if it was on the way or not. Also, Michael was an extraordinarily strong swimmer. If land was in sight, there was a good chance he might make it. Having spent the last months paddling around all the villages of the vicinity, it is doubtful it crossed his mind that if found by natives, he would not be well treated.

René, however, tried desperately to dissuade him.

"This is our last chance," Michael argued. "If we don't take it, we'll just float farther and farther out to sea."

"We had a very long discussion," Wassing says, "and I tried very hard to talk that plan out of his head. I talked about the dangerous tides and the swift currents." Swimming, they would have no chance at all, Wassing argued; also, there was always the danger of sharks, crocodiles and sea serpents.

"He listened to me, but I knew in advance that he would go ahead. It was always very difficult to make him change his mind."

At this point Wassing estimated the distance to shore as about four to seven miles—a distance which would have been impossible for Wassing, the novice swimmer, even under ideal conditions.

"Bluntly I said to him, 'Michael, you are mad.' I also told him that I certainly would not try to swim, because I knew I had no chance at all."

Michael said that he would have to try it, that he was an

excellent swimmer and would also use the jerricans as Simon and Leo had.

"Again I tried to make him change his mind," Wassing told me, "but without any result. He was a brave man, but also very unreasonable. We had been floating farther as we argued, and now I saw that Michael was making preparations to go. I said, 'Michael, I don't take any responsibility for what you are going to do.' "

But Michael didn't answer. Suddenly he stood up, took the red gasoline tank from the outboard motor, and strapped it with his belt to another green jerrican that they had apparentlly salvaged when the boat overturned to form a sort of improvised water wings. Then he took off his trousers and shoes, threw the cans overboard, and jumped in after them.

His last words, that Wassing can recall, were: "I think I can make it."

The time was by now about 7 A.M. Wassing watched the young swimmer until all he could see was three dots made by Michael and the two cans, and then finally—nothing. "That was the last I saw of Michael Rockefeller," he states.

"I don't know what happened to him, but I am almost certain that he didn't get to shore. He really didn't have much time to get solid ground under his feet before the outgoing tide would be on him again. Even if you are only thirty feet from the shore, you don't stand a chance against that abnormally heavy tide."

28

Now Wassing was alone. He was depressed and in a state of near desperation. The boat kept drifting without incident until about four that afternoon, when suddenly he was awakened from his sun-drugged torpor by the clear sound of an airplane engine. It was a Dutch Navy PBY sent from Hollandia as soon as word had been radioed there. Frantically he waved his shirt at the plane, which now slowly and incredibly turned in a tight circle and dropped several flares to show that they had spotted him. A few minutes later a parachute blossomed in the air, and dangling from it was a rubber survival dinghy. It landed only a few dozen yards from the catamaran. This time Wassing did not think of his limited swimming talents or of the sharks but jumped in and swam without hesitation the 75 feet to the drifting life raft.

But when he got there, he was hardly better off than he had been on the catamaran. The dinghy had landed upside down, and all its food and survival gear, including the oars, were underneath. Frantically Wassing tried with his hands to paddle the dinghy back to the capsized catamaran, but it was impossible. He consoled himself with the cheering thought that at least he had been spotted. Help would be on the way.

But a new crisis arose. Slowly Wassing became aware of a hissing and gurgling noise and realized with horror that the rubber raft was losing air at a dangerous rate. He suspected that the flying boat would have to return for fuel before coming back to find him, and how could he be positive they would find him again? After all, his position was not actually fixed.

"It was a severe situation," Wassing says.

But just before dark, only a few hours after he had been spotted, Wassing again heard the reassuring buzz of the Neptune's motors. Turning its powerful searchlights on the water, the flying boat flew several times over the area, but apparently was unable to find the raft. Heartbreakingly the plane disappeared into the darkness, and Wassing was alone again with only the hissing sound of escaping air for company. "It was a terrible hard night," he commented.

Somehow (understandably Wassing isn't entirely clear on many details) he had lost all his clothing. Now in the night it was cold, and it started to rain. It was in fact a near cloudburst. Desperately Wassing clung to the craft as it now sank perceptibly deeper into the sea.

Soon Wassing had the sensation that he was floating in the bottom of a sack. The raft had sunk so low and had so little air left that he was slung into the bottom at an angle from which he could no longer see the sea around him. Once in a while he would raise himself to peer over the sides, but there was nothing in sight but the pulsing sea. Now five large porpoises began to play around the raft, adding to Wassing's fears. "I couldn't even let myself think what might happen if they accidentally rammed that sack I was suspended in."

Wassing's hopes, almost at their nadir, were revived by the sound of humming aircraft motors. But his brief moment of happiness turned to despair when the noise faded again. Couldn't they see him? But a little while later, the plane, apparently flying a search pattern, returned and dropped flares to show they had seen him. Now the PBY vanished again, but shortly afterward the government launch *Tasman* appeared and picked up the nearly delirious anthropologist.

"I was very happy that they found me, but that happiness was overshadowed by knowing that Michael, my friend, probably was lost," Wassing said.

"We had such high expectations of the expedition. We enjoyed the primitive living and didn't even really resent the fact that we wouldn't be home for Christmas. He told me that he had a girl in America, but I never heard anything more of that subject."

Wassing recalled Michael wrote many letters during the expedition. To whom? "I don't know. Perhaps it was a diary. He often spoke about his home in America. He was very upset by the divorce of his mother and father. He spoke often about his mother also."

By the time Wassing got back to Merauke the tiny frontier outpost had been turned into a madhouse. A score of journalists had flown in on a chartered plane from Australia and New Guinea, and soon the number of newsmen tripled. Shortly afterward Goveror Rockefeller arrived in his chartered DC-3.

"Most of the newsmen," Peter Hastings recalls, "didn't realize that this singularly unattractive tropical garrison town hardly had the facilities to accommodate the sixty-odd newsmen who soon jammed the area, packed four to a room in the tiny ramshackle hotel which was the only facility the capital boasted." According to one reporter, there was ultimately a total of ninety-three newsmen on the scene.

One Sydney newspaper sent its top police reporter, on the theory that all that was called for was a little know-how and organization. "He was nearly shot the first night by a trigger-happy young Dutch national serviceman," Hasting recalls wryly.

The situation in regard to press coverage was a delicate

one not only for Rockefeller, but also for Plateel, the Dutch governor. The Dutch were deep in the throes of a toe-to-toe confrontation with Indonesia over who would control western New Guinea. Any signs of poor administration or maltreatment of the native population would furnish ammunition to the Sukarno government. On the other hand, if the situation were handled properly, Plateel might benefit from the publicity. It is problematic whether he felt any guilt or remorse over the fact that his administration had allowed two totally unprepared young people to undertake a highly dangerous expedition without being accompanied by at least a patrol officer. (During my stay in New Guinea the Australian government did not overly concern itself either, but at all times I went with experienced jungle-wise companions.) Nelson Rockefeller, at any rate, uttered no word of criticism of the Dutch officials.

Immediately on their arrival, Elisofon, who had some experience with PBY's in World War II, went out on a search mission, manning binoculars in the waist blister of an Australian Catalina.

"Though I was familiar with New Guinea, having been there several times before, what I saw of the Asmat from the PBY was discouraging," he said. "Endless miles of mud and swamp, and a shocking number of sharks and crocodiles."

Hastings also commented that during his search runs on each leg out from the shore "it wasn't unusual to see between ten and twenty schools of gray nurse sharks, some of prodigious size, perhaps twelve to twenty to a school, all nose to center feeding.

"Giant sea serpents were equally common," Hastings recalls, "and as the Cat roared low over the desolate tidal shores, enormous estuarine crocodiles plowed their way down to the shallow sea, their tails thrashing up a miniature surf.

"Nobody," Hastings concluded, "could have jumped that raft some way at sea and survived those hazards."

On the second day the governor and Mary went out with Elisofon on the search in the DC-3, separated from the newsmen by the forward cabin door. Rockefeller had given out the word: "No pictures."

There had not been such a fuss in the foreign press about a missing American since the Lindbergh kidnapping.

Elisofon was careful not to take advantage of his position as unofficial press secretary, a fact the tough and aggressive newsmen found hard to believe. Several even tried to force their way past him into the forward cabin and had to be restrained by the governor's bodyguard.

"I bet we'll be seeing it in *Life!*" one of them jeered bitterly.

Most of the people on the plane, Elisofon recalls, were cranky from lack of sleep and tense from overcrowding. The governor and his guard couldn't stay awake, but Elisofon, who was wide-awake, was asked to see that no photos were taken in the plane.

"We were bound back to Merauke, and the governor and his daughter were seated together just aft of the passenger door, giving them some room in front," he says. "While I was watching, they both fell asleep. There were binoculars on the governor's chest, and he and Mary were both holding hands. It was a pathetic picture with just enough light from the oval plane window to create an effect. How I wanted to take that picture! But I didn't."

Back in Merauke, the two governors held at least one, sometimes two press conferences a day, though there was little for them to say. Rockefeller was obviously anguished, but maintained an optimistic front. Plateel was correct, but not very hopeful.

Heat, frustration and forced proximity raised the tempers of all concerned to a boiling point. In addition, there was an underlying hostility toward Rockefeller, based partly on his bad recent publicity and partly on the fact that he was an American millionaire.

On one occasion a reporter boldly asked the governor, "Do you have any idea how much this search has cost you?"

"No. Have you?" Rockefeller snapped irritably. (The jet chartered to bring Rockefeller to Biak had cost $38,000, according to one press report.)

Another reporter asked whether the huge search wasn't in fact a political stunt to mitigate publicity over the governor's upcoming divorce.

Rockefeller, understandably, flared into a fit of temper.

"You come here!" he shouted.

Unintimidated, the Australian reporter stood his ground.

"You bloody well come *here*," the newsman replied.

The confrontation was a standoff, but the press continued to spare the governor nothing in needling him about his wealth and his romance with Happy.

Meanwhile, all sorts of bizarre cable communications were reaching Mary, who was known to have a deep interest in spiritualism. People claimed they had seen Michael in dreams, alive, dead, still at sea, adopted as a native god. The letters were ignored by the searchers. It is not known what Mary thought of them. Oddly, in writing this book, I received a number of similar letters, most of them stressing the idea that Michael was a captive native god—a theory not unlike Donahue's.

At first Rockefeller had depended much on his son's known talents as a strong swimmer, but after a week he began to lose his confidence. He had made plans to return and postponed them when a new clue appeared.

A jerrican was found; a gaunt-eyed Wassing identified it

at first as being from his catamaran. Later, however, he wasn't so positive, and still later became certain that it wasn't Michael's.

Rockefeller, still clinging to hope, told Wassing, "I have complete confidence in Michael's stamina and resourcefulness."

By this time the search had reached really mammoth proportions. Australian helicopters were flown in a giant Hercules cargo plane and cooperated with Dutch naval units crisscrossing the endless swamp. The U.S. Pacific Fleet offered to send an aircraft carrier, but the governor declined. Thousands of native canoes combed the shoreline, perhaps impelled by the governor's offer of 250 sticks of tobacco for clues to Michael's whereabouts. Rob Eibrink Jansen, the Dutch resident general who was in charge of the search operation, was frankly pessimistic. "It would be a miracle if Michael is found alive," he said.

At one point Governor Rockefeller expressed a desire for a look at the area where his son might have come ashore. Father Zegwaard, who had been in close touch with Michael just before his departure and had been helpful in guiding the Rockefellers during their stay in Merauke, accompanied them to Piramapoen, where the DC-3 put down on a primitive grass strip. Among those there to greet them was Father Van Kessel, who was also assisting in the search. It was Van Kessel, in fact, whom Michael had been coming to see. The governor was given a chance to talk through an interpreter to some of the natives, but no pertinent information was picked up at the time. Zegwaard, however, had a hunch there was something strange and asked to stay on when the governor and his crew flew on to Merauke.

Wassing, too, tried to help pinpoint the area where Michael might have gone ashore by attempting to retrace their route from the air, but there were so few landmarks that it

224

was difficult, if not impossible, to choose the exact spot at which Michael had jumped overboard.

Wassing later said in a letter to Father Pitka: "If we had only known that Simon and Leo had safely reached shore and had immediately warned the HPB Michael would never have jumped into the sea. . . ."

With the letter he enclosed a watch as a thank-you gift for Simon.

But in all the searching, no one visited Otsjanep. First, it was a village with a known dangerous reputation, which even the missionaries and patrol officers avoided. Second, the ever-suspicious Otsjanep villagers had thrown a tree barricade across the river approaches to their settlement, making them impassable. Of course, Otsjanep itself was too far upriver to be considered a place where Michael could have landed, but canoeists from the village ranged far up and down the coast and had sago growing and fishing areas staked out in the coastal areas which were very likely places for Michael to have gone ashore.

Finally, after ten days, the governor of New York accepted what everybody in Merauke had come to feel was the unavoidable truth. Michael Rockefeller would never be seen again and probably had drowned at sea or been eaten by sharks or crocodiles. President Kennedy sent condolences. The governor held a final press conference, acknowledging that his son was probably lost, and glumly departed with his group aboard the DC-3 for Hollandia and eventually home. Those close to the family say that Michael was the closest to Nelson of all his children and the one in whom he had the greatest hopes for the future. But the future for Michael had apparently been all too short. The reporters left Merauke, the missionaries settled down to their work, and all returned to normality in the Asmat—until about two weeks after the search certain rumors began to filter out of the bush.

As early as March, 1962, about four months after the end of the search, Willem Hekman, one of the Dutch missionaries who knew the area best and was one of Rockefeller's consultants during his visit to the Asmat, wrote to his family in Holland that Rockefeller had been killed by Otsjanep villagers as he swam ashore. Hekman said in his letter that he had been told the whole story by natives and that they had even named people who had Rockefeller's skull and bones.

"The missionaries, white officials and even members of other tribes are afraid to go near Otsjanep village," Hekman wrote to his family. The *Haagsche Courant* in The Hague reported that an American friend of Hekman's sister had earlier been killed by the natives of Otsjanep.

The report caused a stir in Holland but was immediately denied by a spokesman for the Dutch government Department of New Guinea Affairs. Because of this, the report was given little credibility by U.S. news services, though it was picked up and distributed by the Australian Associated Press.

The Rockefeller story, however, refused to die. When Keith Willey visited Daru, in New Guinea, near the West Irian border in 1964, he encountered many refugees coming over the border from the Indonesian side who assured him that most people in West Irian were certain that Rockefeller had been killed, "cooked with sago" and eaten by the Asmat tribesmen. Willey's report was published in Australia, and apparently nowhere else (except briefly in his book *Assignment New Guinea,* which was not published in America).

In 1965 the Dutch newspaper *De Telegraaf* found still another authoritative supporter for the murder theory. Father Jan Smit, a Dutch missionary working at Piramapoen, near the Otsjanep area, had written to his brother in Heerhugowaard his theory of the American scion's death.

226

The brother had made no public statement until Smit himself was killed in a shocking conflict with the Indonesian officials, who had permitted many of the Dutch missionaries to remain and continue their work, provided they did not interfere with the political annexation of West Irian by Indonesia. Campbell provided this account of Smit's death.

Fimbai, an Indonesian official at Agats, administrative headquarters for the village of Piramapoen, where Smit had his Catholic school, was friendly with the missionaries at first but soon decided that it would be a better policy to establish his own school in Piramapoen. When the villagers, who after all had known the Dutch fathers for many years, refused to go to the new government schoolhouse, Fimbai became enraged. He ordered out the occupants of the Catholic school at gunpoint. Smit protested strongly but to no avail. That night at a local party Fimbai was heard boasting that he would shoot and kill Smit the following day.

In the morning Father Smit was summoned to the local pier for a hearing at Agats on the school matter. Friends of the Dutch father warned him that he might be going to his death.

"What can I do?" Smit asked. "He is in authority, and he has summoned me."

Fimbai was waiting in Agats at the foot of the pier with a squad of armed policemen. When the Dutch priest arrived, he accused him of being an American spy. He was marched to the end of the pier where a boat carrying another armed police squad was embarking to seek out Father Anthony Van Der Wouw, the Dutch priest who had replaced Father Van Kessel shortly after Rockefeller's disappearance, and execute him as a spy.

Smit was ordered to kneel at the end of the jetty, and three fatal shots were fired into his head. According to the official announcement, the Dutch missionary had been executed for "insulting the honor of the Indonesian Republic." The decision to execute Van Der Wouw that same day was apparently abandoned, or possibly the Indonesian patrol was unable to penetrate the well-guarded village.

Smit's body is buried at Agats. The Dutch missionaries who gave Campbell the story are reluctant to discuss the affair. It is another case where they feel that further probing would only stir up trouble, this time with the Indonesian government with which they exist in a state of tenuous equilibrium.

Following the "execution" of Smit, Dutch newsmen interviewed the missionary's brother, who revealed the contents of a letter he had received from Smit some years before his death.

"My brother," he said, "was the last man who had contact with the American millionaire's son, Michael Rockefeller, who was missing in New Guinea."

In his letters, the missionary's surviving brother said: "My brother later said that Michael Rockefeller was eaten by native tribes. He had seen tribe members wearing the clothes of Rockefeller, and also bones were found."

What happened to these bones and clothes Smit didn't say. He died before he could be questioned.

29

THE EVENTS that led to Rockefeller's alleged murder went years back in local history and were rooted in the traditional rivalry between the villages of Otsjanep and

Omadesep, with which Michael was familiar from his last trip there.

As far back as 1952, almost ten years before Michael arrived on the Casuarinen coast, Chinese crocodile hunters had visited Otsjanep with rowers from Omadesep. A violent battle ensued, with the Chinese taking the part of their Omadesep paddlers. Six women and two Otsjanep boys were killed—four of them by gunshot.

In December, 1955, Rob Eibrink Jansen—the same man who had directed the Rockefeller search—was sent to investigate the killings. Unfortunately he too was using rowers from Omadesep. Spying the canoes coming up the river paddled by their traditional enemies, the Otsjanep people prepared for bloody combat. Jansen sized up the situation and realized that it would be much too dangerous to attempt a contact at that time, so he returned without completing his investigation.

Toward the end of 1957 the situation was exacerbated when the Omadesep warriors succeeded in killing seven Otsjanep men returning from a canoe trip to one of their coastal outposts. In retaliation Otsjanep tribesmen came down the Ewta River and scored an ambush in which a dozen Omadesep fighters were killed. Actually on the whole expedition, which had started out as an ostensibly combined and friendly trip with the Omadesep flotilla, 124 Otsjanep men had set out, but only 24 returned alive, the rest having been slain by various hostile tribes en route.

Ultimately this endless cycle of killing became a deep concern of the Dutch government, which felt something had to be done to bring peace to the area. But at the same time the fierce reputation of the Otsjanep villagers made the Dutch move with extreme caution—one possible reason for the scattered dates involved. In January, 1958, a police superintendent named Dias arrested eleven men in the village of Omadesep, charging them with the murder of Otsjanep tribesmen, possibly in the hope that this would head off what seemed a certain payback raid. He emphasized the government's displeasure by cutting up all their large canoes, burning down their *yeu* houses and confiscating their weapons.

Word of this punitive raid, of course, percolated through the bush to neighboring villages and no doubt added to the tension.

A week later a nervous young patrol officer named Lapre was sent in to clear up the problem with the Otsjaneps. Who was Lapre? What was his experience? The sometimes-meticulous Dutch records seem strangely silent on the details. The consensus of missionaries and government officials reveal only that he was relatively new to the job and clearly nervous about confronting a village known up and down the coast for its acts of violence.

On his first trip in January Lapre was apparently so intimidated by the bellicose attitude of the Otsjanep villagers that he retreated without taking any action at all.

The following month he returned with Superintendent Dias and several native policemen armed with submachine guns.

Even the missionaries admitted that he had good reason to be nervous. Father Zegwaard told Campbell: "The village expected that this patrol was going to do the same thing they had done at Omadesep—namely, burn down their houses and cut their canoes to pieces. They certainly didn't like the patrol coming in. They had a hostile attitude."

It must have added to the tension in Lapre's mind to find his way barricaded by trees felled across the river, a clear sign that Otsjanep was preparing for battle.

On either bank the forest came down to the water, shutting out any possible view of armed spear and bowmen who could have been waiting in ambush—and such ambushes were a known technique of the Otsjanep tribesmen. As the village was approached, the river grew narrower and narrower, making the small government team an even surer target for the short-ranged accuracy of the tribal bows. What use was a submachine gun and several rifles against a shower of lethal arrows from the shelter of the mangroves? Indications are that Lapre's police escort was no less apprehensive than he.

Finally, the small flotilla of canoes turned one last bend and found themselves confronted by at least two hundred hot-eyed Otsjanep warriors, armed and seemingly ready to fight.

Of course, such a sight is not uncommon. When notified of the approach of strangers by scouts, the warriors traditionally massed, either for battle or for greeting. Possibly the Asmat warriors even may have launched a flight of warning arrows.

Lapre, Dias and the rest of the Dutch patrol apparently snapped under the now-oppressive tension. They opened fire into the massed ranks of the villagers.

According to reports gathered for me by Campbell in the Asmat, three Otsjanep warriors were killed. Patrol Officer Lapre shot a man named Osom, Superintendent Dias shot a fight chief named Foretbai, and one of the policemen shot another warrior named Samat. It is believed that one of these three men was related to Ajam, who succeeded Foretbai as fight chief. At least two women were also reportedly hit and killed in the exchange.

Lapre, apparently horrified by the bloody skirmish, immediately turned his canoes around and fled the scene. Thoughts of pacifying Otsjanep were dropped, at least for the moment.

But two years later, Father Zegwaard told Campbell,

desire for revenge for these killings of Otsjanep villagers by white men were "still embedded in their heads and in their hearts."

To the primitive villagers of course all whites were the same. They could hardly be expected to understand the difference between a Dutchman and an American.

But before revenge could be taken, a *bis* pole had to be built and dedicated. This was the pole photographed by *The Sky Above and the Mud Below* team before their hasty departure from Otsjanep. Beltgens, the policeman, was well aware of the trouble that had occurred only a year earlier and surely knew what he was doing when he advised the group to leave.

This brings us to the Rockefeller expedition the following year. Were the Otsjanep villagers planning revenge even as they traded with Rockefeller and Wassing? Did Rockefeller actually *buy* the *bis* pole which may have predicted his own end? Nobody can say authoritatively.

The first inkling of such a possible violent fate for Rockefeller came when Zegwaard remained behind at Piramapoen after seeing Governor Rockefeller's DC-3 off on its return to Merauke. He noticed Otsjanep tribesmen in the area, in itself a rare occurrence unless a battle was under way. The tribesmen were curious about the story of Rockefeller's disappearance. "They were there," Zegwaard told Campbell, "and I think they just wanted to find out if there was any suspicion or anything. What . . . they always do is send people around—sort of spies to look around and just feel what is going on and listen to the talks of the people and whether there are any suspicions. . . . I am not sure but I thought that might be the case that people are there to find out."

During the search Zegwaard approached police officials and actually asked if they were aware of the possibility that Michael Rockefeller had been killed in revenge for what had happened two years before. But the people he spoke to were new to Merauke and perhaps didn't realize the seriousness of what the missionary was telling them. In any event, the possibility was played down. Zegwaard speculates that they might have been inspired, too, by some feeling of guilt.

"Before Mike Rockefeller got permission from his father to go to West Irian," he says, "Nelson Rockefeller talked with Mr. Joseph Luns, minister of foreign affairs of Holland about Mike going to West Irian. Luns said, 'All right, let him go and I'll take care of him, and I'll take care of everything.' He contacted the governor [Plateel], the governor contacted other people, and everybody gave assurances and guaranteed that everything would be nice and OK, no trouble . . . no danger, nothing. So after a while . . . when it happened, the responsibility was passed from the lower people to the resident [Rob Eibrink Jansen] and from the resident to the governor and from the governor to the minister of foreign affairs."

One wonders whether Jansen, who well knew the hostility of Otsjanep village, was aware that Michael intended to visit this warlike and much aggrieved group. It hardly seems possible he would let them travel without an armed escort if he did know.

Whatever the reason, Zegwaard's theory was ignored at the time, although he was not the only one to give some thought to the people of Otsjanep.

A Father Lommertzen commented that if Michael had reached shore, "he might have reached the shore at a place that was not the best place for him."

"What do you mean, a hostile place?" Campbell asked.

"Hostile, yes," Father Zegwaard answered. "We all knew what happened a couple of years before. There is a possibility that people seeing this man coming out of the sea completely alone, no protection, very quiet, nobody . . . looking around they saw that it was a good chance to take revenge for what happened to their people."

"Otsjanep—do you think that's a possibility?" Campbell asked.

"Yes. I think that happened," Zegwaard replied. "Here on a Sunday morning, a very quiet morning, here is a man coming out of the sea, swimming all the time. So he arrived —Mike Rockefeller—and he would be tired, of course, after the long time of swimming. He is quite alone. No protection. . . . Now imagine . . . that is the nicest opportunity for the Asmat men to take revenge. No defense. He was an easy prey. . . . So, if he swam ashore, and I think he did, the most probable thing is that he fell in the hands of the people that were fishing over there and recalled what had happened two years ago."

In addition to asserting his belief that Michael had been killed by Otsjanep, Father Zegwaard offered some interesting corroborative statements. Asked about the theory of Gerbrands, Hastings and several others that nobody could make it through a sea so teeming with crocodiles and sharks, Zegwaard backed up the opinion of Father Van Kessel vigorously.

Here is the transcript on this point:

CAMPBELL: And it's very unlikely that there could have been sharks or crocodiles or something that could have caused it [Rockefeller's death]?

ZEGWAARD: No. . . . I sort of investigated this possibility. I asked all of the fathers who were having a meal in Merauke . . . fathers that had been all over on this south New Guinea coast altogether for more than one hundred years—I added up all the years they had been living there, there were seven or eight fathers—I asked them: "Have you ever had a case of people that were killed by sharks?" None of them had heard of any cases of natives ever killed by sharks in this particular area. Maybe other areas, I don't know. So sharks don't seem to be very dangerous or attack people in this area.

CAMPBELL: Any crocodiles?

ZEGWAARD: Crocodiles, could be. But crocodiles—it's different also. Though some of them are man hunters, most of them are not. . . . So a crocodile that man-eats is known to other people. . . . So some places are very famous because there is a dangerous crocodile there. But there aren't many crocodiles that are that dangerous or at all dangerous if people don't go close to them. There are always certain crocodiles . . . that are known all over. We had one, I know in Atupa when I was there, very famous. They had been hunting that one for years. Finally they got him. . . . I heard that story about the crocodile that was killed in Atupa everywhere— one hundred miles to the east. . . . But not all crocodiles are that aggressive . . . and there are few of them, of course in the open sea.

I have had a little experience with crocodiles, so if a crocodile gets a human being, he brings him ashore as far as the . . . tide goes—just pulls him a little out of the reach of the water . . . he brings the body to shore, and then he kills him.

The father went on to tell of a boy in one of his villages who had been killed by a crocodile, making the point that the crocodile always drags his victim, often alive, as far on dry land as possible and then kills it and lets it decay before eating it. "It takes a couple of days, maybe a week, maybe weeks to finish the whole corpse," Zegwaard said. In view of the intensive search of the shoreline and the rarity of man-eating crocodiles or sharks, it hardly seems likely that Michael was eaten by a sea predator.

Zegwaard also confirmed that in his opinion and in the judgment of nautical people he worked with during the search, it was entirely feasible that Michael would have reached shore near Otsjanep. The land with a single tree that had been spotted by Michael and Wassing early in their drift, he identifies fairly definitely as a point near Omadesep, a familiar navigational reference.

In regard to Wassing himself, Zegwaard agreed with certain other critics in feeling that it had been poor judgment to give him the sole responsibility of accompanying Michael.

"There was another mistake. . . . Wassing was a man working in a museum. . . . He was not a practical man like a patrol officer. So it was another thing the government was blamed for. They needed to appoint a practical man who is able to handle the situation. But he [Wassing] wasn't the company he [Rockefeller] needed. But here there was an appointment made that this man and Mike would go after these woodcrafts together. . . . So the Dutch officials . . . sent a man, scientific type of man with an interest and an eye for the local woodcraft. He was acquainted with, and he could pick out the good ones and leave the worse ones."

30

FROM HIS interviews with a number of people who were closely involved with the Rockefeller affair in the Asmat, Father Van Zegwaard, Father Van Der Wouw and Dr. Kenneth Dresser, a medical missionary from America attached to The Evangelical Alliance Mission (TEAM), Campbell added details which filled out the picture and helped make this apparent act of senseless violence understandable.

According to his informants, Otsjanep villagers were

boasting of the revenge—and it must be remembered that boasting of a revenge killing is part of the cultural pattern in the Asmat—the *day* after Michael's disappearance and long before the actual search was mounted. How could they have known he was even missing if their story was not based in fact?

The story first emerged when a certain Father Van Pey in the village of Atsj heard that two Otsjanep tribesmen named Bere and Bewor had been boasting that the men of their tribe had intercepted Michael as he was crawling ashore near one of their fishing grounds.

Unfortunately, in those primitive areas, it was not possible to send for police and mount an immediate investigation, especially since chances were good that any police trying to penetrate Otsjanep might be killed.

Also, as Van Pey wrote in his report, Otsjanep became alarmed by the extent of the search for Rockefeller and put up barriers of fallen trees to prevent access by river.

Discreetly Van Pey continued to question natives about what had actually happened.

He learned that a group from Otsjanep, which included the fight chief Ajam and two other chiefs named Fin and Pep, were fishing at one of their coastal bivouacs at a small river between the Ewta and the Otsjanep rivers.

Here is a transcript of part of Campbell's tape with Father Van Der Wouw who had spoken to Van Pey:

CAMPBELL: Where was this? Up the coast?

VAN DER WOUW: Yes, up the coast, near the Fajit River. Before you come to the Ewta River [on which Otsjanep is located, a few miles upstream], there is a very small river, Jowor is the name of it. The chiefs, I think there was Fin, Pep and Ajam, were over there with the women, fishing. . . . And then Rockefeller came drifting to the shore, and they told me, there he was, panting, kind of exhausted, and then as they say, Fin, he speared him with his fish spear—he fish-speared

237

Rockefeller with his fish spear and after that they took him ashore and killed him.

CAMPBELL: Who told you this?

VAN DER WOUW: From Father Van Kessel. Father Van Pey was living in Atsj . . . so as soon as Rockefeller was killed by Otsjanep, the next day Omadesep knew it already because it was such—I mean. . . .

CAMPBELL: Prestige.

VAN DER WOUW: Prestige. They never could keep that quiet, and straight on told it to Omadesep. So first of all Father Van Pey heard about it.

CAMPBELL: In Atsj?

VAN DER WOUW: In Atsj. And he sent a letter to Father Van Kessel.

Father Van Kessel's reactions have been reported earlier. He filed a report to his superiors as soon afterward as he could get enough confirming information. The actual report was dated January 23, 1962, about two months after Michael's disappearance. Father Van Pey himself had left for Holland when Campbell visited the Asmat Coast, so he was unable to interview him personally.

But the interview with Van Der Wouw, who arrived just after the search, confirmed many other points, including the fact that in 1970 the Otsjanep villagers were still considered a problem because of their violence.

"It's the most difficult village to deal with, isn't it?" Campbell asked.

"Yes," said Father Van Der Wouw. "I almost got shot there myself once."

It seems he had gone to Otsjanep to try to persuade a chief named Urum that he should let his children attend the mission school.

"I told him, 'You are a big warrior. You wear that bamboo thing [decoration symbolizing number of enemies killed]; it means that you have killed quite a few people.

Why can't you let the little kids come to school?' So he stood there very ashamed, and soon I heard his wife who, when she saw him standing there ashamed and shy and doing nothing, started hitting the walls of the house with a stick. So he ran away and got his bow and arrow and came back and pulled the bow. I didn't know what he was doing. I didn't think. I just ran straight forward and grabbed him and didn't let him go."

It wasn't Van Der Wouw's only such brush with the Otsjanep tribesmen, but in most other cases his close calls had involved trying to break up fights between the Asmat tribesmen, *whose bellicosity continued unabated in the years following the Rockefeller affair.*

The government did not consider it tactful at the time to ask too many questions about the story of Michael's killing by Otsjanep. Tension with the Otsjaneps had never really abated, and there was a general feeling that questions might only stir up new violence. More important, there was a reluctance to reveal the details of the shooting of the Otsjanep villagers by the Dutch patrol—an incident of which the administrators were thoroughly ashamed.

Father Van Zegwaard commented: "That is why everyone wanted to cover everything up . . . to bury all these things, because the whole thing was rotten."

Even so, Inspector J. Heemskerk, now a policeman in The Netherlands, was given a special assignment to investigate the reports. He remembers today that the Otsjanep tribe was then reputed to be "pretty dangerous."

Although warned by missionaries that a trip to the region was risky, following orders as a policeman should, he questioned tribesmen in the immediate area shortly after the alleged killing and became convinced that the natives who claimed to have slain Rockefeller were telling the truth. His report, however, was deleted from the official government account of the incident. Heemskerk inter-

239

preted this as a matter of delicacy on the part of the officials.

"I understood why this had not to be put in the report," he commented. "It was bad enough for the family what happened."

It is less clear why Van Kessel's religious superiors did not act further on his report, but that may have been out of fear of becoming embroiled with the government officials. Despite the many differences between the government and the missionaries, each must to a large extent depend on the other.

The government finally asked Father Van Der Wouw, who had at least managed to get the village to accept a Catholic school, whether he could persuade the villagers to permit several police officers to spend some time in the village. "They just wanted to stay there for months and months, just to try to contact the people, not to tell them they had in mind to find out anything about Rockefeller," Van Der Wouw said.

Van Der Wouw was afraid at first that the presence of the police officers would cause the people to abandon the village entirely, but with some difficulty he was able to persuade them to stay.

"So then after months and months they [Otsjanep villagers] kind of suspected that these people were looking for Rockefeller's skull, and they thought perhaps they could get some money out of it, so at midnight one night a few fellows came over to the district officer and said, 'We will take you over to the place where the skull is.' So they brought him far back into a muddy place and they dug up a skull . . . and sent it to Merauke, and after all, we heard it was just a regular Papuan skull. Then for sure they destroyed it [Rockefeller's skull], I think. They were too afraid. It seems they still have pieces of his eyeglasses."

"How did you find this out?" Campbell asked.

"I was told by the new chief of the village. But I hadn't

dared even to bring up the subject for five or six years later. *Then something terrible happened.*"

Resident Jansen had already heard the rumor before Van Kessel's report.

"From the day of Michael's disappearance," Jansen told a reporter, "tens of such rumors reached me. Most of them I knew beforehand could not be based on truth, but I investigated every message and every rumor by patrols. I did not like to miss one chance in a million. There were many stories of murder and cannibalism. There was also a rumor that a Papuan headman was walking around in Rockefeller's pants. The most romantic sory was that Michael Rockefeller was still alive—or is—and was kept as a white idol by a tribe near the coast."

Now we come to the reluctant American medical missionary Dresser who, it will be remembered, had also sent a note to Van Kessel at the time of the disappearance saying he believed that Rockefeller had been killed.

Around five o'clock Sunday afternoon he had heard over the radio that Mike's catamaran was in trouble. He, a patrol officer and another missionary named Don Gregory set out in a flat-bottomed fiber-glass boat to help in the search for the catamaran, which by now had been spotted by the Neptune. But it was almost sundown by the time they were able to actually put to sea, and just before dark, they spotted the Neptune with its searchlights. It tried to show them the location of the raft by flying level and then zooming up as it came to the catamaran's position. When the three men saw the life raft dropped, they were positive it was the catamaran.

But just as they felt they had a good chance to reach it, the Neptune apparently ran out of fuel and had to return. All they had aboard the boat as a navigational aid was one tiny pocket compass, so they doubted that they would be able to find the raft or the catamaran in the dark.

Finally, after weaving uncertainly back and forth in the dark for quite a long while in the face of a rising wind, Dresser says he figured: "There's not much point in losing three more lives too," and decided to return. It was two in the morning by the time they got back. By then the boat from Agats which had had to turn back for fuel arrived. Exhausted as they were, the men took off along with the *Tasman* at daybreak again to continue the search.

About nine o'clock Monday morning the Neptune sighted the raft again, and Wassing was picked up and brought to Merauke. Wassing was in surprisingly good shape considering his ordeal and, except for a raging thirst, seemed to have no complaints.

Of course, they all noted the ironic fact that Wassing apparently didn't realize that on the bottom of his flipped-over raft was a complete supply of chocolate, water, food and first-aid supplies.

His principal comment was: "I nearly died in that swim!"—meaning the 75 yards from the catamaran to the raft.

After more discussion of the sea conditions at the time and the reasons for Rockefeller's marine disaster, Campbell asked Dresser bluntly, "Do you think Michael was killed by the natives of Otsjanep?"

"Turn off that thing," Dresser said, indicating the tape recorder, "and I'll tell you." Campbell did as he asked, but as soon as he was finished listening to Dresser, he went to his hut and narrated on tape the content of their conversation. Here is the transcript of what he sent me:

CAMPBELL: As you've just heard, Dr. Dresser didn't want to discuss his views about the disappearance of Michael Rockefeller. He seems to think that discussing it any further would serve no useful purpose, and I guess he certainly doesn't want to bring up the whole matter again. His next words were:

"He was killed by people of Otsjanep." When I asked him how he knew about this he said that shortly after Rockefeller disappeared, Don Gregory, the missionary who works further up the Cook River, who is a linguist also with the TEAM, the Evangelical Mission, had been told by the people of his village, who had heard from Otsjanep itself, that Rockefeller had been killed and eaten. Gregory also said that a year later when he was in Omadesep during the outbreak of cholera, he heard exactly the same story almost word for word from the teacher of the Omadeseps down to the details of where he was killed, and what sort of spear was used and he even said that the skull had been kept but that Hekman, another missionary working for the TEAM, had offered quite a large reward in axes for the skull, but this had been turned down. And nothing has ever been found since. He does agree that it's supposition but he strongly believes that Rockefeller was killed. Both Dr. Dresser and his wife mentioned that the fight leaders from Otsjanep had been here at Piramapoen I think on [that] Sunday. They didn't say why they were down here, but the story that I gathered is they were here delivering wood or firewood, I'm not sure which, and were on their way back to Otsjanep at the same time that Mike himself was swimming toward shore. Dr. Dresser seems to believe it was a payback for the killings of several people by a Dutch patrol some years earlier in Otsjanep itself, and his story seems to coincide with what we heard from Father Zegwaard, from Van Kessel, the Catholic missionary who was here at Piramapoen, from Father Van Der Wouw, who came here in 1962, who himself seems to have heard rumors since Rockefeller disappeared. Ari, the new young chief of Otsjanep, has told Van Der Wouw basically the same story that Otsjanep killed and ate Rockefeller. I think certainly the only missionary who doesn't believe it and who was here at the time is Father Hesch . . . and his main assumption is that no white man has ever been killed and eaten in the Asmat before, so he doesn't see why Otsjanep should break the sort of arbitrary rule. It is a fact that Otsjanep has been extremely difficult to deal with. Dr. Dresser mentioned this, Van Der Wouw has certainly found it so, and this village seems to have a whole history of trouble behind it. And the more I listen to people talking, the more I begin to believe that it is possible, in fact it is probable, that Mike Rockefeller was killed and was eaten by Otsjanep, but there is no definite proof. In conclusion, Dr. Dresser's wife, Sophie, said it was a pure fluke. Just a chance in a million. If Rockefeller had come ashore maybe a little farther up the coast or a little farther down the coast, he would not have been killed; it was just pure chance that he happened to land opposite Otsjanep, which had this grudge to settle with the white people, and it was just a chance in a million that he landed there and was killed.

31

WHAT ABOUT a confession? The Indonesian doctor claimed he had got one in 1968, but the actual document seemed impossible to nail down. At least my Indonesian sources at the consulate had been unable to find it.

I had specifically requested Campbell to try to find Ajam —the only one of the alleged killers whose name I knew at the time—and get a new confession from him. There again I was stopped cold. Campbell came up with the disappointing news that every one of the three chiefs alleged to have killed Michael Rockefeller—Ajam, Fin and Pep—had themselves been killed in another outbreak of tribal violence in 1967.

Just after the cholera epidemic which produced the confession allegedly made to the Indonesian doctor, two sections of Otsjanep itself began an internecine fight within their own tribe. This is the incident Van Der Wouw referred to when he said "something terrible happened." Scores were killed in fierce battles, including five local chiefs and Ajam's wife. Leader of the opposition was Urum, the irascible chief who once tried to shoot Father Van Der Wouw.

As a result, no one will be able to question any of these key people.

Campbell asked the new chief, Ari, about the events of 1961, but the chief told him that nobody now in Otsjanep knew anything about Rockefeller.

Van Der Wouw spoke to Ari, too. Since he knew the language and had worked with the village for more than five years, presumably the missionary could inspire greater confidence.

"I told him I would not tell anybody about it, but I just wanted to talk it over," he said.

What Van Der Wouw heard seemed to convince him of Rockefeller's murder.

CAMPBELL: They must have recognized Rockefeller when he came ashore. He'd been to Otsjanep before, hadn't he? He'd been collecting things.

VAN DER WOUW: Yes, he was there, but I don't know whether or not they recognized him, because . . . according to what they tell me he had only a singlet on and his underpants. This is what they tell me. I don't know. The other reason is what happened in fifty-eight. The Dutch officer killed quite a few people in Otsjanep, and this is just for the payback.

CAMPBELL: But there have been cases before—people, Dutch patrol officers killing people—but there's never been a payback.

VAN DER WOUW: No, but they never had the opportunity, I think. This man came all by himself, no boat around, no nothing around. This happened before I came and Father

Van Pey and Father Van Kessel both . . . think for sure it happened that way, because the next day they were already talking before they started searching for him.

CAMPBELL: You think they just got rid of the skull and so forth?

VAN DER WOUW: Oh, yes. When they started looking for him. They should have kept them, but they were afraid to keep them. They are not around anymore.

CAMPBELL: The only thing that might exist are his eyeglasses?

VAN DER WOUW: Yes, that is what they say. But I never will ask these fellows again because it just upsets the people again. So I leave it as it is.

For ten years the world had generally accepted the idea that Michael Rockefeller was drowned in a tidal bore at the mouth of the Eilanden River.

But now we have an accumulation of information indicating that he suffered a much different and more shocking fate—a fate caused by the enormous gap in customs and understanding between the world Michael knew and that of the Asmat tribesmen. To them his family wealth, his years of education, his goodwill and innocence meant nothing. To Ajam and his war chiefs Michael represented only the color of his skin. He represented outside mankind; he was a member of the tribe that brought unavenged deaths to their village. Even if he could have spoken to them, expained that he had come only to help and study their ways, it would have made no difference. The Asmats did not regard killing Michael as a personal matter; it was a question of tribal honor. Ajam would have been as puzzled by Michael's failure to understand this as Michael would have been by their desire to take their revenge on him.

The drowning theory persisted for a decade because those who knew the truth were afraid to talk—afraid of reprisals from the government, afraid to hurt the feelings of the Rockefellers, afraid, most of all, to stir up further tribal violence. But violence continued anyway, the government lost its power, and the Rockefellers, many suspect, came to know the truth long ago.

Eight missionaries of three different sects agree that Michael was the victim of an Asmat payback: Van Pey, Dresser, Van Kessel, Van Der Wouw, Zegwaard, Hekman, Smits and Gregory.

With few exceptions veteran settlers and members of the search party also agree. Gerbrands' statements that no one could swim through the shark- and crocodile-infested waters were refuted by the two Asmat swimmers who safely made it to shore. Statements by Gerbrands and Father Hesch that the people of Otsjanep would not kill a white are easily refuted by the history of the village. Statements by Peter Hastings that the natives of the area were too controlled and pacified to have committed such an act are challenged by the continued behavior of this rebellious village —documented, though reluctantly, by the record of the Dutch and Indonesian governments.

The classic requirements for a murder were present—the motive, the opportunity. Dresser even stated he actually saw the party of killers en route to their accidental rendezvous with Rockefeller. The natives' boasts of the killing, days before they could have possibly known of Rockefeller's disappearance, are impressive evidence. In his devotion to the drowning theory Gerbrands hinted that all the stories might be a hoax cooked up by the missionaries for whom he has such animosity. Not only does this attack not merit refutation, but the fact that at least three of these missionaries even now have refused to talk for publication pretty well answers that argument.

We must also give serious weight to the opinions of people like John Ryan and Tim Ward, who have maintained a keen interest in the subject through the years, and to the members of *The Sky Above and the Mud Below* team, who accept the murder theory unanimously and have good reason to understand its basis.

We cannot actually even call men like Ajam murderers. By their own laws—and what right have we to impose our rules on them?—they behaved in the only way possible: with honor and courage.

We belong to a different civilization. If any of Michael's murderers are still alive and should be convicted and receive the supreme punishment, capital punishment would be one of the few aspects of our civilization that an Otsjanep villager could comprehend—a death for a death.

If we can place the blame for Michael's death anywhere, it must be with the Dutch administration. Certainly the Dutch knew the violent character of the Otsjanep villagers. The fact is in their own records. They also knew the treacherous character of the Eilanden River. The fact that Michael was allowed to enter the swamp and jungle without a bush-wise patrol officer seems a case of serious negligence. Had Michael been accompanied by a properly qualified officer, undoubtedly he would be alive today.

Even as disturbing is the covenant of silence surrounding the murders of the Otsjanep villagers by Officer Lapre. From the villagers' point of view the death of one American chief's son does not necessarily compensate even now for the deaths inflicted on their village, which after all did not ask foreigners to penetrate their privacy and impose on them a set of rules designed for people of another world.

The story as now told is the way I believe it actually happened.

There are those who will be made uncomfortable by it, whose consciences will be disturbed even now.

Perhaps this is as it should be.

But this is the story I believe Michael Rockefeller would have wanted told.

248

BIBLIOGRAPHY

ANDERSON, JAMES L., and HOGG, DONALD, *New Guinea*. Sydney, A. H. and
A. W. Reed, 1969.
———, with Tom McMorrow and Bob Hamilton, "Cannibal!" *Argosy*
magazine (February, 1971).
BJERRE, JENS, *Savage New Guinea*. New York, Hill and Wang, 1964.
BURRIDGE, K. O. L., *Mambu*. London, Methuen and Company, 1960.
ELISOFSON, ELIOT, *Java Diary*. New York, Macmillan, 1969.
GARDNER, ROBERT, and HEIDER, KARL G., *Gardens of War*. New York,
Random House, 1968.
GODWIN, JOHN, "Where Is Michael Rockefeller?" *Argosy* magazine (Oc-
tober, 1968).
HASTINGS, PETER, "Looking for Rockefeller." *New Guinea* magazine (June-
July, 1968).
HEIDER, KARL G., *The Dugum Dani*. Chicago, Aldine Press, 1970.
LAWRENCE, PETER, *Road Belong Cargo*. Manchester, Manchester University
Press, 1964.
———, and PEGGETT, M. J., *Gods, Ghosts and Men in Melanesia*. Mel-
bourne, Oxford University Press, 1965.
MCCARTHY, J. K., *Patrol into Yesterday*. Sydney, F. W. Cheshire, 1963.
MALINOWSKI, BRONISLAW, *Argonauts of the Western Pacific*. New York,
E. P. Dutton, 1961.
MATTHIESSEN, PETER, *Under the Mountain Wall*. New York, Viking, 1962.
Pacific Islands Monthly. Sydney, various issues.
PUTNAM, SAMUEL, "Under the Mountain Wall," *Harvard Medical School,
Alumni Bulletin* (Winter, 1963).
ROCKEFELLER, MICHAEL, *The Asmat*. New York, New York Museum of
Primitive Art, n.d.
ROWLEY, C. D., *The New Guinea Villager*. Sydney, F. W. Cheshire, 1965.
RYAN, PETER, *Fear Drive My Feet*. Melbourne, Melbourne University
Press, 1959.

SAULNIER, TONY, *Les Papous Coupeurs de Têtes*. Paris, Éditions Pont Royal, 1961.

SINCLAIR, J. P., *Beyond the Ranges*. Melbourne, Melbourne University Press, 1966.

WILLEY, KEITH, *Assignment New Guinea*. Brisbane, Jacaranda Press, 1965.

Index

Agats, 135
Ajam, 194–96; death of, 244
Algemeen Dagblatt, 211
Amanamki, 172
Anderson, Jim, 41–42, 51
ANGAU, 29
Angoram, 101
Arafura Sea, 178
Asmat Coast, 9–10, 74; art carvings in, 147, 163–64, 190; cannibalism in, 142; language, 134; local myths, 147, 185; native leadership, 196; white man's effect on, 179
Asmat of New Guinea: The Journal of Michael Clark Rockefeller, The, 146–47
Atjametsj, 179
Atsj, 192
Australian Special Branch, 44, 45
Ave, Joop, 37, 38

Baliem Valley, 8; as an agricultural society, 152–53; death ceremonies in, 171–72; description of, 153, 171–72; history of, 153
Basim, 197
Berita Yudha, 194
Bis poles, 177, 195; as symbols for revenge, 199, 232; ritual of, 174
Broekhuyse, Jan, 155, 157

Campbell, John, 195
Cannibalism, 42, 197; bones as tools, 142–43; cultural, 148–49; governmental denials of, 199; missionary diary of, 200–5; as a ritual, 173
Cargo cult, 53–54, 96, 196–97; denials of, 96, 199
Carstensz Toppen, 50
Christian and Missionary Alliance, 157
Coast watchers, 67–68
Contraband. *See* Smuggling
Cook Bay, 209
Crocodile hunting, 69–70, 74–77
Cruickshank, Ian, 105–7

Dale, Stan, 199; missionary diary of, 200–5
De Bruyn, Dr. Victor, 153
Delloye, Gerard: on Michael, 196
De Maigret, Count Hervé, 195
Djayapura, 38, 169
Dobu Islands, 71; natives of, 64
Donahue, John, conversation with, 14–28
Donaldson, M. G., 33, 68
Dresser, Dr. Kenneth, 139, 236; on Michael, 241–44
Dutch Administrative Headquarters (HPB), 208

Dutch government, 40, 140, 143–44; and Indonesia, 221
Dutch New Guinea. *See* West Irian

Egloff, Brian, 65
Eilanden River, 10, 207
Elisofon, Elliot, 165, 168, 213
Emak tsjem, 147

Fairbridge expedition, 59, 66
Fergusson Island, 71–72
Flaherty Award, Robert, 183
Free Choice, Act of, 37–38, 89–90, 140, 194
Fumeripits, 185–86

Gabwina Island, 84–86
Gaisseau, Pierre, 196
Gardner, Robert, 152; on Michael, 184
Gerbrands, Adrian, 146; conversation with, 148–50
Godwin, John, 31
Grasmeri River, 103
Gwimi, 113–15

Hanuabada, 49
Hansen, Warren, 107
Harvard. *See* Peabody expedition; Peabody Museum; Rockefeller, Michael
Hastings, Peter, 45, 179–82; on Michael, 182–83
Haus tambaran, 103
Headhunters of Papua, 195
Headhunting, 148–49; denials of, 199; penalty for, 104; preparation of skulls, 101–2, 117–18; as power and prestige, 28, 47; as ritual, 173, 186–87. *See also Bis* poles; *Emak tsjem*
Healy, Mike, 91, 93–94
Heemskerk, J., 239
Heider, Karl, 155

Hekman, Father Willem, 46, 185, 226
Hesch, Father Delmar, 185, 243
Hogg, Donald, 53, 55
Hollandia. *See* Djayapura
Homuak, 163
Huxley, Tom, 96–97

Interpol, 36

Jansen, Rob Eibrink, 187, 224, 229
Johnson cult, 91–95

Kanapa, 35
Kanapu, 35, 43, 64, 86–88
Kanganomon, 108
Kavieng, 91
Kennedy, David, 51
Kiap, 113
Kiriwina, 43, 52, 61
Kukukuku, 30, 124–26; family life of, 119–20; war dances of, 127
Kula trading ring, 63–64
Kurelu, 157–58
Kwita, 78

Lang, Mel, 69
Lawes, Bruce, 101
Loosjes, Pat, 44
Luns, Joseph, 233

Madang, 33, 96
Magic, 64, 71, 91, 200; and disease, 194; and human sacrifice, 79–80; and spirits, 54; white man as "big medicine," 20, 22–23. *See also* Headhunting; Natives, primitive; Revenge killing
Malik, Adam, 38, 45
Malinowski, Bronislaw, 71–72
Marawaka, 119
Masters, Phil, 199, 204
Matthiessen, Peter, 155, 165
McCarthy, Jack, 97

McCarthy, Keith, 119
McKenzie, C. J., 187
Mead, Margaret, 61
Medwick, 22, 32–33, 34–35, 59
Merauke, 11, 37
Money-growing cult, 97–100
Moresby, Port, 49

Nance, John, 130
Natives, primitive, 22, 27–28, 53–56; and death, 139; and fear of white man, 28, 31, 51, 126, 160; and language, 51, 158; and warfare with other tribes, 103–4, 113–14, 119–23, 228–34. See also Cargo cult; Gwimi; Headhunting; Kavieng; Kukukuku; Magic; Osulumani; Otsjanep; Revenge killing; River people; Sepik; Trobriand Islands; Yali
New Guinea: description of, 7, 21, 42, 50; House of Assembly, 93; political history of, 37–38; transportation in, 43, 106, 120
New York Post, 39
Ninia, 199
Normanby Island, 199

O'Hara, J. S., 68–69
Orangwoks, 50
Osulumani, 115–18
Otsjanep, 139, 173–77, 185. See also Ajam; Bis poles

Payback. See Revenge killing
Peabody expedition: and Dutch government, 9, 170, 181; effect on natives, 166; purpose of, 8, 160–61; preliminary arrangements, 156–63
Peabody Museum, 7, 155
Pearl divers, 47
Piracy, 58
Pitka, Father Superior Francis, 185; on Michael, 206–11

Plateel, P. J., 11, 214
Putnam, Sam, 154
Primitive Art, Museum of, 146, 174

Revenge killing, 53, 141, 197; and culture, 55–56, 148, 236–37; examples of, 55, 121–24, 179; and innocent victims, 145, 150; Dutch intervention, 123. See also Natives, primitive
Rijksmuseum Voor Volkenkunde, 146
River people, 106–7
Robbins, Albie, 129
Rockefeller, Mary (Mrs. Mary Strawbridge), 11, 137, 223
Rockefeller, Michael: at Harvard, 154; in military service, 156; and his restless nature, 7, 172; in Baliem Valley, 165, 167, 172; in Agats, 191; on Asmat Coast, 178–79, 188, 190; and Wassing, 10, 192; rumors about the fate of, 19–25, 57, 105, 170, 223. See also Asmat Coast; Peabody expedition; Wassing, René
Rockefeller, Nelson A., 11–12, 32, 220–21, 223
Ryan, John, 128–29

Saulnier, Tony, 195
Sepik: and haus tambaran, 103, 109–11; headhunting and cannibalism, 199
Shurum, 206
Sinclair, Jim, 123
Singina, Yali, 91–93, 95
Smith, Vince, 96
Smit, Father Jan, 226–28
Smuggling, 36, 44, 58, 83
Sorcery. See Magic
Soulship, 147
South Pacific Post, 51–52
Steeger, Hal, 31, 36

Sukarno, 37
Sukarnapura. *See* Djayapura
Sydney *Morning Herald,* 194

Thursday Island, 47
Time magazine, 170
Tjemor, 190
Trade goods, 18, 48, 58; most prized, 160–63
Trobriand Islands, 21, 61, 78; communication and transportation, 53; and local myths, 78–80; and native sailors, 34, 57

Usher, L. G., 36

Van Der Wouw, Father Anthony, 227; conversations with, 237–38, 245–46; at Otsjanep, 239

Van Kessel, Reverend Corneles, 39, 132, 185; conversation with, 135–45
Van Pey, 139

Wamena, 168
Ward, Tim, 43, 56–57, 129–30
Waro, 158
Wassing, René, 8, 35; and Michael, 211–12, 214–20
West Irian, 38
Wewak, 101
Willey, Keith, 45–47, 194, 226

Yalis, 200–5

Zegwaard, Father Gerald, 185–86, 224, 234–35

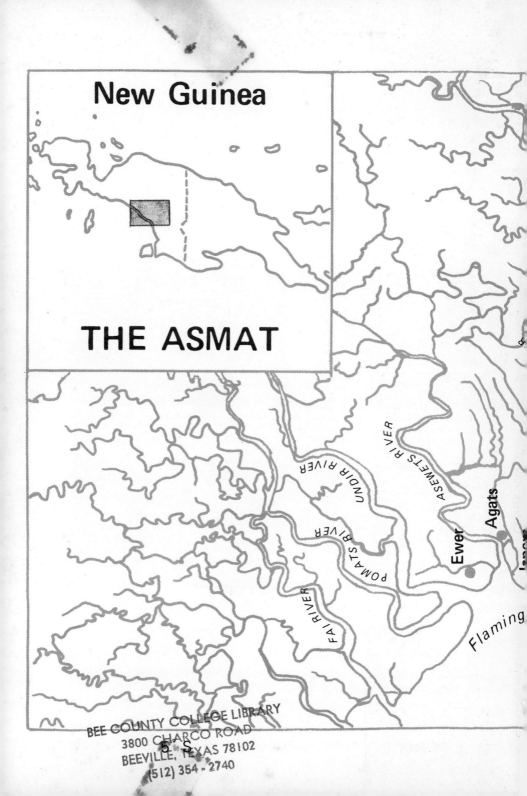

New Guinea

THE ASMAT

FAI RIVER

POMATS RIVER

UNDIR RIVER

ASEMETS RIVER

Ewer

Agats

Flaming